# SYMBOLISM AND HINDU WORSHIP

# SYMBOLISM AND HINDU WORSHIP

*Editor-in-Chief*
**Swami Chidatman Jee Maharaj**

**ANMOL PUBLICATIONS PVT. LTD.**
**NEW DELHI - 110 002 (INDIA)**

**ANMOL PUBLICATIONS PVT. LTD.**
**H.O.:** 4374/4B, Ansari Road, Daryaganj,
New Delhi-110 002 (India)
Ph.: 23278000, 23261597
**B.O.:** No. 1015, Ist Main Road, BSK IIIrd Stage
IIIrd Phase, IIIrd Block,
Bangalore - 560 085 (India)
*Visit us at*: www.anmolpublications.com



*Symbolism and Hindu Worship*


First Published, 2009
ISBN 978-81-261-3628-5



PRINTED IN INDIA

Printed at Mehra Offset Press, Delhi.

# Contents

# Preface

India colourful and vibrant, a land as diverse as its people. A mosaic of faiths, cultures, customs and languages that blend harmoniously to form a composite whole. One of the world's oldest living civilizations—which gave to the world—the concept of zero, the primordial sound Aum..., Yoga and Buddhism.

She is old. She is young. The two diametrically opposite, different yet unique and dynamic faces of India coexist even at this turn of the millennium. With a history of heritage, learning and civilisation dating back to almost 5000 years or perhaps even more, the modern India presents itself as an ideal country. From snow clad mountains to breezy sparkling blue sea side. From arid deserts with shifting sand dunes to lush green country sides. From ancient relics and architectural ruins dating back into antiquity to modern cities, India has it all.

To the north it is bordered by the world's highest mountain chain, where foothill valleys cover the northernmost of the country's maximum states. Further south, plateaus, tropical rain forests and sandy deserts are bordered by palm fringed beaches. Its southernmost tip is the meeting point of three Oceans.

India is a land of staggering contrast with a mingling of the tradition and modernity that is an unique experience to be in India. One will forever remember the stay in this wonderful Homeland-a land truly of mystery and enchantment. Only India can offer such an astonishing variety of contrasts.

She has given birth to numerous spiritual leaders and founders of some of the popular religions of the present day world. India probably has the most religious diversity in any country. It's the birthplace of Hinduism, Buddhism, Sikhism and Jainism and is among the few places to have a resident

Zoroastrian population. India with her veritable treasure trove of culture, mysticism, philosophy, art, music and architecture to name a few. Much of India's classical music is devotional and the North Indian Hindustani and South Indian Carnatic streams are distinct and both have a complex 'raga' framework. The legacy of dance in India is tremendous. The classical dances of India are numerous such as Kathakali of Kerala, Bharatnatyam of Tamil Nadu, Kuchipudi of Andhra Pradesh, Manipuri and Odissi from Orissa are the prominent dance forms in this country that sways to an altogether novel beat. The Yakshagana, nautanki and puppetry are ancient folk forms that live on till date. The earliest specimens of Indian painting are the ones on the walls of the Ajanta Caves dating back to 2nd century BC. The Mughals had a huge impact on Indian art. The influence of Persian art brought placid garden scenes, illustrations from myths, legends and history into Indian art. Word craft, handicrafts, architecture and sculpture all contribute to this rich and varied domain. Indian literature, both in English and in the vernacular, is ever more popular around the world.

The book aims at presenting perspectives of different aspects of Indian culture. It has topics on Indian classical music and dance, painting, ayurveda and yoga which are traditional and indigenous system of physical and mental wellbeing, language, philosophy and excellence achievements by Indian in the different branches of science and social sciences. It also includes our ancient religious and classic literature.

It is hoped that this book will be welcomed by the general readers as also scholars who are interested in the Indian heritage.

—*Editors*

# 1

# Hindu Religious Tradition

Silent adorations to *Sachidananda Para-Brahman,* Who is the silent Witness of all minds, Who is the Indweller in all beings, Who has projected this world for His own *Lila* or sport, Who is the support for this world, body and mind and all movements, and Who is the foundation for all societies and their activities.

## Purpose of Religion

The word Religion comes from the Latin word *religio* which consists of two words, *viz.*, *re* (back) and *ligare* (to bring or bind). That which binds the soul back to God is religion. Religion shows the way for the attainment of God-realisation.

Religion satisfies the deep inward craving in man who is not always content with leading merely an animal existence and wants spiritual consolation, solace and peace. Man cannot live by bread alone. A time comes in the life of many of us when mere worldly prosperity does not satisfy us and we hanker after something more. In the case of many more, trials and tribulations of life turn their attention to spiritual solace.

## Distinguishing Features of Hinduism

***A Revealed Religion:*** Hinduism is the religion of the Hindus, a name given to the Universal Religion which hailed supreme in India. It is the oldest of all living religions. This is not founded by any prophet. Buddhism, Christianity and Mohammedanism owe their origin to the prophets. Their dates are fixed. But no such date can be fixed for Hinduism. Hinduism is not born of the teachings of particular prophets. It is not based on a set of dogmas preached by a particular set of teachers. It is free from religious fanaticism.

Hinduism is also known by the names *Sanatana-Dharma* and *Vaidika-Dharma*.

Sanatana-Dharma means eternal religion. Hinduism is as old as the world itself. Hinduism is the mother of all religions. Hindu scriptures are the oldest in the world, Sanatana-Dharma is so called, not only because it is eternal, but also because it is protected by God and because it can make us eternal.

Vaidika-Dharma means the religion of the Vedas. The Vedas are the foundational scriptures of Hinduism. The ancient Rishis and sages of India have expressed their intuitive spiritual experiences *(Aparoksha-Anubhuti)* in the Upanishads. These experiences are direct and infallible. Hinduism regards the spiritual experiences of the Rishis of yore as its authority. The priceless truths that have been discovered by the Hindu Rishis and sages through millennia constitute the glory of Hinduism. Therefore, Hinduism is a revealed religion.

***A Religion of Freedom:*** Hinduism, unlike other religions, does not dogmatically assert that the final emancipation is possible only through its means and not through any other. It is only a means to an end and all means which will ultimately lead to the end are equally approved.

Hinduism allows absolute freedom to the rational mind of man. Hinduism never demands any undue restraint upon the freedom of human reason, the freedom of thought, feeling and will of man. It allows the widest freedom in matters of faith and worship. Hinduism is a religion of freedom.

It allows absolute freedom to the human reason and heart with regard to questions such as nature of God, soul, creation, form of worship and the goal of life. Hinduism does not lie in the acceptance of any particular doctrine, nor in the observance of some particular rituals or form of worship. It does not force anybody to accept particular dogmas or forms of worship. It allows everybody to reflect, investigate, enquire and cogitate. Hence, all sorts of religious faiths, various forms of worship or

Sadhana, and diverse kinds of rituals and customs, have found their honourable places side by side within Hinduism and are cultured and developed in harmonious relationship with one another.

Hinduism does not condemn those who deny God as the creator and ruler of the world, who do not accept the existence of an eternal soul and the state of Moksha or state of liberation. Hinduism does not render the upholders of such views unfit to be recognised as pious and honourable members of the Hindu religious society.

The religious hospitality of Hinduism is proverbial. Hinduism is extremely catholic and liberal. This is the fundamental feature of Hinduism. Hinduism pays respects to all religions. It does not revile any other religion. It accepts and honours truth—wherever it may come from and whatever garb it may put on. There are considerable numbers of the followers of other religions in India. And yet, the Hindus live in perfect harmony, peace and friendship with all of them. Their tolerance and fellow-feeling towards the followers of other religions is remarkable.

Despite all the differences of metaphysical doctrines, modes of religious discipline and forms of ritualistic practices and social habits prevalent in the Hindu society, there is an essential uniformity in the conception of religion and in the outlook on life and the world, among all sections of Hindus.

### *The Glory of Vedanta and Yoga*

Vedanta, or the philosophy of the Upanishads, is lofty, sublime and unique. The Western philosophers have paid their tribute to the ancient seers of the Upanishads. They have been amazed at the lofty heights scaled by them. Schopenhauer studied the Upanishads and meditated on the thoughts of the Upanishads just before going to bed. He said: "The Upanishads are the solace of my life and they will be solace to me after my death also."

The Raja-Yoga system of Hinduism is also splendid and unique. The lessons are immensely practical and highly instructive. No system of physical exercise on the surface of the earth can compete with Hatha-Yoga. Kundalini-Yoga is wonderful. Hence the Americans and Europeans are in search of Hindu Sannyasins and Yogins. They visit the Himalayas frequently in quest of Yoga teachers. Some are living under Hindu Yogins as disciples and are practising Yoga. Many Europeans and Americans are even now Hindus by faith and practice, though they are born Christians. They practise Raja-Yoga and Vedanta.

## Emphasis on Practice

Hinduism provides spiritual food and Yoga Sadhana for all sorts of people to suit their temperaments, capacities, tastes, stages of spiritual development and conditions of life. It prescribes Yoga Sadhana even for a scavenger or a cobbler to attain God-realisation, while doing his ordinary avocation in the world.

Hindu Yoga and Vedanta teachers lay great stress on self-restraint, Tapas, renunciation and practical Sadhana which is best calculated to control the mind and the senses and unfold the divinity or attain Self-realisation. Hinduism is not a religion of mere theories. It is eminently practical. In no religion you will find such a variety of practical Yoga practised and such sublime unique philosophy expounded. That is the reason why India is the only glorious land of sages, Rishis, Yogins and saints.

Religion is practical aspect of philosophy. Philosophy is rational aspect of religion. The philosophy of Hinduism is not arm-chair philosophy. It is not meant for intellectual curiosity and vain discussion. Hindu philosophy is a way of life. The philosopher of Hinduism seriously reflects after hearing the Srutis, does Atma-Vichara, constantly meditates, and then attains Self-realisation or Atma-Sakshatkara. Moksha is his goal. He attempts to attain Jivanmukti now and here.

Religion is spiritualisation of human life for a Hindu. Religious culture is really the culture of freedom for him. Religion governs all the departments of Hindu life. He must realise the freedom of the soul in every department of life. Religion affords the greatest scope for him for the culture of true freedom. Religion is the only way to him for the realisation of perfect freedom in life.

It is in India alone that every man knows something of philosophy. The cowherd who tends the cattle, the peasant who ploughs the fields, the boat-man who pulls at his oar, sing songs replete with philosophical truths. Even the barber repeats OM NAMAH SHIVAYA, SIVOHAM before he takes up the razor. The Paramahamsa Sannyasins, the itinerant monks of Hinduism, have disseminated the highest of Vedanta from door to door. In exchange for a handful of rice, they have distributed from door to door, through religious songs, the priceless gems of Hindu religion and philosophy.

## Who is a Hindu?

In a meeting of the Sanatana Dharma Sabha, Lokamanya Tilak said: "A Hindu is he who believes that the Vedas contain self-evident and axiomatic truths."

The Hindu Maha Sabha has given another definition: "A Hindu is one who believes in a religion which has originated in India."

"Those who burn the dead are Hindus." This is another definition given by some.

"He who protects the cows and the Brahmins is a Hindu." This is another definition given by some.

Some define: "A Hindu is one who regards India as his motherland and the most sacred spot on earth."

Some others define: "He who calls and considers himself a Hindu is a Hindu."

Some define: "He who accepts the Vedas, the Smritis, the Puranas and the Tantras as the basis of religion and of the rule of conduct, and believes in one Supreme God (Brahman), in the Law of Karma or retributive justice, and in reincarnation *(Punarjanma),* is a Hindu."

"He who follows the Vedic or Sanatana-Dharma is a Hindu." This is the definition by some.

"He who is a follower of the Vedanta is a Hindu." This is another definition given by some others.

"He who has perfect faith in the Law of Karma, the law of reincarnation *Avatara,* ancestor worship, *Varnashrama Dharma, Vedas* and existence of God, he who practises the instructions given in the Vedas with faith and earnestness, he who does *Sandhya, Shradha, Pitri-Tarpana* and the *Pancha-Maha-Yajnas,* he who follows the Varnashrama Dharmas, he who worships the Avataras and studies the Vedas, is a Hindu." This is the definition given by some highly cultured men. This is the only correct and complete definition.

### *Origin and Significance of the Term*

That part of the great Aryan race which migrated from Central Asia, through the mountain passes into India, settled first in the districts near the river Sindhu, now called the Indus, on the other side of the river. The Persians pronounced the word Sindhu as Hindu, and named their Aryan brethren Hindus. *Hindu* is only a corrupt form of *Sindhu.*

The Hindu Aryans spread themselves over the plains of the Ganga. Then the Persians gave the name Hindusthan, or abode of the Hindus, to the whole of those districts between Punjab and Benaras. (Latest *historical researches have now proved that the Aryans did not come from outside India, but were the original inhabitants of India.*)

The classical name for India which is used in Sanskrit literature is *Bharata-Varsha* or *Bharata-Khanda,* after the name of Bharata who ruled over a large extent of territory in days of yore. Manu's name for the whole central region between the Himalayas and the Vindhya mountains is *Aryavarta,* Abode of the Aryans. Another name for the whole of India is *Jambu-Dvipa.* The Greeks gave the name Indu to the whole of this country. It was on account of this *India* became popular as the name of this country throughout Europe.

*Hindu* is not a mere name. This name *Hindu* is not only of geographical, but also of national and racial importance. The whole history of our nation from the very beginning is bound up with it. All our ideas and ideals are so intimately connected with it that it is difficult to give a simple definition of it. Poets, prophets and Avataras came to sing the praises and glory of this name. Rishis, sages and saints took their birth to compile the *Shastras* and *Darshanas* for this nation.

Heroes and warriors have fought for its honour and laid down their very lives for it. Piety, nobility, generosity, philosophy, religious bent of mind, Yoga, religious tolerance, wisdom, devotion, renunciation, Self-realisation. Ahimsa, Satya and purity are associated with the name 'Hindu'.

***The Spiritual Soil of India***

India is the sacred land which has given birth to countless sages, Rishis, Yogins, saints and prophets. India is the land that has produced many Acharyas or spiritual preceptors like Sri Shankara and Sri Ramanuja; many saints like Kabir, Ramdas, Tukaram and Gauranga Mahaprabhu; many Yogins like Jnana Dev, Dattatreya and Sadashiva Brahman; and many prophets like Buddha and Nanak. Buddha is our flesh and blood.

India is proud of Guru Govinda Singh and Shivaji. India is proud of king Bhoja and Vikramaditya. India is proud of Shankara and Kabir. India is proud of Valmiki and Kalidasa. Krishna, Rama and all Avataras were born in India. How sacred is India! How sublime is India!

The dust of Brindavan and Ayodhya, the land trodden by the sacred feet of Krishna and Rama, still purifies the heart of countless people. Even Jesus, during the missing period of His life, lived in Kashmir and learnt Yoga from the Indian Yogins. Glory to Mother India!

India is a spiritual country. India never conquered territories or annexed dominions. Military conquest is not her ambition. She wants her children to have *Atma-Svarajya* or Absolute Independence. She does not call upon them to rule over others. She wants them to have conquest over internal and external nature. She wants them to possess brilliant divine virtues, moral stamina and inner spiritual strength born of wisdom of the soul. Ahimsa is her weapon to have the spiritual conquest and the conquest of the minds of others.

People of India have Self-realisation as their goal. They do not, generally, bestow too much attention on material prosperity and advancement. They want Yoga or communion with the Supreme Being. They practise Ahimsa, Satya and Brahmacharya. They wish to enjoy the eternal bliss of the Absolute. They are always ready to renounce worldly possessions in order to possess or realise the inner Atman or Brahman. They will sacrifice anything and everything in order to attain the immortal Atman. They are always spiritual-minded.

India is the sacred land with several holy rivers and powerful spiritual vibrations. The hoary Himalayas attract the people of the whole world. It is a land peculiarly suitable for divine contemplation and Yogic practices. Every country has its own special attractive features. India is the land of Yogins and sages. This is the special attractive feature of India. This is the reason why people from America, England and all parts of the world come to India for the practice of Yoga.

### *The Facts of History*

India is the most tolerant country in the world. She has a very expansive heart. She includes all nations in the embrace of her love.

The Western nations are the descendents of the original Hindus or Aryans. They might have forgotten their old connections with the Aryans and Hindu culture. They might have forgotten all about their ancestors. But this cannot be effaced from the annals of history. Mother India, the repository of Hindu culture, cannot forget her children beyond the seas. They are always dear to her.

Hindu culture and Hindu civilisation were at their zenith in the days of yore. Greeks and Romans imitated the Hindus and absorbed Hindu thoughts. Even now Hindu culture and Hindu civilisation stand foremost in the world. No religion has produced so many great saints, sages, Yogins, Rishis, Maharishis, prophets, Acharyas, benefactors, heroes, poets, statesmen and kings as Hinduism. Each and every province of the country has produced intellectual giants, poets and saints. Even now India abounds in Rishis, philosophers, saints and high intellectuals. Even now she abounds in sages and great souls.

The Hindus had to undergo severe hardships and tortures. They had to face fierce battles and cruelties and yet they live today. Some mysterious power has preserved them. Some invisible force has protected them. That power will protect them for ever.

## Reasons for Survival of the Hindu Religion

Hinduism is neither asceticism nor illusionism, neither polytheism nor pantheism. It is the synthesis of all types of religious experiences. It is a whole and complete view of life. It is characterised by wide toleration, deep humanity and high spiritual purpose. It is free from fanaticism. That is the reason why it has survived the attacks of the followers of some of the other great religions of the world.

No religion is so very elastic and tolerant like Hinduism. Hinduism is very stern and rigid regarding the fundamentals. It is very elastic in readjusting to the externals and non-essentials. That is the reason why it has succeeded in living through millennia.

The foundation of Hinduism has been laid on the bedrock of spiritual truths. The entire structure of Hindu life is built on eternal truths, the findings of the Hindu Rishis or seers. That is the reason why this structure has lasted through scores of centuries.

***Its Future:*** The glory of Hinduism is ineffable. It has within it all the features of a universal religion. Its Dharmas are universal. Its doctrines are sublime. Its philosophy is grand. Its ethics is soul-elevating. Its scriptures are wonderful. Its Sadhanas or Yoga-Vedantic practices are unique. Glorious has been the past of this religion; still more glorious is its future. It has a message to give to a world rent asunder by hatred, dissension and war—the message of cosmic love, truth and non-violence, the gospel of unity of Self or Upanishadic oneness.

The more you know of India and Hinduism, the more will you come to regard and love it and the more grateful to the

Lord will you be in that you have got a taste for practising Yoga and that you are imbibing the teachings and spirit of Hinduism.

Glory to India! Glory to Hinduism! Glory, glory to the Rishis and the seers who have kept burning the flame of Hinduism with its extreme effulgence and splendour!

## Hindu Scriptures

### *Sanskrit Literature*

Sanskrit literature can be classified under six orthodox heads and four secular heads. The six orthodox sections form the authoritative scriptures of the Hindus. The four secular sections embody the later developments in classical Sanskrit literature.

The six scriptures are: (i) Srutis, (ii) Smritis, (iii) Itihasas, (iv) Puranas, (v) Agamas and (vi) Darshanas.

The four secular writings are: (i) Subhashitas, (ii) Kavyas, (iii) Natakas and (iv) Alankaras.

### *The Scriptures*

***The Srutis:*** The *Srutis* are called the *Vedas,* or the *Amnaya.* The Hindus have received their religion through revelation, the Vedas. These are direct intuitional revelations and are held to be *Apaurusheya* or entirely superhuman, without any author in particular. The Veda is the glorious pride of the Hindus, nay, of the whole world!

The term *Veda* comes from the root *Vid,* to know. The word *Veda* means knowledge. When it is applied to scripture, it signifies a book of knowledge. The Vedas are the foundational scriptures of the Hindus. The Veda is the source of the other five sets of scriptures, why, even of the secular and the materialistic. The Veda is the storehouse of Indian wisdom and is a memorable glory which man can never forget till eternity.

***Revealed Truths Without Beginning or End:*** The Vedas are the eternal truths revealed by God to the great ancient Rishis of India. The word *Rishi* means a seer from *dris,* to see. He is the *Mantra-Drashta,* a seer of Mantra or thought. The thought was not his own. The Rishis saw the truths or heard them. Therefore, the Vedas are what are heard (Sruti). The Rishi did not write. He did not create it out of his mind. He was the seer of thought which existed already. He was only the spiritual discoverer of the thought. He is not the inventor of the Veda.

The Vedas represent the spiritual experiences of the Rishis of yore. The Rishi is only a medium or an agent to transmit to people the intuitional experiences which he received. The truths of the Vedas are revelations. All the other religions of the world claim their authority as being delivered by special messengers of God to certain persons, but the Vedas do not owe their authority to any one. They are themselves the authority as they are eternal, as they are the Knowledge of the Lord.

Lord Brahma, the Creator, imparted the divine knowledge to the Rishis or seers. The Rishis disseminated the knowledge. The Vedic Rishis were great realised persons who had direct intuitive perception of Brahman or the Truth. They were inspired writers. They built a simple, grand and perfect system of religion and philosophy from which the founders and teachers of all other religions have drawn their inspiration.

The Vedas are the oldest books in the library of man. The truths contained in all religions are derived from the Vedas and are ultimately traceable to the Vedas. The Vedas are the fountain-head of religion. The Vedas are the ultimate source to which all religious knowledge can be traced. Religion is of divine origin. It was revealed by God to man in the earliest times. It is embodied in the Vedas.

The Vedas are eternal. They are without beginning and end. An ignorant man may say how a book can be without beginning or end. By the Vedas, no books are meant. Vedas came out of the breath of the Lord. They are the words of God. The Vedas are not the utterances of persons.

They are not the composition of any human mind. They were never written, never created. They are eternal and impersonal. The date of the Vedas has never been fixed. It can never be fixed. Vedas are eternal spiritual truths. Vedas are an embodiment of divine knowledge. The books may be destroyed, but the knowledge cannot be destroyed. Knowledge is eternal. In that sense, the Vedas are eternal.

***The Four Vedas and Their Sub Divisions:*** The Veda is divided into four great books: the Rig-Veda, the Yajur-Veda, the Sama-Veda and the Atharva-Veda. The Yajur-Veda is again divided into two parts, the Sukla and the Krishna. The Krishna or the Taittiriya is the older book and the Sukla or the Vajasaneya is a later revelation to sage Yajnavalkya from the resplendent Sun-God.

The Rig-Veda is divided into twenty-one sections, the Yajur-Veda into one hundred and nine sections, the Sama-Veda into one thousand sections and the Atharva-Veda into fifty sections. In all, the whole Veda is thus divided into one thousand one hundred and eighty recenssions.

***Each Veda Consists of Four Parts:*** the Mantra-Samhitas or hymns, the Brahmanas or explanations of Mantras or rituals, the Aranyakas and the Upanishads. The division of the Vedas into four parts is to suit the four stages in a man's life.

The Mantra-Samhitas are hymns in praise of the Vedic God for attaining material prosperity here and happiness hereafter. They are metrical poems comprising prayers, hymns and incantations addressed to various deities, both subjective and objective. The Mantra portion of the Vedas is useful for the Brahmacharins.

The Brahmana portions guide people to perform sacrificial rites. They are prose explanations of the method of using the Mantras in the Yajna or the sacrifice. The Brahmana portion is suitable for the householders.

The Aranyakas are the forest books, the mystical sylvan texts which give philosophical interpretations of the rituals. The Aranyakas are intended for the Vanaprasthas or hermits who prepare themselves for taking Sannyasa.

The Upanishads are the most important portion of the Vedas. The Upanishads contain the essence or the knowledge portion of the Vedas. The philosophy of the Upanishads is sublime, profound, lofty and soul-stirring. The Upanishads speak of the identity of the individual soul and the Supreme Soul. They reveal the most subtle and deep spiritual truths. The Upanishads are useful for the Sannyasins.

The subject matter of the whole Veda is divided into *Karma-Kanda, Upasana-Kanda* and *Jnana-Kanda.* The Karma-Kanda or Ritualistic Section deals with various sacrifices and rituals. The Upasana-Kanda or Worship-Section deals with various kinds of worship or meditation. The Jnana-Kanda or Knowledge-Section deals with the highest knowledge of Nirguna Brahman. The Mantras and the Brahmanas constitute Karma-Kanda; the Aranyakas Upasana-Kanda; and the Upanishads Jnana-Kanda.

***The Mantra-Samhitas*:** The Rig-Veda Samhita is the grandest book of the Hindus, the oldest and the best. It is the Great Indian Bible, which no Hindu would forget to adore from the core of his heart. Its style, the language and the tone are most beautiful and mysterious. Its immortal Mantras embody the greatest truths of existence, and it is perhaps the greatest treasure in all the scriptural literature of the world. Its priest is called the Hotri.

The Yajur-Veda Samhita is mostly in prose and is meant to be used by the Adhvaryu, the Yajur-Vedic priest, for superfluous explanations of the rites in sacrifices, supplementing the Rig-Vedic Mantras.

The Sama-Veda Samhita is mostly borrowed from the Rig-Vedic Samhita and is meant to be sung by the Udgatri, the Sama-Vedic priest, in sacrifices.

The Atharva-Veda Samhita is meant to be used by the Brahma, the Atharva-Vedic priest, to correct the mispronunciations and wrong performances that may accidentally be committed by the other three priests of the sacrifice.

***The Brahmanas and the Aranyakas*:** There are two Brahmanas to the Rig-Veda—the Aiteriya and the Sankhayana. "The Rig-Veda," says Max Muller, "is the most ancient book of the world. The sacred hymns of the Brahmanas stand unparalleled in the literature of the whole world; and their preservation might well be called miraculous." (History of Ancient Sanskrit Literature) The Satapatha Brahmana belongs to the Sukla Yajur-Veda. The Krishna-Yajur-Veda has the Taittiriya and the Maitrayana Brahmanas.

The Tandya or Panchavimsa, the Shadvimsa, the Chhandogya, the Adbhuta, the Arsheya and the Upanishad Brahmanas belong to the Sama-Veda. The Brahmana of the Atharva-Veda is called the Gopatha. Each of the Brahmanas has got an Aranyaka.

***The Upanishads*:** The Upanishads are the concluding portions of the Vedas or the end of the Vedas. The teaching based on them is called Vedanta. The Upanishads are the gist and the goal of the Vedas. They form the very foundation of Hinduism.

There are as many Upanishads to each Veda as there are Sakhas, branches or recenssions, *i.e.*, 21, 109, 1000 and 50 respectively to the four Vedas, the Rig-Veda, the Yajur-Veda, the Sama-Veda and the Atharva-Veda.

The different philosophers of India belonging to different schools, such as Monism, Qualified Monism, Dualism, Pure Monism, Difference-cum-non-difference, etc., have acknowledged the supreme authority of the Upanishads. They have given their own interpretations, but they have obeyed the authority. They have built their philosophy on the foundation of the Upanishads.

Even the Western scholars have paid their tribute to the seers of the Upanishads. At a time when the Westerners were clad in barks and were sunk in deep ignorance, the Upanishadic seers were enjoying the eternal bliss of the Absolute, and had the highest culture and civilisation.

The most important Upanishads are Isa, Kena, Katha, Prasna, Mundaka, Mandukya, Aiteriya, Taittiriya, Chhandogya, Brihadaranyaka, Kaushitaki and Svetasvatara and Maitrayani. These are supremely authoritative.

May the fundamental truths of the Vedas be revealed unto you all, like the Amalaka fruit in the palm of your hand. May

Gayatri, the blessed Mother of the Vedas, impart to you the milk of Knowledge, the ancient wisdom of the Upanishads.

***The Upa-Vedas*:** There are four *Upa-Vedas* or subsidiary Vedas, *viz.*, the Ayurveda, the Dhanurveda, the Gandharva Veda and the Arthashastra, forming auxiliaries to the four Vedas, which mean, respectively, the science of health, the science of war, the science of music and the science of polity.

***The Vedangas*:** There are six *Angas* or explanatory limbs, to the Vedas: the *Siksha* and *Vyakarana* of Panini, the *Chhandas* of Pingalacharya, the *Nirukta* of Yaska, the *Jyotisha* of Garga, and the *Kalpas* (Srauta, Grihya, Dharma and Sulbha) belonging to the authorship of various Rishis.

Siksha is a knowledge of phonetics. Siksha deals with pronunciation and accent. The text of the Vedas is arranged in various forms or *Pathas*. The Pada-patha gives each word its separate form. The Krama-patha connects the word in pairs.

Vyakarana is Sanskrit grammar. Panini's books are most famous. Without knowledge of Vyakarana, you cannot understand the Vedas.

Chhandas is metre dealing with prosody.

Nirukta is philology or etymology.

Jyotisha is astronomy and astrology. It deals with the movements of the heavenly bodies, planets, etc., and their influence in human affairs.

Kalpa is the method of ritual. The Srauta Sutras which explain the ritual of sacrifices belong to Kalpa. The sulbha Sutras, which treat of the measurements which are necessary for laying out the sacrificial areas, also belong to Kalpa. The Grihya Sutras which concern domestic life, and the Dharma Sutras which deal with ethics, customs and laws, also belong to Kalpa. The Pratishakhyas, Padapathas, Kramapaṭhas, Upalekhas, Anukramanis, Daivatsamhitas, Parishishtas, Prayogas, Paddhatis, Karikas, Khilas and Vyuhas are further elaborations in the rituals of the Kalpa Sutras.

Among the Kalpa Sutras, the Asvalayana, Sankhyana and the Sambhavya belong to the Rig-Veda. The Mashaka,

Latyayana, Drahyayana, Gobhila and Khadira belong to the Sama-Veda. The Katyayana and Paraskara belong to the Sukla Yajur-Veda.

The Apastamba, Hiranyakesi, Bodhayana, Bharadvaja, Manava, Vaikhanasa and the Kathaka belong to the Krishna Yajur-Veda. The Vaitana and the Kaushika belong to the Atharva-Veda.

***The Smritis***

Next in importance to the Sruti are the Smritis or secondary scriptures. These are the ancient sacred law-codes of the Hindus dealing with the Sanatana-Varnashrama-Dharma. They supplement and explain the ritualistic injunctions called *Vidhis* in the Vedas. The Smriti Shastra is founded on the Sruti. The Smritis are based on the teachings of the Vedas. The Smriti stands next in authority to the Sruti. It explains and develops Dharma. It lays down the laws which regulate Hindu national, social, family and individual obligations.

The works which are expressly called Smritis are the law books, Dharma Shastras. Smriti, in a broader sense, covers all Hindu Shastras save the Vedas. The laws for regulating Hindu society from time to time are codified in the Smritis. The Smritis have laid down definite rules and laws to guide the individuals and communities in their daily conduct and to regulate their manners and customs. The Smritis have given detailed instructions, according to the conditions of the time, to all classes of men regarding their duties in life.

The Hindu learns how he has to spend his whole life from these Smritis. The duties of Varnashrama and all ceremonies are clearly given in these books. The Smritis prescribe certain acts and prohibit some others for a Hindu, according to his birth and stage of life. The object of the Smritis is to purify the heart of man and take him gradually to the supreme abode of immortality and make him perfect and free.

These Smritis have varied from time to time. The injunctions and prohibitions of the Smritis are related to the particular social surroundings. As these surroundings and essential conditions of the Hindu society changed from time to time, new

Smritis had to be compiled by the sages of different ages and different parts of India.

***The Celebrated Hindu Law-Givers*:** From time to time, a great law-giver would take his birth. He would codify the existing laws and remove those which had become obsolete. He would make some alterations, adaptations, readjustments, additions and subtractions, to suit the needs of the time and see that the way of living of the people would be in accordance with the teachings of the Veda. Of such law-givers, Manu, Yajnavalkya and Parasara are the most celebrated persons.

Hindu society is founded on, and governed by, the laws made by these three great sages. The Smritis are named after them. We have Manu Smriti or Manava Dharma-Shastra (the Laws of Manu or the Institutes of Manu), Yajnavalkya Smriti and Parasara Smriti. Manu is the greatest law-giver of the race. He is the oldest law-giver as well. The Yajnavalkya Smriti follows the same general lines as the Manu Smriti and is next in importance to it. Manu Smriti and Yajnavalkya Smriti are universally accepted at the present time as authoritative works all over India. Yajnavalkya Smriti is chiefly consulted in all matters of Hindu Law. Even the Government of India are applying some of these laws.

There are eighteen main Smritis or Dharma Shastras. The most important are those of Manu, Yajnavalkya and Parasara. The other fifteen are those of Vishnu, Daksha, Samvarta, Vyasa, Harita, Satatapa, Vasishtha, Yama, Apastamba, Gautama, Devala, Sankha-Likhita, Usana, Atri and Saunaka.

The laws of Manu are intended for the Satya Yuga, those of Yajnavalkya are for the Treta Yuga; those of Sankha and Likhita are for the Dvapara Yuga; and those of Parasara are for the Kali Yuga.

The laws and rules which are based entirely upon our social positions, time and clime, must change with the changes in society and changing conditions of time and clime. Then only the progress of the Hindu society can be ensured.

***Need for a New Law-Code*:** It is not possible to follow some of the laws of Manu at the present time. We can follow their spirit and not the letter. Society is advancing. When it advances, it outgrows certain laws which were valid and helpful at a particular stage of its growth. Many new things which were not thought out by the old law-givers have come into existence now. It is no use insisting people to follow now those old laws which have become obsolete.

Our present society has considerably changed. A new Smriti to suit the requirements of this age is very necessary. Another sage will place before the Hindus of our days a new suitable code of laws. Time is ripe for a new Smriti. Cordial greetings to this age.

***The Inner Voice of Dharma*:** He who is endowed with a pure heart through protracted Tapas, Japa, Kirtana, meditation and service of Guru and who has a very clear conscience, can be guided by the inner voice in matters of Dharma or duty or moral action. The inner voice that proceeds from a clean heart filled with Sattva is, indeed, the voice of God or Soul or Antaryamin or Inner Ruler. This voice is more than Smriti. It is Smriti of Smritis. Purify your heart and train yourself to hear this inner voice. Keep your ear in tune with the 'voice'.

***The Sruti and the Smriti*:** The Sruti and the Smriti are the two authoritative sources of Hinduism. *Sruti* literally means what is heard, and *Smriti* means what is remembered. Sruti is revelation and Smriti is tradition. Upanishad is a Sruti. Bhagwad Gita is a Smriti.

Sruti is direct experience. Great Rishis heard the eternal truths of religion and left a record of them for the benefit of posterity. These records constitute the Vedas. Hence, Sruti is primary authority. Smriti is a recollection of that experience. Hence, it is secondary authority. The Smritis or Dharma Shastras also are books written by sages, but they are not the final authority. If there is anything in a Smriti which contradicts the Sruti, the Smriti is to be rejected.

***The Itihasas***

***The Friendly Treatises and the Commanding Treatises*:** There are four books under this heading: The

Valmiki-Ramayana, the Yogavasishtha, The Mahabharata and the Harivamsa. These embody all that is in the Vedas, but only in a simpler manner. These are called the Suhrit-Samhitas or the Friendly Treatises, while the Vedas are called the Prabhu-Samhitas or the Commanding Treatises with great authority. These works explain the great universal truths in the form of historical narratives, stories and dialogues. These are very interesting volumes and are liked by all, from the inquisitive child to the intellectual scholar.

The Itihasas give us beautiful stories of absorbing interest and importance, through which all the fundamental teachings of Hinduism are indelibly impressed on one's mind. The laws of Smritis and the principles of the Vedas are stamped firmly on the minds of the Hindus through the noble and marvellous deeds of their great national heroes. We get a clear idea of Hinduism from these sublime stories.

The common man cannot comprehend the high abstract philosophy of the Upanishads and the Brahma Sutras. Hence, the compassionate sages Valmiki and Vyasa wrote the Itihasas for the benefit of common people. The same philosophy is presented with analogies and parables in a tasteful form to the common run of mankind.

The two well-known Itihasas (histories) are the epics (Mahakavyas), *Ramayana* and *Mahabharata*. They are two very popular and useful Shastras of the Hindus. The Ramayana was written by the sage Valmiki, and the Mahabharata by Vyasa.

***The Ramayana:*** The Ramayana, the Adi-Kavya or the first epic poem, relates the story of Sri Rama, the ideal man. It is the history of the family of the solar race descended from Ikshvaku, in which was born Sri Ramachandra, the Avatara of Lord Vishnu, and his three brothers. The ideal characters like Rama, Sita, Lakshmana, Bharata and Sri Hanuman that we find in Ramayana firmly establish Hindu Dharma in our minds. The story of the birth of Rama and his brothers, their education and marriages, the exile of Sri Rama, the carrying off and recovery of Sita, his wife, the destruction of Ravana, the Rakshasa King of Lanka, and the reign of Sri Rama, are described in detail in Ramayana. How a man should behave towards his superiors, equals and inferiors, how a king ought to rule his kingdom, how a man should lead his life in this world, how he can obtain his release, freedom and perfection, may be learnt from this excellent epic.

The Ramayana gives a vivid picture of Indian life. Even today our domestic, social and national ideals are copied from the noble characters in the Ramayana and the Mahabharata. The great national heroes stand even today as beacon-lights to guide and inspire the people of the whole world. The lives of Rama, Bharata and Lakshmana provide a model of fraternal affection and mutual service. Sri Hanuman stands as an ideal unique Karma Yogin. The life of Sita is regarded as the most perfect example of womanly fidelity, chastity and sweetness. The Ramayana is written in twenty-four thousand verses by Sri Valmiki.

***The Mahabharata*:** The Mahabharata is the history of the Pandavas and the Kauravas. It gives a description of the great war, the Battle of Kurukshetra, which broke out between the Kauravas and the Pandavas who were cousins and descendants of the lunar race. The Mahabharata is an encyclopaedia of Hindu Dharma. It is rightly called the fifth Veda. There is really no theme in religion, philosophy, mysticism and polity which this great epic does not touch and expound. It contains very noble moral teachings, useful lessons of all kinds, many beautiful stories and episodes, discourses, sermons, parables and dialogues which set forth the principles of morals and metaphysics. The Pandavas obtained victory through the grace of Lord Krishna. The Mahabharata is written in one hundred thousand verses by Sri Krishnadvaipayana Vyasa.

***The Bhagwad Gita*:** The most important part of the Mahabharata is the *Bhagwad Gita*. It is a marvellous dialogue between Lord Krishna and Arjuna on the battle-field, before the commencement of the great war. Bhagavan Sri Krishna became the charioteer of Arjuna. Sri Krishna explained the essentials of Hindu religion to Arjuna. Just as the Upanishads contain the cream of the Vedas, so does the Gita contain the cream of the Upanishads. The Upanishads are the cows. Lord

Krishna is the cowherd. Arjuna is the calf. The Gita is the milk. The wise men are those who drink the milk of the Gita.

The Gita is the most precious jewel of Hindu literature. It is a universal gospel. The Gita teaches the Yoga of Synthesis. It ranks high in the religious literature of the world.

Arjuna saw before him his dear relatives and teachers in the battle-field. He fainted and refused to fight against them. Then Lord Krishna imparted knowledge of the Self to Arjuna and convinced him that it was his duty to fight regardless of consequences. Afterwards Arjuna gave up his *Moha,* or delusion. All his doubts were cleared. He fought against the Kauravas and achieved victory.

***Knowledge of Ancient Indian History and Culture*:** The Mahabharata contains also the immortal discourse of Bhishma on Dharma, which he gave to Yudhishthira, when he was lying on the bed of arrows. The whole Mahabharata forms an encyclopaedia of history, morals and religion unsurpassed by any other epic in the world.

The Ramayana and the Mahabharata speak to us clearly about the ancient India, about her people, her customs, her ways of living, her arts, her civilisation and culture, her manufactures, etc. If you read these two books, you will come to know how great India once was, and you will be inspired to make her great once more. No other country has produced so many great men, great teachers, great Yogins, great Rishis, great prophets, great Acharyas, great kings, great heroes, great statesmen, great patriots and great benefactors, as India. The more you know of India and Hinduism, the more you will honour and love it and the more thankful to the Lord you will be that you were born in India as a Hindu. Glory to India! Glory to Hinduism! Glory to the seers of the Upanishads! Glory, glory to Lord Krishna, the author of the Song Divine!

## *The Puranas*

The Puranas are of the same class as the Itihasas. They have five characteristics *(Pancha-Lakshana) viz.*, history, cosmology (with various symbolical illustrations of philosophical principles), secondary creation, genealogy of kings and of

Manvantaras. All the Puranas belong to the class of Suhrit-Samhitas.

Vyasa is the compiler of the Puranas from age to age; and for this age, he is Krishnadvaipayana, the son of Parasara.

The Puranas were written to popularise the religion of the Vedas. They contain the essence of the Vedas. The aim of the Puranas is to impress on the minds of the masses the teachings of the Vedas and to generate in them devotion to God, through concrete examples, myths, stories, legends, lives of saints, kings and great men, allegories and chronicles of great historical events. The sages made use of these things to illustrate the eternal principles of religion. The Puranas were meant, not for the scholars, but for the ordinary people who could not understand high philosophy and who could not study the Vedas.

The Darshanas are very stiff. They are meant only for the learned few. The Puranas are meant for the masses with inferior intellect. Religion is taught in a very easy and interesting way through these Puranas. Even to this day, the Puranas are popular. The Puranas contain the history of remote times. They also give a description of the regions of the universe not visible to the ordinary physical eye. They are very interesting to read and are full of information of all kinds. Children hear the stories from their grandmothers. Pundits and Purohits hold Kathas in temples, on banks of rivers and in other important places. Agriculturists, labourers and bazaar people hear the stories.

***The Eighteen Puranas*:** There are eighteen main Puranas and an equal number of subsidiary Puranas or Upa-Puranas. The main Puranas are: Vishnu Purana, Naradiya Purana, Srimad Bhagavata Purana, Garuda (Suparna) Purana, Padma Purana, Varaha Purana, Brahma Purana, Brahmanda Purana, Brahma Vaivarta Purana, Markandeya Purana, Bhavishya Purana, Vamana Purana, Matsya Purana, Kurma Purana, Linga Purana, Shiva Purana, Skanda Purana and Agni Purana. Of these, six are Sattvic Puranas and glorify Vishnu; six are Rajasic and glorify Brahma; six are Tamasic and they glorify Shiva.

Neophytes or beginners in the spiritual Path are puzzled when they go through Shiva Purana and Vishnu Purana. In Shiva Purana, Lord Shiva is highly eulogised and an inferior position is given to Lord Vishnu. Sometimes Vishnu is belittled. In Vishnu Purana, Lord Hari is highly eulogised and an inferior status is given to Lord Shiva. Sometimes Lord Shiva is belittled. This is only to increase the faith of the devotees in their particular Ishta-Devata. Lord Shiva and Lord Vishnu are one.

The best among the Puranas are the Srimad Bhagavata and the Vishnu Purana. The most popular is the Srimad Bhagavata Purana. Next comes Vishnu Purana. A portion of the Markandeya Purana is well known to all Hindus as *Chandi,* or Devimahatmya. Worship of God as the Divine Mother is its theme. Chandi is read widely by the Hindus on sacred days and Navaratri (Durga Puja) days.

***The Srimad Bhagavata Purana and the Ten Avataras*:** The Srimad Bhagavata Purana is a chronicle of the various Avataras of Lord Vishnu. There are ten Avataras of Vishnu. The aim of every Avatara is to save the world from some great danger, to destroy the wicked and protect the virtuous. The ten Avataras are: Matsya (The Fish), Kurma (The Tortoise), Varaha (The Boar), Narasimha (The Man-Lion), Vamana (The Dwarf), Parasurama (Rama with the axe, the destroyer of the Kshatriya race), Ramachandra (The hero of Ramayana—the son of Dasaratha), who destroyed Ravana, Sri Krishna, The teacher of the Gita, Buddha (The prince-ascetic, founder of Buddhism) and Kalki (The hero riding on a white horse, who is to come at the end of the Kali-Yuga).

The object of the Matsya Avatara was to save Vaivasvata Manu from destruction by a deluge. The object of Kurma Avatara was to enable the world to recover some precious things which were lost in the deluge. The Kurma gave its back for keeping the churning rod when the Gods and the Asuras churned the ocean of milk. The purpose of Varaha Avatara was to rescue, from the waters, the earth which had been dragged down by a demon named Hiranyaksha. The purpose of Narasimha Avatara, half-lion and half-man, was to free the world from the oppression of Hiranyakasipu, a demon, the father of Bhakta

Prahlada. The object of Vamana Avatara was to restore the power of the gods which had been eclipsed by the penance and devotion of King Bali. The object of Parasurama Avatara was to deliver the country from the oppression of the Kshatriya rulers. Parasurama destroyed the Kshatriya race twenty-one times.

The object of Rama was to destroy the wicked Ravana. The object of Sri Krishna Avatara was to destroy Kamsa and other demons, to deliver His wonderful message of the Gita in the Mahabharata war, and to become the centre of the Bhakti schools of India. The object of Buddha Avatara was to prohibit animal sacrifices and teach piety. The object of the Kalki Avatara is the destruction of the wicked and the re-establishment of virtue.

***The Tamil Puranas*:** Lord Shiva incarnated himself in the form of Dakshinamurti to impart knowledge to the four Kumaras. He took human form to initiate Sambandhar, Manikkavasagar, Pattinathar. He appeared in flesh and blood to help his devotees and relieve their sufferings. The divine Lilas of Lord Shiva are recorded in the Tamil Puranas like Shiva Purana, Periya Purana, Shiva Parakramam and Tiruvilayadal Purana.

***The Upa-Puranas*:** The eighteen Upa-Puranas are: Sanatkumara, Narasimha, Brihannaradiya, Shivarahasya, Durvasa, Kapila, Vamana, Bhargava, Varuna, Kalika, Samba, Nandi, Surya, Parasara, Vasishtha, Devi-Bhagavata, Ganesha and Hamsa.

***Utility of the Puranas*:** Study of the Puranas, listening to sacred recitals of scriptures, describing and expounding of the transcendent Lilas of the Blessed Lord—these form an important part of Sadhana of the Lord's devotees. It is most pleasing to the Lord. *Sravana* is a part of *Navavidha-Bhakti. Kathas* and *Upanyasas* open the springs of devotion in the hearts of hearers and develop *Prema-Bhakti* which confers immortality on the *Jiva*.

The language of the Vedas is archaic, and the subtle philosophy of Vedanta and the Upanishads is extremely difficult to grasp and assimilate. Hence, the Puranas are of special value as they present philosophical truths and precious teachings in an easier manner. They give ready access to the mysteries of life and the key to bliss. Imbibe their teachings. Start a new life of Dharma-Nishtha and Adhyatmic Sadhana from this very day.

### *The Agamas*

Another class of popular scriptures are the Agamas. The Agamas are theological treatises and practical manuals of divine worship. The Agamas include the Tantras, Mantras and Yantras. These are treatises explaining the external worship of God, in idols, temples, etc. All the Agamas treat of (i) *Jnana* or Knowledge, (ii) *Yoga* or Concentration, (iii) *Kriya* or Esoteric Ritual and (iv) *Charya* or Exoteric Worship. They also give elaborate details about ontology and cosmology, liberation, devotion, meditation, philosophy of *Mantras,* mystic diagrams, charms and spells, temple-building, image-making, domestic observances, social rules, public festivals, etc.

The Agamas are divided into three sections: The *Vaishnava,* the *Shaiva* and the *Shakta.* The three chief sects of Hinduism, *viz.*, Vaishnavism, Shaivism and Shaktism, base their doctrines and dogmas on their respective Agamas. The Vaishnava Agamas or Pancharatra Agamas glorify God as Vishnu. The Shaiva Agamas glorify God as Shiva and have given rise to an important school of philosophy known as Shaiva-Siddhanta, which prevails in South India, particularly in the districts of Tirunelveli and Madurai. The Shakta Agamas or Tantras glorify God as the Mother of the Universe, under one of the many names of *Devi.*

The Agamas do not derive their authority from the Vedas, but are not antagonistic to them. They are all Vedic in spirit and character. That is the reason why they are regarded as authoritative.

***The Vaishnava Agamas*:** The Vaishnava Agamas are of four kinds: the Vaikhanasa, Pancharatra, Pratishthasara and Vijnanalalita. The Brahma, Shaiva Kaumara, Vasishtha, Kapila, Gautamiya and the Naradiya are the seven groups of the Pancharatras. The Naradiya section of the Santi-Parva of the

Mahabharata is the earliest source of information about the Pancharatras.

Vishnu is the Supreme Lord in the Pancharatra Agamas. The Vaishnavas regard the Pancharatra Agamas to be the most authoritative. They believe that these Agamas were revealed by Lord Vishnu Himself. Narada-Pancharatra says: "Everything from Brahma to a blade of grass is Lord Krishna." This corresponds to the Upanishadic declaration: "All this is, verily, Brahman—*Sarvam Khalvidam Brahma.*"

There are two hundred and fifteen of these Vaishnava texts. Isvara, Ahirbudhnya, Paushkara, Parama, Sattvata, Brihad-Brahma and Jnanamritasara Samhitas are the important ones.

***The Shaiva Agamas*:** The Shaivas recognise twenty-eight Agamas, of which the chief is Kamika. The Agamas are also the basis of Kashmir Shaivism which is called the Pratyabhijna system. The latter works of Pratyabhijna system show a distinct leaning to Advaitism. The Southern Shaivism, *i.e.*, Shaiva Siddhanta and the Kashmir Shaivism, regard these Agamas as their authority, besides the Vedas. Each Agama has Upa-Agamas. Of these, only fragmentary texts of twenty are extant. Lord Shiva is the central God in the Shaiva Agamas. They are suitable to this age, Kali Yoga. They are open to all castes and both the sexes.

***The Shakta Agamas*:** There is another group of scriptures known as the *Tantras.* They belong to the Shakta cult. They glorify Shakti as the World-Mother. They dwell on the Shakti (energy) aspect of God and prescribe numerous courses of ritualistic worship of the Divine Mother in various forms. There are seventy-seven Agamas. These are very much like the Puranas in some respects. The texts are usually in the form of dialogues between Shiva and Parvati. In some of these, Shiva answers the questions put by Parvati, and in others, Parvati answers, Shiva questioning. Mahanirvana, Kularnava, Kulasara, Prapanchasara, Tantraraja, Rudra-Yamala, Brahma-Yamala, Vishnu-Yamala and Todala Tantra are the important works. The Agamas teach several occult practices some of which confer powers, while the others bestow knowledge and freedom. Shakti is the creative power of Lord Shiva. Shaktism is really a supplement to Shaivism.

Among the existing books on the Agamas, the most famous are the Isvara-Samhita, Ahirbudhnya-Samhita, Sanatkumara-Samhita, Narada-Pancharatra, Spanda-Pradipika and the Mahanirvana-Tantra.

### *The Six Darshanas*

These are the intellectual section of the Hindu writings, while the first four are intuitional, and the fifth inspirational and emotional. Darshanas are schools of philosophy based on the Vedas. The Agamas are theological. The Darshana literature is philosophical. The Darshanas are meant for the erudite scholars who are endowed with acute acumen, good understanding, power of reasoning and subtle intellect. The Itihasas, Puranas and Agamas are meant for the masses. The Darshanas appeal to the intellect, while the Itihasas, Puranas, etc., appeal to the heart.

Philosophy has six divisions—*Shad-Darshana*—the six Darshanas or ways of seeing things, usually called the six systems or six different schools of thought. The six schools of philosophy are the six instruments of true teaching or the six demonstrations of Truth. Each school has developed, systematised and correlated the various parts of the Veda in its own way. Each system has its *Sutrakara*, *i.e.*, the one great Rishi who systematised the doctrines of the school and put them in short aphorisms or Sutras.

The Sutras are terse and laconic. The Rishis have condensed their thoughts in the aphorisms. It is very difficult to understand them without the help of commentaries by great sages or Rishis. Hence, there arose many commentators or *Bhashyakaras*. There are glosses, notes and, later, commentaries on the original commentaries.

The Shad-Darshanas (the six schools of philosophy) or the Shat-Shastras are: the NYAYA, founded by Gautama Rishi, the VAISESHIKA by Kanada Rishi, the SANKHYA by Kapila Muni, the YOGA by Patanjali Maharshi, the PURVA MIMAMSA by

Jaimini, and the UTTARA MIMAMSA or VEDANTA by Badarayana or Vyasa. The Darshanas are divided into three pairs of aphoristic compositions which explain the philosophy of the Vedas in a rationalistic method of approach. They are: the Nyaya and the Vaiseshika, the Sankhya and the Yoga, and the Mimamsa and the Vedanta. Each set of Sutras has got its *Bhashya, Vritti, Varttika, Vyakhyana* or *Tika* and *Tippani.*

***Sutra***

*Svalpaksharam-asandigdham*
*Saravad-visvatomukham*
*Astobham-anavadyam cha*
*Sutram sutravido viduh*

A Sutra or an aphorism is a short formula with the least possible number of letters, without any ambiguity or doubtful assertion, containing the very essence, embracing all meanings, without any stop or obstruction and absolutely faultless in nature.

The Sutrakara or the composer of the aphorisms is said to be as happy as one would be while getting the first male child, if he is but able to reduce one letter in his abstruse Sutra of far-fetched words and ideas. The best example of the greatest, the tersest and the most perfect of Sutra literature is the series of aphorisms called the *Ashtadhyayi* composed by Panini. Panini is the father of all Sutrakaras from whom all others seem to have borrowed the method of composition.

The Sutras are meant to explain a big volume of knowledge in short assertions suitable to be kept in memory at all times. The six Vedangas and the six systems of Hindu philosophy form the twelve sets of Sutra literature of the world. In addition to these, there are later compositions like the Narada-Bhakti Sutras, the Sandilya-Bhakti Sutras, etc., which also wish to assume an equal form with the famous Sutras mentioned above.

***Bhashya***

*Sutrartho varnyate yatra*
*Padaih sutranusaribhih*
*Svapadani cha varnyante*
*Bhashyam bhashyavido viduh*

A Bhashya is an elaborate exposition, a commentary on the Sutras, with word by word meaning of the aphoristic precepts, their running translation, together with the individual views of the commentator or the Bhashyakara. The best and the exemplary Bhashya in Sanskrit literature is the one written by Patanjali on the Vyakarana Sutras of Panini.

This Bhashya is so very famous and important that it is called the MAHABHASHYA and its celebrated author is specially called the BHASHYAKARA. Patanjali is the father of Bhashyakaras. The next important Bhashya is the one on the Mimamsa Sutras written by Sabara-Swamin who learnt the art from Patanjali's commentary.

The third important Bhashya was written by Shankara on the Brahma Sutras, in close following with the Sabara-Bhashya. The Bhashyas on the six sets of aphorisms dealing with Indian philosophy were written by Vatsyayana, Prasastapada, Vijnanabhikshu, Vyasa, Sabara and Shankara. On the Vedanta or Brahma Sutras, there are about sixteen Bhashyas, like those of Ramanuja, Madhva, Vallabha, Nimbarka, etc.

***Vritti***

*Sadvrittih sannibandhana*

A Vritti is a short gloss explaining the aphorisms in a more elaborate way, but not as extensively as a Bhashya. An example is Bodhayana's Vritti on the Brahma Sutras.

***Varttika***

*Uktanuktaduruktanam*
*Chinta yatra pravartate*
*Tam grantham varttikam prahuh*
*Varttikajnavichakshanah*

A Varttika is a work where a critical study is made of that which is said and left unsaid or imperfectly said in a Bhashya, and the ways of making it perfect by supplying the omissions therein, are given. Examples are the Varttikas of Katyayana on Panini's Sutras, of Suresvara on Shankara's Upanishad-Bhashyas, and of Kumarila Bhatta on the Sabara-Bhashya on the Karma-Mimamsa.

***Vyakhyana or Tika***: A Vyakhyana is a running explanation in an easier language of what is said in the original, with little elucidations here and there. A Vyakhyana, particularly of a Kavya, deals with eight different modes of dissection of the Sloka, like Pada-Chheda, Vigraha, Sandhi, Alankara, Anuvada, etc. This forms an important aspect in the study of Sanskrit Sahitya Shastra. An Anu-Vyakhyana—like the one written by Sri Madhva—is a repetition of what is already written, but in greater detail. An Anuvada is merely a running translation or statement of an abstruse text of the original. Tika is only another name for Vyakhyana. The best Vyakhyanas are of Vachaspati Mishra on the Darshanas, especially on Shankara's Brahmasutra-Bhashya.

***Tippani***: Tippani is just like a Vritti, but is less orthodox than the Vritti. It is an explanation of difficult words or phrases occurring in the original. Examples are Kaiyata's gloss on the Mahabhashya of Patanjali, Nagojibhatta's gloss on Kaiyata's gloss, or Appayya's gloss on Amalananda's gloss on the Bhamati of Vachaspati Mishra.

### *Other Scriptures*

The Tevaram and the Tiruvachakam which are the hymns of the Shaiva saints of South India, the Divya-Prabandham of the Alwar saints of South India, the songs of Kabir, the Abhangas of Tukaram and the Ramayana of Tulasi Das—all of which are the outpourings of great realised souls—are wonderful scriptures. They contain the essence of the Vedas.

### *The Secular Writings*

***The Subhashitas***: The Subhashitas are wise sayings, instructions and stories, either in poetry or in prose. Examples are Bhartrihari's three centuries of verses, the Subhashita-Ratna-Bhandagara and Somadeva Bhatta's Katha-Sarit-Sagara or Kshemendra's Brihat-Katha-Manjari. The Panchatantra and the Hitopadesa also belong to this category.

***The Kavyas***: These are highly scholarly compositions in poetry, prose or both. The greatest of poetical Kavyas are those of Kalidas *(The Raghuvamsa* and *Kumarasambhava),* Bharavi

*(The Kiratarjuniya),* Magha *(The Sisupalavadha),* Sri Harsha *(The Naishadha).* The best prose Kavyas in the whole of Sanskrit literature were written by Bhattabana *(The Kadambari* and *Harshacharita),* the great genius in classical Sanskrit. Among those containing both poetry and prose, the Champu-Ramayana and the Champu-Bharata are most famous. These are all wonderful masterpieces which will ever remain to glorify India's literary calibre.

***The Natakas*:** These are marvellously scholastic dramas embodying the *Rasas* of Sringara, Vira, Karuna, Adbhuta, Hasya, Bhayanaka, Bibhatsa and Raudra. It is told that none can write on the ninth Rasa, *viz.*, Santi. It is attainable only on final Liberation. The best dramas are written by Kalidasa *(Sakuntala),* Bhavabhuti *(Uttara-Rama-Charita),* and Visakhadatta *(Mudrarakshasa).*

***The Alankaras*:** These are grand rhetorical texts, treating of the science of perfection and beauty of ornamental language and of effective composition with elegance and force, both in poetry and in prose. These are the fundamentals of Sanskrit Sahitya, even superior to the Kavyas and the Natakas. The best Alankara-Granthas are those of Mammata *(Kavyaprakasa)* and Jagannath *(Rasagangadhara).*

### *Conclusion*

These constitute the entirety of Sanskrit literature—sacred and secular. The Sruti is the root; the Smritis, Itihasas and Puranas are the trunk; the Agamas and Darshanas are the branches; and the Subhashitas, Kavyas, Natakas and Alankaras are the flowers of the tree of India's Culture.

The Smritis, the Itihasas, the Puranas, the Agamas and the Darshanas are only developments of the Veda. Their ultimate source is the Veda. Their one common aim is to enable man to annihilate his ignorance and attain perfection, freedom, immortality and eternal bliss through knowledge of God or the Eternal. Their purpose is to make man like God and one with Him.

# 2

# Hindu Dharma

Silent adorations to the Lord, the Embodiment of Dharma, the Controller and Protector of Dharma and the Fountain-head of Dharma. What is Dharma? Dharma is so called, because it *holds;* Dharma alone holds the people, etc. The word *Dharma* is derived from the root *Dhr*—to hold—and its etymological meaning is 'that which holds' this world, or the people of the world, or the whole creation from the microcosm to the macrocosm. It is the eternal Divine Law of the Lord. The entire creation is held together and sustained by the All-powerful Law of God. Practice of Dharma, therefore, means recognition of this Law and abidence by it.

That which brings well-being to man is Dharma. Dharma supports this world. The people are upheld by Dharma. That which secures preservation of beings is Dharma. Dharma leads to eternal happiness and immortality. That which is Dharma is verily the Truth. Therefore, whosoever speaks the truth is said to speak Dharma, and whosoever speaks Dharma is said to speak the truth. One and the same thing becomes both. Dharma includes all external deeds, as well as thoughts and other mental practices which tend to elevate the character of man. Dharma comes from the Divine and leads you to the Divine.

## Definition of Dharma

No language is perfect. There is no proper equivalent word in English for the Sanskrit term *Dharma.* It is very difficult to define Dharma. Dharma is generally defined as 'righteousness' or 'duty.' Dharma is the principle of righteousness. It is the principle of holiness. It is also the principle of unity. Bhishma says in his instructions to Yudhishthira that whatever creates conflict is Adharma, and whatever puts an end to conflict and brings about unity and harmony is Dharma. Anything that helps to unite all and develop pure divine love and universal brotherhood, is Dharma.

Anything that creates discord, split and disharmony and foments hatred, is Adharma. Dharma is the cementer and sustainer of social life. The rules of Dharma have been laid down for regulating the worldly affairs of men. Dharma brings as its consequence happiness, both in this world and in the next. Dharma is the means of preserving one's self. If you transgress it, it will kill you. If you protect it, it will protect you. It is your sole companion after death. It is the sole refuge of humanity.

That which elevates one is Dharma. This is another definition. Dharma is that which leads you to the path of perfection and glory. Dharma is that which helps you to have direct communion with the Lord. Dharma is that which makes you divine. Dharma is the ascending stairway unto God. Self-realisation is the highest Dharma. Dharma is the heart of Hindu ethics. God is the centre of Dharma.

Dharma means *Achara* or the regulation of daily life. Achara is the supreme Dharma. It is the basis of Tapas or austerity. It leads to wealth, beauty, longevity and continuity of lineage. Evil conduct and immorality will lead to ill-fame, sorrow, disease and premature death. Dharma has its root in morality and the controller of Dharma is God Himself.

Maharshi Jaimini defines Dharma as that which is enjoined by the Vedas and is not ultimately productive of suffering.

Rishi Kanada, founder of the Vaiseshika system of philosophy, has given the best definition of Dharma, in his Vaiseshika Sutras: *"Yato-bhyudayanihsreyasa-siddhih sa dharmah."* "That which leads to the attainment of *Abhyudaya* (prosperity in this world) and *Nihsreyasa* (total cessation of pain and attainment of eternal bliss hereafter) is Dharma."

### *The Sole Authority of the Vedas*

The four Vedas, the Smriti texts, the behaviour of those who have entered into their spirit and act according to their injunctions, the conduct of holy men and satisfaction of one's own self—these are the bases of Dharma, according to Manu.

In the matter of Dharma, the Vedas are the ultimate authority. You cannot know the truth about Dharma through any source of knowledge other than the Vedas. Reason cannot be the authority in the matter of Dharma. Among the scriptures of the world, the Vedas are the oldest. This is supported by all leading scholars and antiquarians of the entire civilised world. They all declare with one voice, that of all books so far written in any human language, the Rig-Veda Samhita is undoubtedly the oldest. No antiquarian has been able to fix the date when the Rig-Veda Samhita was composed or came to light.

## The Changing Dharma

Just as a doctor prescribes different medicines for different people according to their constitution and the nature of their disease, so also Hinduism prescribes different duties for different people. Rules for women are different from the rules for men. The rules for different Varnas and Ashramas vary. But, non-violence, truth, non-stealing, cleanliness and control of the senses, are the duties common to all men.

Dharma depends upon time, circumstances, age, degree of evolution and the community to which one belongs. The Dharma of this century is different from that of the tenth century.

There are conditions under which Dharma may change its usual course. Apad-Dharma is such a deviation from the usual practice. This is allowed only in times of extreme distress or calamity.

What is Dharma in one set of circumstances becomes Adharma in another set of circumstances. That is the reason why it is said that the secret of Dharma is extremely profound and subtle. Lord Krishna says in the Gita: "Let the scriptures be the authority in determining what ought to be done and what ought not to be done" (Ch. XVI, 24). The truth of Dharma lies hidden. Srutis and Smritis are many. The way of Dharma open to all is that which a great realised soul has traversed.

### *Dharma in Other Religions*

All other religions also lay stress on Dharma. Buddhism, Jainism, Christianity, Sikhism, Zoroastrianism, Islam are all remarkably alive to its value. Plato, Socrates, Aristotle, Kant, Swedenborg and Spinoza are all striking examples in the interesting history of Western philosophy for the high pedestal on which they have placed morality, duty and righteousness, and adored them all as the only means to the attainment of the goal of life. Each religion lays greater stress on certain aspects of Dharma.

## Benefits of the Practice of Dharma

Of the four grand objects of human aspiration—*Purusharthas—viz.*, Dharma, Artha, Kama and Moksha, *Dharma* is given the foremost rank in the scriptures. Dharma alone is the gateway to Moksha, to immortality, infinite bliss, supreme peace and highest knowledge. Dharma alone is the primary Purushartha. Dharma is the first and foremost Purushartha. Through the practice of Dharma alone can you ever hope to achieve the crowning glory of all human endeavours, *viz.*, Moksha which is the best and the highest of all desirable things.

Practice of Dharma leads to the perfect realisation of essential unity or the final end, the highest good, namely, Moksha. The practitioner experiences peace, joy, strength and tranquillity within himself. His life becomes thoroughly disciplined. His powers and capacities are exceedingly intensified. He realises that there is one underlying homogeneous essence, a living truth, behind these names and forms. He is transmuted into divinity. His whole nature gets transformed. He becomes one with the Eternal. He beholds Brahman above, Brahman below, Brahman to the right, Brahman to the left, Brahman in front, Brahman at the back, Brahman within, Brahman without and Brahman pervading the whole world.

### *Kinds of Dharma*

Dharma can be classified under two heads: (i) *Samanya* or the general, universal Dharma and (ii) *Visesha* or the specific, personal Dharma. Contentment, forgiveness, self-restraint, non-stealing, purity, control of senses, discrimination between right and wrong, between the real and the unreal, spiritual knowledge, truthfulness and absence of anger come under the general or universal Dharma. The rules of the castes and orders of life are specific Dharmas. These are the tenfold characteristics of Dharma according to Manu.

Dharma assumes various kinds: Sanatana Dharma (Eternal Law), Samanya Dharma (general duty), Visesha Dharma (special duty), Varnashrama Dharma (duties of Caste and Order), Svadharma (one's own duty), Yuga Dharma (duty of the Age), Kula Dharma (duty of family), Manava Dharma (duty of man), Purusha Dharma (duty of male), Stri Dharma (duty of female), Raja Dharma (duty of king), Praja Dharma (duty of subjects), Pravritti Dharma (duty in worldly life) and Nivritti Dharma (duty in spiritual life).

## Sanatana Dharma

Sanatana Dharma means the Eternal Religion, the Ancient Law. This is based on the Vedas. This is the oldest of living religions. Hinduism is known by the name Sanatana Dharma. What the Vedas alone declare to be the means of attaining the *summum bonum* or the final emancipation, is the Sanatana Dharma or Hindu Dharma.

The foundation of Sanatana Dharma is Sruti; Smritis are the walls; the Itihasas and Purnas are the buttresses or supports. In ancient times, the Srutis were learnt by heart. The teacher sang them to his pupils and the pupils sang them after him. They were not written in book form. All the sects, all the philosophical systems, appeal to the Sruti as the final authority. The Smriti stands next in authority to the Sruti.

Hinduism stands unrivalled in the depth and grandeur of its philosophy. Its ethical teachings are lofty, unique and sublime. It is highly flexible and adapted to every human need.

It is a perfect religion by itself. It is not in need of anything from any other religion. No other religion has produced so many great saints, great patriots, great warriors and great Pativratas. The more you know of it, the more you will honour and love it. The more you study it, the more it will enlighten you and satisfy your heart.

### *India—The Home of Religions*

The religious history of the world tells us that from time immemorial, India has been the home of great sages, seers and Rishis. All the grand religious ideals that have moulded the character of men, the loftiest of ethics and morality that have raised human beings to magnanimous heights of divine splendour and all the sublime truths of spirituality that have made men divine and have moulded the spiritual ideals of nations and saviours of mankind, first arose in India.

The spiritual horizon of India has always been illumined with the glory of the self-effulgent sun of wisdom of the Upanishads. Whenever there was any upheaval in any part of the world, the origin of this could be traced to the wave of spirituality caused by the birth of a great soul—a special manifestation of Divinity—in some part of India.

Hindus have had a culture, civilisation and religion millennia older than those of any other country or people. God did speak to the world through India's Rishis, Yogins, Mahatmas, Alvars, prophets, Acharyas, Sannyasins and saints. Their teachings and Puranas are really inspired. God is the one Light and Truth from whom emanate the teachings of all faiths.

India is the home and abode of religions. It occupies the proud first place in religious devotion and godliness. It is famous for its Yogins and saints. The goal of India is Self-realisation or attainment of God-consciousness, through renunciation. The history of India is a history of religion. Its social code and regulations are founded upon religion. Minus its Yoga, religion and its regulations, India will not be what it has been for millennia. Some Hindus are still not aware of the distinguishing features of Sanatana Dharma. If every Hindu knew and understood what Hinduism is, the Hindus of today would all be gods on this earth. May you all be endowed with the knowledge of Sanatana Dharma!

May you all endeavour to protect the Eternal Dharma! May the secrets of Sanatana Dharma be revealed unto you all, like a fruit in the palm of your hand, through the Grace of the Lord! May the blessings of Rishis be upon you all! Glory to the Vedas and Sanatana Dharma! Glory to Brahman, the source for all Vedas and Sanatana Dharma!

### *Samanya Dharma*

Every religion has a generic form or *Samanya-Rupa* and a specific form or *Visesha-Rupa.* The general form remains eternally the same. It is never changed by any circumstance whatsoever. It is not affected at all by changes of time, place, surroundings and individual differences. This aspect of religion is called Sanatana or eternal. That which changes according to the change of time, place and surrounding circumstances is the external aspect or ritual, of Dharma.

Samanya Dharma is the general Dharma or law for all men. Varnashrama Dharmas are special Dharmas which are to be practised by particular castes and by men in particular stages of life. The Samanya Dharmas must be practised by all, irrespective of distinctions of Varna and Ashrama, creed or colour. Goodness is not the property of any one class, creed, sect or community. Every man should possess this virtue.

## Fundamentals of Dharma

The Vishnu Samhita enumerates forgiveness, truthfulness, control of the mind, purity, practice of charity, control of the senses, non-violence, service of the Guru, visiting places of pilgrimage, compassion, simplicity, absence of greed, worship of the gods and the Brahmanas, and absence of malice as the ingredients of Samanya Dharma, the general law for all men.

The Mahabharata enumerates the performance of Shradha or offering oblations to the forefathers, religious austerity, truth, restraint of anger, satisfaction with one's own wife, purity, learning, absence of envy, knowledge of the Self and forbearance as the fundamentals of Dharma.

It is said in Padma Purana that Dharma proceeds from continence, truthfulness, austerity, charity, self-control, forbearance, purity, non-violence, serenity and non-thieving and that one should recognise Dharma by these ten factors. According to this Purana, bestowing gifts on deserving persons, fixing one's thoughts on Lord Krishna, adoration of one's parents, offering a portion of the daily meal to all creatures and giving a morsel of food to a cow are the characteristics of Dharma.

According to Matsya Purana, freedom from malice, absence of covetousness, control of the senses, austerity, celibacy, compassion, truthfulness, forbearance and fortitude constitute the fundamentals of Sanatana Dharma.

Patanjali Maharshi, the exponent of Raja Yoga philosophy, recommends that ten virtues should be practised by all men. The first five are: Ahimsa (non-violence), Satya (truthfulness), Brahmacharya (celibacy in thought, word and deed), Asteya (non-stealing) and Aparigraha (non-covetousness). These constitute Yama or self-restraint. The other five virtues are: Saucha (internal and external purity), Santosha (contentment), Tapas (austerity), Svadhyaya (study of scriptures or recitation of Mantra) and Isvara-pranidhana (consecration of the fruits of all works to the Lord). These constitute Niyama or religious observance.

The Gita enumerates the following virtues as Daivi-Sampat or divine qualities: fearlessness, cleanness of life, steadfastness in the Yoga of Wisdom, alms-giving, self-restraint, sacrifice, study of the scriptures, austerity, straightforwardness, harmlessness, truth, absence of wrath, renunciation, peacefulness, absence of crookedness, compassion to living beings, non-covetousness, mildness, modesty, absence of fickleness, vigour, forgiveness, fortitude, purity and absence of envy and pride. All these virtues are manifestations of the four fundamental virtues: (i) non-violence, (ii) truth, (iii) purity and (iv) self-control. All the above virtues come under the above four cardinal virtues. The virtues that are enumerated under the Noble Eightfold Path of Buddhism and the virtues prescribed by Lord Jesus in his Sermon on the Mount, also come under the above fundamental virtues.

The development of the divine qualities is indispensable for the attainment of Self-realisation. Brahman or the Eternal is purity. The Eternal cannot be attained without the attainment of purity. Brahman is truth. The Eternal cannot be attained without practising truth. Brahman is fearlessness. The Eternal cannot be attained unless you become absolutely fearless. Attachment to the body causes fear and Dehadhyasa. If only you become fearless, then the identification with the body will vanish.

You have rendered the heart harder than flint, steel or diamond through greed, miserliness, harshness and rudeness. You can soften it only through the practice of mercy, sympathy, charity, generosity, magnanimity, harmlessness, mildness, disinterested action and untiring service of the poor. You have made the heart crooked and narrow through hypocrisy, untruthfulness, backbiting and talebearing. You can expand it through the practice of straightforwardness, truthfulness, cleanness of life, alms-giving and non-covetousness. You have rendered the heart impure through lust. You can purify it through the practice of celibacy in thought, word and deed.

***Non-violence*:** Ahimsa or non-violence is the most important virtue. That is the reason why Patanjali Maharshi has placed it first in Yama. Practice of Ahimsa must be in thought, word and deed. Practice of Ahimsa is not impotence or cowardice or weakness. It is the highest type of heroism. The practice demands immense patience, forbearance and endurance, infinite inner spiritual strength and gigantic will-power.

Ahimsa is a modification or expression of truth only. Satyam and Ahimsa always go together. He who is established in Ahimsa can move the whole world. In his presence, all hostilities vanish; lion and cow, cobra and mongoose, live together peacefully. Hinduism, Buddhism and Jainism lay great stress on Ahimsa. Lord Jesus also has emphasised much on Ahimsa in his Sermon on the Mount. He says: "If anyone beats you on one cheek, show him the other cheek also."

He who is firmly established in Ahimsa can hope to attain Self-realisation. He who practises Ahimsa develops cosmic love to a maximum degree. Practice of Ahimsa eventually leads to realisation of oneness or unity of Self. Such a man only can attain self-restraint. Retaliation—tooth for tooth, blow for blow—is the maxim, doctrine or principle of an Asura or a man of diabolic nature. This belongs to the beastly nature. To return good for evil is divine. Constant vigilance and alertness are needed in the practice of Ahimsa. If you are careless even a bit, you will be carried away by the force of previous wrong Samskaras and impulses and will become a victim of Himsa, despite your good intentions.

***Truth***: Brahman is Sat or Existence-Absolute. Truth must be observed in thought, word and deed. If you are established in truth, all other virtues will cling to you by themselves. Harischandra sacrificed everything for the sake of truth. He lives still in our hearts. Yudhishthira was also devoted to truth. There is no virtue higher than truth. Practice of truth and Ahimsa constitute the crown and glory of ethical life. In the Taittiriya Upanishad, the preceptor says in his convocation address to the students: "*Satyam vada*—Speak the truth." The world is rooted in truth. Dharma is rooted in truth. All religions are rooted in truth. Honesty, justice, straightforwardness and sincerity are only modifications or expressions of truth.

***Purity***: Purity comprises both external purity and internal purity. Purity implies both purity of body and purity of mind. Purity of body is only the preliminary to purity of mind.

This body is the temple of God. It should be kept clean by daily bathing and clean dress. Cleanliness is a part of godliness.

The restriction in diet is best calculated to make the mind pure. Food exercises a direct influence on the mind.

Sattvic food makes the mind pure. Purity of food leads to purity of mind. Mind is only made up of the fine essence of food. As the food is, so is the mind.

You must be pure in thought, word and deed. Your heart must be as pure as crystal or the Himalayan snow. Then only the divine light will descend. Purity comprises such virtues as frankness, innocence, straightforwardness and absence of all evil thoughts. He who is endowed with purity will find it easy to tread the spiritual path.

***Self-control***: You must have perfect self-control or self-mastery. Self-control implies both control of the body and control of the mind. Self-control does not mean self-torture. You must lead a well-regulated and disciplined life. You must keep all the senses under your perfect control. The senses are like turbulent and wild horses. This body is like a chariot. Mind is the reins. Intellect is the driver.

The Atman is the Lord of the chariot. If the senses are not kept under proper control, they will throw this chariot into a deep abyss. You will come to ruin. He who keeps the reins firm and drives this chariot intelligently by controlling the horses (senses), will reach the destination (Moksha or the Abode of Eternal Bliss) safely.

Self-control implies self-sacrifice, annihilation of egoism, patience, endurance, forbearance and humility. Overcome Raga or attachment by Vairagya or dispassion. Dispassion will dawn in your mind if you look into the defects of sensual life such as birth, death, disease, old age, pain, sorrow, etc. (Mithya-Drishti and Dosha-Drishti). Overcome anger and hatred by Kshama or forgiveness, love and selfless service. Overcome evil by good. Return good for evil. Overcome lust by the practice of Brahmacharya and regular Japa and meditation. Conquer greed by charity, generosity and disinterested actions. Conquer pride by humility and delusion by discrimination and enquiry. Overcome jealousy by magnanimity, Atma-bhava and nobility. Conquer egoism by self-sacrifice, self-surrender, self-abnegation and meditation on the non-dual, eternal, self-luminous Brahman, the innermost Self, the Inner Ruler, the Immortal.

May you all attain eternal bliss and immortality through the practice of the cardinal virtues or the fundamental Dharma.

## Varnashrama Dharma

The principle of Varnashrama Dharma is one of the basic principles of Hinduism. The Varnashrama system is peculiar to Hindus. It is a characteristic feature of Hinduism. It is also prevalent throughout the world according to Guna-Karma (aptitude and conduct), though there is no such distinct denomination of this kind, elsewhere.

The duties of the castes are Varna Dharma. The four castes are Brahmana, Kshatriya, Vaishya and Sudra. The duties of the stages in life are Ashrama Dharma. The four Ashramas or orders of life are Brahmacharya, Grihastha, Vanaprastha and Sannyasa.

***The Principle:*** Human society is like a huge machine. The individuals and communities are like its parts. If the parts are weak and broken, the machine will not work. A machine is nothing without its parts. The human body also can work efficiently if its parts and organs are in sound and strong condition. If there is pain in any part of the body, if there is disease in any organ or part of the body, this human machine will go out of order. It will not perform its usual function or work.

So is the case with the human society. Every individual should perform his duties efficiently. The Hindu Rishis and sages formed an ideal scheme of society and an ideal way of individual life, which is known by the name Varnashrama Dharma. Hinduism is built on Varnashrama Dharma. The structure of the Hindu society is based on Varnashrama Dharma. Observance of Varnashrama Dharma helps one's growth and self-evolution. It is very indispensable. If the rules are violated, the society will soon perish.

The aim of Varnashrama Dharma is to promote the development of the universal, eternal Dharma. If you defend Dharma, it will defend you. If you destroy it, it will destroy you. Therefore, never destroy your Dharma. This principle holds true of the individual as much as of the nation. It is Dharma alone which keeps a nation alive. Dharma is the very soul of man. Dharma is the very soul of a nation also.

In the West and in the whole world also, there is Varnashrama, though it is not rigidly observed there. Some Western philosophers have made a division of three classes, *viz.*, philosophers, warriors and masses. The philosophers correspond to the Brahmanas, warriors to Kshatriyas and the masses to Vaishyas and Sudras. This system is indispensable to keep the society in a state of perfect harmony and order.

***The Four Castes***

In Purusha-Sukta of the Rig-Veda, there is reference to the division of Hindu society into four classes. It is described there that the Brahmanas came out of the face of the Lord, the Creator, Kshatriyas from His arms, Vaishyas from His thighs, and the Sudras from His feet.

This division is according to the Guna and Karma. Guna (quality) and Karma (kind of work) determine the caste of a man. This is supported by Lord Krishna in the Gita, also. He says in the Gita: "The four castes were emanated by Me, by the different distribution of qualities and actions. Know Me to be the author of them, though the actionless and inexhaustible" (Ch. IV-13).

There are three qualities or Gunas, *viz.*, *Sattva* (purity), *Rajas* (passion) and *Tamas* (inertia). Sattva is white, Rajas is red and Tamas is black. These three qualities are found in man in varying proportions. Sattva preponderates in some persons. They are Brahmanas. They are wise persons or thinkers. They are the priests, ministers or philosophers who guide kings or rulers. In some, Rajas is predominant. They are Kshatriyas. They are warriors or men of action. They fight with the enemies or invaders and defend the country. In some, Tamas is predominant. They are Vaishyas or traders. They do business and agriculture and amass wealth. Sudras are the servants. None of these qualities is highly developed in them. They serve the other three castes.

In a broad sense, a Sattvic man, who is pious and virtuous and leads the divine life, is a Brahmana, a Rajasic man with heroic quality is a Kshatriya, a Rajasic man with business tendencies is a Vaishya and a Tamasic man is a Sudra. Hitler and Mussolini were Kshatriyas. Ford was a Vaishya.

Serenity, self-restraint, austerity, purity, forgiveness, and also, uprightness, knowledge, Realisation and belief in God are the duties of the Brahmanas, born of (their own) nature. Prowess, splendour, firmness, dexterity, and also, not flying from battle, generosity and lordliness are the duties of the Kshatriyas, born of (their own) nature. Agriculture, cattle-rearing and trade are the duties of the Vaishyas, born of (their own) nature. And action consisting of service is the duty of the Sudras, born of (their own) nature.

***The Law of Spiritual Economics*:** The underlying principle in caste system or Varṇa Dharma, is division of labour. Rishis studied human nature carefully. They came to the conclusion that all men were not equally fit for all kinds of work. Hence, they found it necessary to allocate different kinds of duties to different classes of people, according to their aptitude, capacity or quality. The Brahmanas were in charge of spiritual and intellectual affairs. The work of political administration and defence was given to the Kshatriyas. The Vaishyas were entrusted with the duty of supplying food for the nation and administering its economic welfare. The Sudras did menial work. The Rishis felt all these needs of the Hindu nation and started the system of Varnas and Ashramas.

This division of labour began in Vedic times. The Vedas taught that the Brahmana was the brain of the society, the Kshatriya its arms, the Vaishya its stomach, and the Sudra its feet.

There was a quarrel between the senses, the mind and the Prana as to who was superior. There was a quarrel amongst the different organs and the stomach. If the hands quarrel with the stomach; the entire body will suffer. When Prana departed from the body, all the organs suffered. The head or stomach cannot claim its superiority over the feet and hands. The hands and feet are as much important as the stomach or head. If there is quarrel between the different castes as to which is superior, then the entire social fabric will suffer. There will be disharmony, rupture and discord. A scavenger and a barber are as much important as a minister for the running of the society. The social edifice is built on the law of spiritual economics. It has nothing to do with superiority or inferiority. Each class contributes its best to the common weal or world-solidarity. There is no question of higher and lower here.

***Character Determines Caste*:** A Brahmana is no Brahmana if he is not endowed with purity and good character, and if he leads a life of dissipation and immorality. A Sudra is a Brahmana if he leads a virtuous and pious life. What a great soul was Vidura! What a noble, candid, straightforward student was Satyakama Jabala of Chhandogya Upanishad! Caste is a question of character. Varna is no more the colour of the skin, but the colour of one's character or quality. Conduct and character count and not lineage alone. If one is Brahmana by birth and, at the same time, if he possesses the virtues of a Brahmana, it is extremely good, because certain virtuous qualifications only determine the birth of a Brahmana.

***Use and Abuse of the Caste System*:** The Hindus have survived many a foreign conquest on account of their caste system. But they have developed class jealousies and hatred in the name of the caste system. They have not got the spirit of cooperation. That is the reason why they are weak and disunited today. They have become sectarians in the name of the caste system. Hence there is degradation in India.

The caste system is, indeed, a splendid thing. It is quite flawless. But the defect came in from somewhere else. The classes gradually neglected their duties. The test of ability and character slowly vanished. Birth became the chief consideration in determining castes. All castes fell from their ideals and forgot all about their duties. Brahmanas became selfish and claimed superiority over others by mere birth, without possessing due qualifications.

The Kshatriyas lost their chivalry and spirit of sacrifice. The Vaishyas became very greedy. They did not earn wealth by honest means. They did not look after the economic welfare of the people. They did not give charity. They also lost the spirit of sacrifice. Sudras gave up service. They became officers. They wished that others should serve them. The greed and pride of man have created discord and disharmony.

There is nothing wrong in Varnashrama. It is arrogance and haughtiness in men that have brought troubles. Man or the little Jiva is imperfect. He is full of defects. He is simply waiting for claiming superiority over others. The Brahmana thinks that the other three castes are inferior to him. The Kshatriya thinks that the Vaishya and Sudra are inferior to him. A rich Sudra thinks that he is superior to a poor Brahmana or a poor Kshatriya or Vaishya. At the present moment, the Varnashrama system exists in name only.

It has to be rebuilt properly. Brahmanas, Kshatriyas, Vaishyas and Sudras, who have fallen from their ideals and who are not doing their respective duties, must do their respective duties properly. They must be educated on right lines. They must raise themselves to their original lofty level. The sectarian spirit must die. They should develop a new understanding heart of love and devotion, with a spirit of cooperation, sacrifice and service.

### *The Four Ashramas*

There are four Ashramas or stages in life, *viz.*, Brahmacharya or the period of studentship, Grihastha or the stage of the householder, Vanaprastha or the stage of the forest-dweller or hermit, and Sannyasa or the life of renunciation or asceticism. Each stage has its own duties. These stages help the evolution of man. The four Ashramas take man to perfection by successive stages. The practice of the four Ashramas regulates the life from the beginning to the end. The first two Ashramas pertain to Pravritti Marga or the path of work and the two later stages—the life of Vanaprastha and that of Sannyasa—are the stages of withdrawal from the world. They pertain to Nivritti Marga or the path of renunciation.

***Towards Orderly Spiritual Evolution:*** Life is very systematically and orderly arranged in Sanatana Dharma. There is opportunity for the development of the different sides of human activity. Due occupations and training are assigned to each period of life. Life is a great school in which the powers, capacities and faculties of man are to be evolved gradually.

Every man should pass through the different Ashramas regularly. He should not enter any stage of life prematurely. He can enter the next stage, only when each has been completed. In nature, evolution is gradual. It is not revolutionary.

Lord Manu says in his Smriti: "Having studied the Vedas or two Vedas or even one Veda in due order without breaking celibacy, let him dwell in the householder order. When the householder sees wrinkles in his skin and whiteness in his hair and the son of his son, then let him retire to the forest. Having passed the third portion of life in the forests, let him, having abandoned attachments, wander as an ascetic in the fourth portion of life."

In extraordinary cases, however, some of the stages may be omitted. Suka was a born Sannyasin. Shankara took Sannyasa without entering the stage of a householder. In rare and exceptional cases, a student is allowed to become a Sannyasin, his debts to the world having been fully paid in a previous birth. Nowadays, young Sannyasins without qualification are found in abundance. This is contrary to the ancient rules and causes much trouble.

***The Brahmacharin or the Celibate Student*:** The first stage, Brahmacharya, is the period of study and discipline. The student should not indulge in any pleasures. He stays in the house of his preceptor and studies the Vedas and the sciences. This is the period of probation. The teachers in ancient India usually lived in forest hermitages. These hermitages were the Gurukulas or forest universities. The student begged his food. The children of the rich and poor lived together. The student regarded his teacher as his spiritual father and served him with faith, devotion and reverence.

The life of the student begins with the Upanayana ceremony, his second birth. He must be hardy and simple in his habits. He rises early, bathes and does Sandhya and Gayatri Japa. He studies scriptures. He takes simple food in moderation and takes plenty of exercise. He sleeps on a hard mat and does not use soft beds and pillows. He is humble and obedient. He serves and respects elders. He attempts to be chaste in thought, word and deed.

He ever engages himself in doing services to his preceptor. He refrains from wine, meat, perfumes, garlands, tasty and savoury dishes, women, acids, spices and injury to sentient creatures; from lust, anger, greed; dancing, singing and playing on musical instruments; from dice-playing, gossip, slander and untruth. He sleeps alone. After the end of his student career, he gives a present to his preceptor according to his ability and returns home to enter the household life. The preceptor gives the final instruction and sends the student home. The teacher delivers a convocation address to the students at the conclusion of their studentship:

"Speak the truth. Do your duty. Never swerve from the study of the Veda. Do not cut off the line of progeny (after giving the preceptor the fee he desires). Never swerve away from truth. Never swerve from duty. Never neglect your welfare. Never neglect your prosperity. Never neglect the study and the teaching of the Vedas.

"Never swerve from the duties to the gods and the forefathers. Regard your mother as a god *(Matridevo Bhava)*. Regard your father as a god *(Pitridevo Bhava)*. Regard your teacher as a god *(Acharyadevo Bhava)*. Regard your guest as god *(Atithidevo Bhava)*. Let only those actions that are free from blemishes be done and not others. Only those that are good acts to us should be performed by you and not others.

"You should remove the fatigue of Brahmanas who are superior to you by serving them with seats, etc. Gift should be given with faith, in plenty, with modesty and sympathy. If there be any doubt regarding rites or conduct, then look up to the lives of great men and follow their examples. This is the injunction. This is the teaching. This is the secret of the Vedas. This is God's word of command. This should be observed. Thus is this to be meditated upon."

***The Grihastha or the Householder*:** The second stage is that of the Grihastha or householder. The household stage is entered at marriage, when the student has completed his studentship and is ready to take up the duties and responsibilities of householder life. Of all the Ashramas, this is the most important, because it supports all the others. As all creatures live supported by the air, so the other Orders exist supported by the householder. As all streams and rivers flow to rest in the ocean, so all the Ashramas flow to rest in the householder. The Grihastha is the very heart of Aryan life. Everything depends on him.

Marriage is a sacrament for a Hindu. The wife is his partner in life. She is his Ardhangini. He cannot do any religious ritual without her. She stands by his left side when he performs any religious performance. Husband and wife keep Rama and Sita as their ideal.

A householder should earn money by honest means and distribute it in the proper manner. He should spend one-tenth of his income in charity. He should enjoy sensual pleasures within the limits of the moral law. A householder is permitted to enjoy conjugal happiness on one night in a month.

The householder should perform the Pancha Maha Yajnas. The five Yajnas are:

*DEVA-YAJNA—offering oblations unto Devas, with recitation of Vedic Mantras.*

*RISHI-YAJNA—study of Vedas and teaching of Vedas to students, and offering of oblations to Rishis.*

*PITRI-YAJNA—Tarpana or ablutions to departed souls and Shradha or annual religious rites performed for departed souls.*

*BHUTA-YAJNA—distribution of food to cows, crows and animals in general.*

*ATITHI-YAJNA—giving food to guests and honouring them.*

Hospitality is one of the householder's chief duties. He must ever feed first his guests, Brahmanas and his relatives, and then he and his wife should eat.

When the householder sees that his sons are able to bear the burden of his duties, when his grandsons are around him, he should know that the time has come for him and his wife to retire from the world and spend their time in study and meditation.

***The Vanaprastha or the Recluse*:** The next stage is that of the Varnaprastha. Brahmacharya is a preparation for the life of the householder. Even so, Vanaprastha is a preparation for the final stage of Sannyasa. After discharging all the duties of a householder, he should retire to the forest or a solitary country place and begin to meditate in solitude on higher spiritual things. He is now free from social bonds and the responsibilities of life. He has ample time for study of scriptures. His wife may go with him or remain with her sons.

***The Sannyasin or the Renunciate*:** The next stage is that of a Sannyasin. When a man becomes a Sannyasin, he renounces all possessions, all distinctions of caste, all rites and ceremonies and all attachments to any particular country, nation, or religion. He lives alone and spends his time in meditation. He lives on alms. When he attains the sublime state of deep meditation he rejoices in his own Self. He is quite indifferent to sensual pleasures. He is free from likes and dislikes, desires, egoism, lust, anger, greed and pride.

He has equal vision and balanced mind. He loves all. He roams about happily and disseminates Brahma Jnana or Knowledge of the Self. He is the same in honour and dishonour, praise and censure, success and failure. He is now *Ativarnasrami, i.e.*, above Varna and Ashrama. He is quite a free man. He is not bound by any social customs and conventions.

Such a Sannyasin is an ideal man. He has attained perfection and freedom. He is Brahman Himself. He is a Jivanmukta or a liberated sage. Glory to such exalted personages who are living Gods on earth!

### *Ashrama Dharma Under Modern Conditions*

At the present moment, the Ashramas cannot be exactly lived according to the details of the ancient rules, as the conditions have changed very much; but, they may be revived in their spirit, to the great improvement of modern life. In these stages, no one should do the duty of another. The student or Brahmachari should not do the duties of a householder, a recluse or a Sannyasin. The householder must not perform the duties of a Brahmacharin, Vanaprastha or a Sannyasin. A Sannyasin should not seek again the joys of the householder.

Peace and order will prevail in society, only if and when all people do their respective duties efficiently. The abolition of Varnas and Ashramas will cut at the very root of social duties. How can the nation hope to live when Varnashrama Dharma is not rigidly practised?

The students of schools, and colleges should lead a life of purity and simple living. The householder should lead the life of an ideal Grihastha. He should practise self-restraint, mercy, tolerance, non-injury, truthfulness and moderation in everything. Those who find it difficult to lead the life of the third and the fourth Ashramas should, remaining in either of the other two Ashramas, gradually withdraw themselves from worldly life and practise selfless service, study and meditation.

### *The Highest State*

Varnashrama pertains to body alone, but not to the pure, all-pervading, immortal soul or Atman. Attain Knowledge of the Self and become an Ativarnasrami like Lord Dattatreya. Hear what he says:

***Mahadadi Jagat Sarvam***

*Na kinchit pratibhati me*
*Brahmaiva kevalam sarvam*
*Katham varnasramasthitih*

"The whole world, from Mahat downwards, does not shine in Me. Everything is Brahman only. Where then is Varnashrama?"

May you all have comprehensive understanding of Varnashrama Dharma! May you all develop universal love and brotherhood! May all barriers which are made by man for his own self-aggrandisement and self-assertion and which create discord and disunion, be broken asunder!

### *Yuga Dharma*

In Satya-Yuga or the golden age there was a different set of Dharmas or laws; in Treta, they changed into another form; in Dvapara, the Dharmas were different from the Dharmas of other Yugas; and in Kali-Yuga, they assumed still another form. The Dharma changes according to the changes of the cycles. Man is undergoing change. His nature gets transformed through experiences. Hence, his external form of Dharmas also should change. That which is achieved through contemplation in Satya Yuga, through sacrifices in Treta Yuga, and through the worship of Lord Hari in Dvapara Yuga, may be attained through Kirtana or loud chanting of Lord Vishnu's Name in Kali Yuga or Iron age.

In the Satya Yuga, the mind of men was generally pure. They had no distraction of the mind. There were neither cinemas, nor hotels, nor dancing halls and similar other distractions. Hence, meditation was easy and natural for them. That is the reason why contemplation has been prescribed for men of Satya Yuga. In the Treta Yuga, materials for the performance of Yajnas or sacrifices were easily available. The people had active tendencies. Therefore it was easy for them to perform Agnihotra, Jyotistoma, Darsa-Paurnimas and other Yajnas.

That is the reason why Yajna has been described as the external form of Sanatana Dharma in that age. In the Dvapara Yuga, there was the manifestation of Avataras and men could easily have direct worship of God. Hence, worship was prescribed as the principal form of Sadhana in that age. In the Kali Yuga, there are many distractions for the mind. People lack in Brahmacharya, strength of will and power of enquiry or rational investigation. It is very difficult to procure materials for the performance of sacrifices. Therefore, Hari Kirtana or loud chanting of the Divine Name and selfless service of humanity have been recommended as the principal forms of Sadhana.

### *Conclusion*

Follow your Dharma with zeal and enthusiasm. Discharge your duties faithfully. Develop all the virtues which constitute Dharma. Never deviate an inch from the path of righteousness. Stick to Dharma with all your heart, with all your mind and with all your soul. Performance of one's duties brings happiness, quick evolution and freedom. You will soon attain immortality, eternal bliss, supreme peace, perennial joy, absolute freedom and perfection. Glory to Dharma, the supreme light that leads you to the kingdom of eternal bliss and everlasting peace.

May the eternal Dharma of Hinduism be preserved for ever! May all Hindus be consolidated by the bond of true love!!

# 3

# Hindu Worship

## Worship or Upasana

Worship is the expression of devotion, reverence and love to the Lord, of keen yearning to be united with Him and of spiritual thirsting to hold conscious communion with Him. The devotee prays to the Lord for granting him intense devotion and removing the veil of ignorance.

He pines for His benign grace. He constantly remembers His Name. He repeats His Mantra. He sings His praise. He does Kirtana. He hears and recites His Lilas. He lives in His Dhama in the company of His devotees. He meditates on His form, His nature, His attributes and His Lilas. He visualises the form of the Lord with closed eyes and enjoys supreme peace and bliss.

Worship is the effort on the part of the Upasaka, *i.e.*, he who does Upasana or worship, to reach the proximity or presence of God or the Supreme Self. *Upasana* literally means *sitting near God*. Upasana is approaching the chosen ideal or object of worship by meditating on it in accordance with the teachings of the Shastras and the Guru and dwelling steadily in the current of that one thought, like a thread of oil poured from one vessel to another (Tailadharavat).

It consists of all those observances and practices, physical and mental, by which the aspirant or Jijnasu makes a steady progress in the realm of spirituality and eventually realises in himself—in his own heart—the presence of Godhead.

## Benefits of Worship

Worship of the Lord purifies the heart, generates harmonious vibrations, steadies the mind, purifies and ennobles the emotions, harmonises the five sheaths, and eventually leads to communion, fellowship or God-realisation.

Upasana helps the devotee to sit near the Lord or to commune with Him. It fills the mind with Suddha Bhava and Prema or pure love for the Lord. It gradually transmutes man into a divine being.

Upasana changes the mental substance, destroys Rajas and Tamas and fills the mind with Sattva or purity. Upasana destroys Vasanas, Trishnas, egoism, lust, hatred, anger, etc. Upasana turns the mind inward and induces Antarmukha Vritti. It eventually brings the devotee face to face with the Lord, frees the devotee from the wheel of births and deaths, and confers on him immortality and freedom.

The mind becomes that on which it meditates in accordance with the analogy of the wasp and the caterpillar (Bhramara-Kitaka Nyaya). Just as you think, so you become. This is the immutable psychological law. There is a mysterious or inscrutable power (Achintya Shakti) in Upasana which makes the meditator and the meditated identical.

You will find in the Bhagwad Gita: "But by devotion to Me alone, I may thus be perceived, O Arjuna; and known and seen in essence and entered, O Parantapa" (Ch. XI, 54).

Patanjali Maharshi emphasises in various places in his Raja Yoga Sutras, on the importance of Upasana. For even a Raja Yogi, Upasana is necessary. He has his own Ishta Devata or guiding Deity—Yogesvara Krishna or Lord Shiva. Self-surrender to God is an Anga (limb) of Raja Yoga and Kriya Yoga. Patanjali says: "One can enter into Samadhi through Upasana."

Of all those things which are conducive to spiritual advancement, Adhyatmic uplift and the acquisition of Dharma, Upasana is one which is not only indispensably requisite, but eminently beneficial to all classes and grades of people. It is easy too.

Eating, drinking, sleeping, fear, copulation, etc., are common in brutes and human beings, but that which makes one a real man or a God-man is the religious consciousness. He who leads a mere outward sensual life without doing any Upasana is an animal only, though he wears outwardly the form of a human being.

### *Saguna-Upasana and Nirguna-Upasana*

Upasana is of two kinds, *viz.*, Pratika-Upasana and Ahamgraha-Upasana. *Pratika* means *a symbol*. Pratika-Upasana is Saguna-Upasana. Ahamgraha-Upasana is Nirguna-Upasana or meditation on the formless and attributeless Akshara or transcendental Brahman. Meditation on idols, Saligrama, pictures of Lord Rama, Lord Krishna, Lord Shiva, Gayatri Devi, etc., is Pratika-Upasana. The blue expansive sky, all-pervading ether, all-pervading light of the sun, etc., are also *Pratikas* for abstract meditation. Saguna-Upasana is concrete meditation. Nirguna-Upasana is abstract meditation.

Hearing of the Lilas of the Lord, Kirtana or singing His Names, constant remembrance of the Lord (Smarana), service of His feet, offering flowers, prostration, prayer, chanting of Mantra, self-surrender, service of Bhagavatas, service of humanity and country with Narayana-Bhava, etc., constitute Saguna-Upasana.

Chanting of Om with Atma-Bhava, service of humanity and country with Atma-Bhava, mental Japa of Om with Atma or Brahma Bhava, meditation on Soham or Sivoham or on the Mahavakyas such as *Aham Brahma Asmi* or *Tat Tvam Asi* after sublating the illusory vehicles through 'Neti, Neti' doctrine, constitute Ahamgraha-Upasana or Nirguna-Upasana.

Saguna-Upasana is Bhakti Yoga or the Yoga of Devotion. Nirguna-Upasana is Jnana Yoga or the Yoga of Knowledge. Worshippers of Saguna (the qualified) Brahman and of Nirguna (the unqualified) Brahman reach the same goal. But, the latter path is very hard, because the aspirant has to give up attachment to the body (Dehabhimana) from the very beginning of his spiritual practice. The Akshara or the Imperishable is very hard to reach for those who are attached to their bodies. Further, it is extremely difficult to fix the mind on the formless and attributeless Brahman. Contemplation on the Akshara or Nirguna Brahman demands a very sharp, one-pointed and subtle intellect.

## The Bhavas in Bhakti Yoga

The Yoga of Bhakti or Devotion is much easier than Jnana Yoga or philosophical meditations. In Bhakti Yoga, the devotee establishes a near and dear relationship with the Lord. He cultivates slowly any one of the six Bhavas according to his temperament, taste and capacity.

Santa Bhava, Dasya Bhava, Sakhya Bhava, Vatsalya Bhava, Kanta Bhava and Madhurya Bhava are the six kinds of attributes of devotees or Bhavas towards God. The Bhavas differ in type and intensity of feeling. The different Bhavas are arranged in order of their intensity. Dhruva and Prahlada had the feeling of a child to its parents. This is Santa Bhava. In Dasya Bhava, the devotee behaves like a servant. His Lord is his master. Hanuman is an ideal servant of God.

In Sakhya Bhava, there is a sense of equality. Arjuna and Kuchela had this Bhava. In Vatsalya Bhava, the devotee looks upon the Lord as his own child. Yashoda had this Bhava for Sri Krishna. Kausalya had this Bhava for Sri Rama. Kanta Bhava is the love of the wife towards the husband. Sita and Rukmini had this Bhava. The culmination is reached in Madhurya Bhava. The lover and the Beloved become one through the intensity of love. Radha and Mira had this type of love.

The last Bhava is the highest culmination of Bhakti. It is merging or absorption in the Lord. The devotee adores the Lord. He constantly remembers Him. He sings His Name (Kirtana). He speaks of His glories. He repeats His Name. He chants His Mantra. He prays and prostrates. He hears His Lilas. He does total, ungrudging, unconditional surrender, obtains His grace, holds communion with Him and gets absorbed in Him eventually. In Madhurya Bhava, there is the closest relationship between the devotee and the Lord. There is no sensuality in Kanta and Madhurya Bhavas. There is no tinge of carnality in them. Passionate people cannot understand these two Bhavas as their minds are saturated with passion and lower sexual appetite. Sufistic saints also have the Bhava of lover and the Beloved, Madhurya Bhava. The Gita Govinda written by Jaya Deva is full of Madhurya Rasa. The language of love which the mystic uses cannot be comprehended by worldly persons. Only Gopis, Radha, Mira, Tukaram, Narada, Hafiz and similar other great devotees of the Lord can understand this language.

## Puja and Ishta-Devata

*Puja* is the common term for *ritual worship*, of which there are numerous synonyms such as Archana, Vandana, Bhajana, etc., though some of these stress certain aspects of it. The object of worship is the Ishta Devata or guiding Deity or the particular form of the Deity whom the devotee worships—Narayana or Vishnu as such, or His forms as Rama and Krishna in the case of Vaishnavas, Shiva in His eight forms in the case of Saivas and Devi in the case of Saktas.

The devotee selects sometimes his Kuladeva or Kuladevi, family Deva or Devi, for his worship. Sometimes, the Devata is chosen for him by his Guru or spiritual preceptor. Sometimes, he himself chooses that Devata which most appeals to him. This form is his Ishta Devata.

An object is used in the outer Puja such as an image (Pratima), a picture, or an emblem such as Saligrama in the case of Vishnu worship or Linga in the case of worship of Shiva.

Whilst all things may be the objects of worship, choice is naturally made of those objects which, by reason of their effect on the mind, are more fitted for it. An image or one of the useful emblems, is likely to raise in the mind of the worshipper the thought of a Devata. Saligrama stone induces easily concentration of mind. Everybody has got predilection for a symbol, emblem or image. Idol or Murti (Vigraha), sun, fire, water, Ganga, Saligrama and Linga are all symbols or Pratikas of God which help the aspirants to attain one-pointedness of mind and purity of heart. These are all personal inclinations in the worshipper due to his belief in their special efficacy for him. Psychologically, all this means that a particular mind finds that it works best in the direction desired by means of particular instruments or emblems or images.

The vast bulk of humanity are either of impure or of weak mind. Therefore, the object of worship must be pure for these people. The objects that are capable of exciting lust and dislike must be avoided. But, a higher, advanced Sadhaka who has a pure mind and who sees the divine presence everywhere and in everything, can worship any kind of object.

In Puja, an image or picture representing some divine form is used as the object of worship. The image is adored. All image, a Sila or Vigraha or Murti, represents the particular Lord who is invoked in it. A Linga represents Shiva. It represents the secondless, formless Brahman. The Sruti says: "*Ekamevadvitiyam Brahma*—The Brahman is one alone, without a second." There is no duality here. A Linga is shining and attractive to the eyes. It helps concentration. Ravana propitiated Shiva and obtained boons by worshipping the Linga.

A Saligrama is an idol of Vishnu. Saligrama is the symbol of Vishnu. There are images of Sri Rama, Sri Krishna, Karttikeya, Ganesha, Hanuman, Dattatreya, Sita, Lakshmi, Parvati, Durga, Kali, Saraswati, etc., according to the taste of the particular devotee.

The images of Vishnu and of His Avataras, and the images of Shakti and Shiva, are the popular idols that are worshipped both in temples and in the houses. The idols in the temples of Tirupati, Ṗandarpur, Palani, Katirgama, etc., are powerful Deities. They are Pratyaksha Devatas. They grant boons to the devotees, cure their ailments and give Darshana. Wonderful Lilas are associated with these Deities. There is no polytheism in Hinduism. Shiva, Vishnu, Brahma and Shakti are different aspects of one Lord.

God reveals Himself to His devotees in a variety of ways. He assumes the very form which the devotee has chosen for his worship. If you worship Him as Lord Hari with four hands, He will come to you as Hari. If you adore Him as Shiva, He will give you Darshana as Shiva. If you worship Him as Mother

Durga or Kali, He will come to you as Durga or Kali. If you worship Him as Lord Rama, Lord Krishna or Lord Dattatreya, He will come to you as Rama, Krishna or Dattatreya. If you worship Him as Christ or Allah, He will come to you as Christ or Allah.

You may worship Lord Shiva or Lord Hari, Lord Ganesha or Lord Subrahmanya or Lord Dattatreya, or anyone of the Avataras, Lord Rama or Lord Krishna, Saraswati or Lakshmi, Gayatri or Kali, Durga or Chandi. All are aspects of one Isvara or Lord. Under whatever name and form, it is Isvara who is adored. Worship goes to the Indweller, the Lord in the form. It is ignorance to think that one form is superior to another. All forms are one and the same. Shiva, Vishnu, Gayatri, Rama, Krishna, Devi and Brahman are one. All are adoring the same Isvara. The differences are only differences of names due to differences in the worshippers, but not in the object of adoration. It is only out of ignorance that different religionists and different sects fight and quarrel amongst themselves.

## The Philosophy and Significance of Idol-Worship

### *The Idol—A Prop for the Spiritual Neophyte*

Idol is a support for the neophyte. It is a prop of his spiritual childhood. A form or image is necessary for worship in the beginning. It is an external symbol of God for worship. It is a reminder of God. The material image calls up the mental idea. Steadiness of mind is obtained by image-worship. The worshipper will have to associate the ideas of infinity, omnipotence, omniscience, purity, perfection, freedom, holiness, truth and omnipresence. It is not possible for all to fix the mind on the Absolute or the Infinite. A concrete form is necessary for the vast majority for practising concentration. To behold God everywhere and to practise the presence of God is not possible for the ordinary man. Idol-worship is the easiest form of worship for the modern man.

A symbol is absolutely indispensable for fixing the mind. The mind wants a prop to lean upon. It cannot have a conception of the Absolute in the initial stages. Without the help of some external aid, in the initial stages, the mind cannot be centralised. In the beginning, concentration or meditation is not possible without a symbol.

### *Everyone an Idol-Worshipper*

There is no reference to worship of idols in the Vedas. The Puranas and the Agamas give descriptions of idol-worship both in the houses and in the temples. Idol-worship is not peculiar to Hinduism. Christians worship the Cross. They have the image of the Cross in their mind. The Mohammedans keep the image of the Kaba stone when they kneel and do prayers. The people of the whole world, save a few Yogis and Vedantins, are all worshippers of idols. They keep some image or the other in the mind.

The mental image also is a form of idol. The difference is not one of kind, but only one of degree. All worshippers, however intellectual they may be, generate a form in the mind and make the mind dwell on that image.

Everyone is an idol-worshipper. Pictures, drawings, etc., are only forms of Pratima or the idol. A gross mind needs a concrete symbol as a prop or Alambana and a subtle mind requires an abstract symbol. Even a Vedantin has the symbol OM for fixing the wandering mind. It is not only the pictures or images in stone and in wood, that are idols but dialectics and leaders also become idols. So, why condemn idolatry?

### *A Medium for Establishing Communion with God*

Idols are not the idle fancies of sculptors, but shining channels through which the heart of the devotee is attracted to and flows towards God. Though the image is worshipped, the devotee feels the presence of the Lord in it and pours out his devotion unto it. It is the appalling ignorance of the modern sensual man that clouds his vision and prevents him from seeing Divinity in lovely and enchanting idols of His form. The very scientific advances of this century ought to convince you of the glory of idol-worship. How are the songsters and orators confined to a small box-like thing to be called a radio? It is a mere piece of a mechanical lifeless structure which breaks into a thousand pieces if you throw it away violently; and yet, if you know how to handle it, you can hear through it, the music that is being played several thousands of miles away and the discourse that is being delivered in the remotest part of the globe.

Even as you can catch the sound-waves of people all over the world through the radio receiving set, it is possible to commune with the all-pervading Lord through the medium of an idol. The divinity of the all-pervading God is vibrant in every atom of creation. There is not a speck of space where He is not. Why do you then say that He is not in the idols?

There are others who would glibly say: "Oh, God is all-pervading formless Being. How can He be confined to this idol?" Are these people ever conscious of His omnipresence? Do they always see Him and Him alone in everything? No. It is their ego that prevents them from bowing to the idols of God and, with that motive, put this lame excuse forward!

Empty vessels only make much sound. A practical man who does meditation and worship, who is full of knowledge and real devotion, keeps always silence. He influences and teaches others through silence. He only knows whether a Murti is necessary in the beginning for concentration or not.

However intellectual one may be, he cannot concentrate without the help of some symbol in the beginning. An intellectual and learned person, on account of his pride and vanity only says: "I do not like a Murti. I do not wish to concentrate on a form." He cannot concentrate on the formless one. He thinks that people will laugh at him when they come to know that he is meditating on a form. He never does any meditation on the formless one. He simply talks and argues and poses.

He wastes his life in unnecessary discussions only. An ounce of practice is better than tons of theories. Intellect is a hindrance in the vast majority of intellectual persons. They say that the existence of Brahman is a guess-work, Samadhi is a bluff of the mind and Self-realisation is an imagination of the Vedantins. Deluded souls! They are steeped in ignorance. They are carried away by their secular knowledge which is mere husk when compared to the Knowledge of the Self. There is no hope of salvation for such people. First, their wrong Samskaras should be flushed by good Samskaras through Satsanga. Then only they will realise their mistakes. May the Lord bestow on them clear understanding and thirsting for real knowledge!

### *A Symbol of God*

Pratima, the idol, is a substitute or symbol. The image in a temple, though it is made of stone, wood or metal, is precious for a devotee as it bears the mark of his Lord, as it stands for something which he holds holy and eternal. A flag is only a small piece of painted cloth, but it stands for a soldier for something that he holds very dear. He is prepared to give up his life in defending his flag. Similarly, the image is very dear to a devotee. It speaks to him in its own language of devotion. Just as the flag arouses martial valour in the soldier, so also the image arouses devotion in the devotee. The Lord is superimposed on the image and the image generates divine thoughts in the worshipper.

A piece of ordinary white paper or coloured paper has no value. You throw it away. But, if there is the stamp of the Government on the paper (currency note), you keep it safe in your money-purse or trunk. Even so, an ordinary piece of stone has no value for you. You throw it away. But, if you behold the stone Murti of Lord Krishna at Pandarpur or any other Murti in shrines, you bow your head with folded hands, because there is the stamp of the Lord on the stone. The devotee superimposes on the stone Murti his own Beloved Lord and all His attributes.

When you worship an image, you do not say: "This image has come from Jaipur. It was brought by Prabhu Singh. Its weight is 50 lbs. It is made of white marble. It has cost me Rs. 500/-." You superimpose all the attributes of the Lord on the image and pray: "O Antaryamin (Inner Ruler)! You are all-pervading. You are omnipotent, omniscient, all-merciful. You are the source for everything. You are self-existent. You are Sat-Chit-Ananda. You are eternal, unchanging. You are the Life of my life, Soul of my soul! Give me light and knowledge!

Let me dwell in Thee for ever." When your devotion and meditation become intense and deep, you do not see the stone image. You behold the Lord only who is Chaitanya. Image-worship is very necessary for beginners.

### *An Integral Part of Virat*

For a beginner, Pratima is an absolute necessity. By worshipping an idol, Isvara is pleased. The Pratima is made up of five elements. Five elements constitute the body of the Lord. The idol remains an idol, but the worship goes to the Lord. If you shake hands with a man, he is highly pleased. You have touched only a small part of his body and yet he is happy. He smiles and welcomes you. Even so, the Lord is highly pleased when a small portion of His Virat (cosmic) body is worshipped. An idol is a part of the body of the Lord. The whole world is His body, Virat form. The devotion goes to the Lord. The worshipper superimposes on the image the Lord and all His attributes. He does Shodasopachara for the idol, the sixteen kinds of paying respects or service to the Lord.

The presence of the Deity is invoked (Avahana). Then a seat (Asana) is offered. Then the feet are washed (Padya). Then offering of water is given (Arghya). Arghya is offering hospitality. Then comes bathing (Snana). Then the image is dressed (Vastra). Then comes the investiture with the sacred thread (Yajnopavita). Then sandal paste (Chandana) is offered. Then comes offering of flowers (Pushpa). They are the symbols of the heart-flowers of devotion, love and reverence. Then incense is burnt (Dhupa). Then a lamp is lit and waved before the Deity (Dipa). Then food is offered (Naivedya). Then betel is offered (Tambula). Then camphor is burnt (Nirajana).

Then Svarnapushpa (gift of gold) is offered. In the end, the Deity is bidden farewell to (Visarjana). In these external forms of worship, the inner love finds expression. The wandering mind is fixed now in this form of worship. The aspirant gradually feels the nearness of the Lord. He attains purity of heart and slowly annihilates his egoism.

To the worshipper who believes the symbol, any kind of image is the body of the Lord under the form of stone, clay, brass, picture, Saligrama, etc. Such worship can never be idolatry. All matter is a manifestation of God. God is present in everything which exists. Everything is an object of worship, for all is a manifestation of God who is therein worshipped. The very act of worship implies that the object of worship is superior and conscious. This way of looking at things must be attained by the devotee. The untutored mind must be trained to view things in the above manner.

### *Idol-Worship Develops Devotion*

Idol-worship makes concentration of man simpler and easier. You can bring before your mind's eye the great Lilas the Lord has played in His particular Avatara in which you view Him. This is one of the easiest modes of Self-realisation.

Just as the picture of a famous warrior evokes heroism in your heart, so also a look at the picture of God will elevate your mind to divine heights. Just as the child develops the maternal Bhava (mother-feeling) of the future caressing, nursing, protecting mother by playing with its imaginary toy-child made up of rags and suckling the child in an imaginary manner, so also the devotee develops the feeling of devotion by worshipping the Pratima and concentrating on it.

### *Regular Worship Unveils the Divinity in the Idol*

Regular worship (Puja) and other modes of demonstrating our inner feeling of recognition of Divinity in the idol unveil the Divinity latent in it. This is truly a wonder and a miracle. The picture comes to life. The idol speaks. It will answer your questions and solve your problems. The God in you has the power to awaken the latent Divinity in the idol.

It is like a powerful lens that focuses the sun's rays on to a bundle of cotton. The lens is not fire and the cotton is not fire either nor can the sun's rays, by themselves, burn the cotton. When the three are brought together in a particular manner, fire is generated and the cotton is burnt. Similar is the case with the idol, the Sadhaka and the all-pervading Divinity. Puja makes the idol shine with the divine resplendence. God is then enshrined in the idol. From here, He will protect you in a special manner. The idol will perform miracles. The place where it is installed is at once transformed into a temple, nay, a Vaikuntha or Kailasa in reality. Those who live in such a place are freed from miseries, from diseases, from failures and from Samsara itself. The awakened Divinity in the idol acts as a guardian angel blessing all, conferring the highest good on those who bow to it.

### *The Image, A Mass of Chaitanya*

The idol is only a symbol of the Divine. A devotee does not behold therein a block of stone or a mass of metal. It is an emblem of God for him. He visualises the Indwelling Presence in the Murti or image. All the Shaiva Nayanars, saints of South India, attained God-realisation through worship of the Linga, the image of Lord Shiva. For a devotee, the image is a mass of Chaitanya or consciousness. He draws inspiration from the image. The image guides him. It talks to him. It assumes human form to help him in a variety of ways. The image of Lord Shiva in the temple at Madurai in South India helped the fuel-cutter and the old woman. The image in the temple at Tirupati assumed human form and gave witness in the court to help His devotees. There are marvels and mysteries. Only the devotees understand these.

### *When Idols became Alive?*

For a Bhakta or a sage, there is no such thing as *Jada* or insentient matter. Everything is Vasudeva or Chaitanya—*Vasudevah Sarvam Iti*. The devotee beholds actually the Lord in the idol. Narsi Mehta was put to the test by a king. The king said: "O Narsi, if you are a sincere devotee of Lord Krishna, if as you say the idol is Lord Krishna Himself, let this idol move." According to the prayer of Narsi Mehta, the idol moved. The sacred bull Nandi before Shiva's idol took the food offered by Tulsidas. The Murti played with Mira Bai. It was full of life and Chaitanya for her.

When Appayya Dikshitar went to the Tirupati temple in South India, the Vaishnavas refused him admission. The next morning they found the Vishnu Murti in the temple changed into Shiva Murti. The Mahant was much astonished and startled, asked pardon and prayed to Appayya Dikshitar to change the Murti again into Vishnu Murti.

Kanaka Dasa was a great devotee of Lord Krishna in Udipi, in the district of South Kanara, in South India. He was not allowed to enter the temple on account of his low birth. Kanaka Dasa went round the temple and saw a small window at the back of the temple. He seated himself in front of the window. He was soon lost in singing songs in praise of Lord Krishna. Many people gathered round him.

They were very much attracted by the sweet melody of his music and the depth of his devotion. Lord Krishna turned round to enable Kanaka Dasa to get His Darshana. The priests were struck with wonder. Even today, pilgrims are shown the window and the place where Kanaka Dasa sat and sang.

The Murti is the same as the Lord, for it is the vehicle of the expression of the Mantra-Chaitanya which is the Devata. The same attitude should the devotee have in regard to the Murti in the temple, which he would evince if the Lord would appear before him in person and speak to him in articulate sound.

## Vedanta and Idol-Worship

A pseudo-Vedantin feels himself ashamed to bow or prostrate himself before an idol in the temple. He feels that his Advaita will evaporate if he prostrates himself. Study the lives of the reputed Tamil saints, Appar, Sundarar, Sambandhar, etc. They had the highest Advaitic realisation. They saw Lord Shiva everywhere and yet they visited all temples of Shiva, prostrated before the idol and sang hymns which are on record now.

The sixty-three Nayanar saints practised *Charya* and *Kriya* only and attained God-realisation thereby. They swept the floor of the temple, collected flowers, made garlands for the Lord and put on lights in the temple. They were illiterate, but attained the highest realisation. They were practical Yogis and their hearts were saturated with pure devotion. They were embodiments of Karma Yoga. All practised the Yoga of

Synthesis. The idol in the temple was all Chaitanya or Consciousness for them. It was not a mere block of stone.

Madhusudana Swami, who had Advaitic realisation, who beheld oneness of the Self and who had Advaitic Bhava, was intensely attached to the form of Lord Krishna with flute in His hands.

Tulasidas realised the all-pervading essence. He had cosmic consciousness. He communed with the all-pervading, formless Lord. And yet, his passion for Lord Rama with bow in His hand did not vanish. When he had been to Vrindavana and saw the Murti of Lord Krishna with flute in His hands, he said: "I will not bow my head to this form." At once Lord Krishna's form assumed the form of Lord Rama. Then only he bowed his head. Tukaram also had the same cosmic experience as that of Tulasidas. He sings in his Abhanga: "I see my Lord all-pervading, just as sweetness pervades the sugar-cane;" and yet, he always speaks of his Lord Vitthala of Pandarpur with His hands on the hips. Mira also realised her identity with the all-pervading Krishna, and yet she was not tired of repeating again and again: "My Giridhara Nagar."

From the above facts, we can clearly infer that one can realise God through worship of Murti or idol; that the worship of the Lord in Saguna form is a great aid for the realisation of the Lord in His all-pervading, formless aspect also; that the worship of the Murti is very essential for the purpose of concentration and meditation in the beginning and that such a worship is not in anyway a hindrance to the attainment of God-consciousness.

Those who vehemently attack Murti Puja are groping in extreme darkness and ignorance, and they have no real knowledge of Puja and worship. They enter into unnecessary vain debates and discussion against Murti Puja to show that they are learned persons. They have not done any real Sadhana at all. They are persons who have made idle talking and tall talk their habit and profession. They have ruined themselves. They have unsettled the minds of countless persons and ruined them also. The whole world worships symbols and Murtis only in some form or the other. The mind is disciplined in the beginning by fixing it on a concrete object or symbol. When it is rendered steady and subtle, it can be fixed later on, on an abstract idea such as *'Aham Brahma Asmi.'* When one advances in meditation, the form melts in the formless and he becomes one with the formless essence. Image worship is not contrary to the view of Vedanta. It is rather a help.

Those who have not understood the philosophy and significance of idol-worship will have, now at least, a clear understanding of them. Their eyes will be opened now. Ignorant persons only, who have not studied Shastras and who have not associated with Yogis, sages and Bhaktas, raise unnecessary arguments against idol-worship.

### *From Ritualistic Bhakti to Para-Bhakti*

Bhakti is of two kinds, *viz.*, higher Bhakti or Para-Bhakti, and lower Bhakti or ritualistic Bhakti. Ritualistic worship is Vaidhi or Gauni Bhakti. It is formal Bhakti. Vaidhi Bhakti is the lower type of devotion depending on external aids. The mind becomes purer and purer. The aspirant gradually develops love for God through ritualistic worship. He who does ritualistic worship rings bells, adores a Pratika (symbol) or Pratima (image), does Puja with flowers and sandal paste, burns incense, waves light before the image, offers Naivedya or food for God, etc.

Mukhya Bhakti or Para Bhakti is advanced type of devotion. It is higher Bhakti. It transcends all convention. A devotee of this type knows no rule. He does not perform any external worship. He beholds his Lord everywhere, in every object. His heart is saturated with love for God. The whole world is Vrindavana for him. His state is ineffable. He attains the acme of bliss. He radiates love, purity and joy wherever he goes and inspires all who come in contact with him.

The aspirant who worships the idol in the beginning beholds the Lord everywhere and develops Para Bhakti. From Vaidhi Bhakti, he passes on to Ragatmika Bhakti or Prema Bhakti. He beholds the whole world as the Lord. The ideas of good and bad, right and wrong, etc., vanish. He sees the Lord in a rogue, dacoit, cobra, scorpion, ant, dog, tree, log of wood, block of stone, sun, moon, stars, fire, water, earth, etc. His vision or experience baffles description. Glory to such exalted Bhaktas who are veritable Gods on earth, who live to lift others from the quagmire of Samsara and save them from the clutches of death!

Hinduism leads the aspirants gradually from material images to mental images, from the diverse mental-images to the one Personal God, and from the Personal God to the Impersonal Absolute or the Transcendental Nirguna Brahman.

### *The Glory of Hindu Philosophy and Hindu Mode of Worship*

How sublime is Hindu philosophy and Hindu mode of worship! It does not stop or end with worship of idol alone. The Sadhaka is taken, step by step, to higher stages of devotion and Samadhi or communion, through the worship of the idol. Though he worships the idol, he has to keep before his mental eye the all-pervading Lord. He has to feel His presence in his heart and in all objects also. Even in worshipping a small idol, he has to repeat the Purusha-Sukta and to think of the Virat Purusha with countless heads, countless eyes, countless hands, etc., who extends beyond the universe, the Lord or the Atman who dwells in the hearts of all beings.

The same man who burns incense, scented sticks and camphor before the idol says: "The sun does not shine there nor the moon nor the stars nor the lightning. How then could the little fire shine there? All shine after Him. His effulgence alone illumines the whole world." The ways and rules of worship—Puja Vidhi—and the secrets of worship that are described in the Hindu scriptures, are scientifically accurate and highly rational. It is only ignorant people who have not studied the scriptures and who have not associated with the devotees and great souls, who vilify worship of idols or Murtis.

Every other religion lays certain fixed dogmas and attempts to force people to follow them. It has only one kind of drug to treat several diseases. It gives only one kind of food for all and for all conditions. It places before the followers only one coat. It must fit Albert, Atkinson, Ahluwalia, Antony and Abdul

Rehman. The Hindus know that the images, crosses and crescents are simply so many symbols to fix the mind in the beginning for developing concentration, so many concrete pegs to hang their spiritual ideas and convictions on. The symbol is not necessary for everyone. It is not compulsory in Hinduism. It is not needed for an advanced Yogi or sage. Symbol is like the slate which is useful for a boy of the first standard. Those who are not in need of it have no right to say that it is wrong. If they say that it is wrong, they only betray their ignorance.

***Conclusion***

There is nothing wrong in worshipping an idol in the beginning. You must superimpose God and His attributes on the idol. You must think of the Antar-Atman hidden in the idol. The aspirant gradually begins to feel that the Lord he worships is in the idol, in the hearts of all creatures and in all the names and forms of this universe. He begins to feel His presence everywhere.

Idol-worship is only the beginning of religion. Certainly it is not its end. The same Hindu scriptures, which prescribe idol-worship for beginners, speak of meditation on the Infinite or the Absolute and contemplation of the significance of *Tat Tvam Asi* Mahavakya, for advanced aspirants.

There are different stages of worship. The first is the worship of idols. The next is recitation of Mantras and offering of prayers. Mental worship is superior to worship with flowers. Meditation on the Absolute or the attributeless Nirguna Brahman is the best of all.

The supreme state is Self-realisation or Brahma-sakshatkara. The second in rank is meditation. The Yogi practises Sadhana or unceasing meditation on the Supreme Self. The third is the worship of symbols. The fourth is the performance of rituals and pilgrimages to holy places. The Shastras and Gurus are like kind mothers. They take hold of the hands of the aspirants, take them step by step, stage by stage, till they are established in Nirvikalpa Samadhi or superconscious state. They prescribe gross forms of Sadhana or spiritual practices for the neophytes or beginners with gross mind and give lessons on abstract meditation for the advanced aspirants who are endowed with pure, subtle and sharp intellect.

Each marks a stage of progress. The human soul makes different kinds of attempts to grasp and realise the Infinite or the Absolute according to his strength or degree of evolution. He soars higher and higher, gathers more and more strength, and eventually merges himself in the Supreme and attains oneness or identity.

Glory to the Hindu Rishis and the Hindu scriptures who take the aspirants from the lower to the higher form of worship, stage by stage, step by step, and ultimately help them to rest in the attributeless, all-pervading, formless, timeless, spaceless Brahman or the infinite and unconditioned Brahman of the Upanishads.

Beloved children of the Lord! Shed your ignorant disbelief this moment. Enshrine supreme, unshakable, living faith in your heart this very moment. Recall to your mind the glorious examples of Sri Mira, Sri Ramakrishna Paramahamsa and the South Indian Alvars and Nayanars. They believed and they reaped the rich spiritual harvests. You too can enjoy great peace, happiness and prosperity here, and attain Him here and now, if you have this faith in idol-worship.

Though you may perform external worship at regular intervals, let the internal worship of the Lord in your heart be constant and unbroken. Here worship attains completeness. Life is divine worship. May you realise the significance of the universal worship of the *Virat* in daily life, and performing it, attain the *summum bonum* of life. May the Lord bless you all.

# 4

# Hindu Mythology and Symbols

Mythology is a part of every religion. Mythology is concretised philosophy. Mythology is the science which investigates myths or fables or legends founded on remote events, especially those made in the early period of a people's existence. Mythology inspires the readers through precepts and laudable examples and goads them to attain perfection or the highest ideal. The abstract teachings and high subtle ideas are made highly interesting and impressive to the masses through the garb of stories, parables, legends, allegories and narratives. The sublime and abstract philosophical ideas and ideals of Hinduism are taken straight to the heart of the masses through impressive stories.

All religions have their own mythology. Mythology is slightly mixed up with a little history. It is difficult to make a fine distinction between history and mythology. If a Christian stands up and says: "My prophet did such and such a marvellous thing," others will say: "This is only a myth. Our prophets did still more marvellous things which are really historical." It is not easy to differentiate the two into watertight compartments.

The doctrine of Avatara of the Hindus is a myth for the people of other religions. To worship a cow is superstition for the followers of other religions. The beautiful image or idol of Lord Krishna, which captivates the hearts of the sincere devotees and inspires them to enter into Bhava Samadhi, is horrible to look at for some other religionists. A Christian, a Jew and all others have their own various superstitions and myths. But these myths are really historical for each of them, severally.

Mythology has no reference to anything 'unreal', but presents truths as clothed in conceptual categories.

### *Philosophy, Mythology and Ritual*

In every religion there are three parts, *viz.*, philosophy, mythology and ritual. Philosophy is the essence of religion. It sets forth its basic principles or fundamental doctrines or tenets, the goal and the means of attaining it. Mythology explains and illustrates philosophy by means of legendary lives of great men or of supernatural beings. Ritual gives a still more concrete form to philosophy so that everyone may understand it. Ritual consists of forms, ceremonies, etc. Puranas contain various myths. The cosmogonic myths of the Puranas are very interesting. A certain portion of Hindu mythology is even now presented to the public in the form of dramas during days of Hindu festivals. Thus the minds of the people are saturated with sublime ideas and ideals and lifted to great spiritual heights.

### *Study of Mythology and its Advantages*

There are great truths behind the ancient mythology of Hinduism. You cannot ignore a thing simply because it has a garb of mythology. Do not argue. Shut up your mouth. Keep your intellect at a respectable distance when you study mythology. Intellect is a hindrance. It will delude you. Give up arrogance and vanity. Cultivate love for imagery. Sit like a child and open your heart freely. You will comprehend the great truths revealed by mythology. You will penetrate into the hearts of the Rishis and sages who wrote the mythology. You will really enjoy mythology now.

You study geography through maps. There is no real country or town in a map, but it helps you to know a great deal about the different countries. Similar is the case with myths. You can grasp the subtle philosophical truths through myths.

By studying mythology, you will get several object lessons for moulding your character and leading an ideal divine life. The lives of Sri Rama, Sri Krishna, Bhishma, Nala, Harischandra, Lakshmana, Bharata, Hanuman, Yudhishthira,

Arjuna, Sita, Savitri, Damayanti, Radha, etc., are sources of great spiritual inspiration for moulding your life, conduct and character. When you are in a dilemma as to what to do in puzzling situations and when there is conflict of duties, you will get the exact solutions through study of mythology.

Thus, mythology has its own benefits and advantages. It stamps on the minds the subtle and abstract teachings of the Vedas through instructive stories and illuminating discourses and paves the way for men to lead a divine life and attain perfection, freedom and immortality.

### *Hindu Symbols*

Outward symbols are necessary and beneficial. When viewed from the right angle of vision, you will find that they play a very important part in your material as well as spiritual life. Though they may look very simple and unimportant, they are very scientific and effective.

### *Tilaka—A Mark of Auspiciousness*

Tilaka is a mark of auspiciousness. It is put on the forehead with sandal paste, sacred ashes or Kumkuma. The devotees of Shiva apply sacred ashes (Bhasma) on the forehead, the devotees of Vishnu apply sandal paste (Chandana), and the worshippers of Devi or Shakti apply Kumkuma, a red turmeric powder.

The scriptures say: "A forehead without a Tilaka, a woman without a husband, a Mantra the meaning of which is not known while doing Japa, the head that does not bend before holy personages, a heart without mercy, a house without a well, a village without a temple, a country without a river, a society without a leader, wealth that is not given away in charity, a preceptor without a disciple, a country without justice, a king without an able minister, a woman not obedient to her husband, a well without water, a flower without smell, a soul devoid of holiness, a field without rains, an intellect without clearness, a disciple who does not consider his preceptor as a form of God, a body devoid of health, a custom (Achara) without purity, austerity devoid of fellow-feeling, speech in which truth is not the basis, a country without good people, work without wages,

Sannyasa without renunciation, legs which have not performed pilgrimages, a determination unaided by Viveka or discrimination, a knife which is blunt, a cow which does not give milk, a spear without a point—all these are worthy of condemnation. They exist for name's sake only." From this you can imagine the importance of Tilaka or the sacred mark.

Tilaka is applied at the Ajna Chakra, the space between the two eyebrows. It has a very cooling effect. Application of sandal paste has great medicinal value, apart from the spiritual influence. Application of sandal paste will nullify the heating effect when you concentrate and meditate at the Bhrumadhya. Tilaka indicates the point at which the spiritual eye opens.

Lord Shiva has a third eye at the Bhrumadhya. When He opens the third eye, the three worlds are destroyed. So also, when the third eve of the Jiva is opened, the three kinds of afflictions—Adhyatmika, Adhidaivika and Adhibhautika—are burnt to ashes. The three Karmas—Sanchita, Prarabdha and Agami—and also all the sins committed in the countless previous births, are burnt. When you apply the Tilaka, you mentally imagine: "I am the one non-dual Brahman free from all duality. May my eye of intuition open soon." You should remember this every time you apply a Tilaka.

There are various methods of applying Tilaka. Saivas apply three horizontal lines with the sacred ashes. The Vaishnavas apply three vertical lines (Tripundra) on the forehead. When they apply Tilaka, they say: "O Lord, protect me from the evil effects of the Trigunatmika Maya which has Sattva, Rajas and Tamas as its binding cords." Some Vaishnavas apply only one vertical line. Only the method of application differs, but the significance is the same in both the Vaishnavas and the Saivas.

### *The Tuft—Its Utility and Significance*

Brahmins (Brahmanas) as well as the other castes grow Choti or Sikha, a tuft of hair. This tuff of hair was not so small in olden days, as seen in the present day. It covered the whole brain. They allowed the hair to grow. They never cut the tuft. It protects the brain from any sudden stroke and keeps it cool. The heat of the sun does not affect the head directly. Lack of this tuff has necessitated the use of umbrellas, etc. The tuft is most scientific as well as religious. Any religious act should be performed after tying the tuft. Only the funeral and death anniversaries are performed with tuft untied or with dishevelled hair. It is very inauspicious to remain with dishevelled hair. It is done only in times of great sorrow or calamity. Draupadi took an oath in the assembly of the Kurus when she was molested by Dussasana that she would remain with dishevelled hair until the enemies were properly revenged.

Kaikeyi remained with dishevelled hair in her apartment with the object of getting two boons from Dasaratha which were detrimental to the interests of Rama, the favourite of Dasaratha. Auspicious acts are never undertaken with tuft untied. Nowadays, very few people wear tuft, and even women are neglecting this vital point in their feverish anxiety to copy the West. The tuft of hair has a salutary effect on the essential parts of the brain and the central nervous system.

## Significance of the Sacred Thread

Yajnopavita or the sacred thread is worn by the Brahmins, Kshatriyas and the Vaishyas. Wearing the sacred thread is a very holy and sacred ceremony amongst the Hindus. Brahmin boys between the ages of five and eight are invested with the sacred thread on a very auspicious day. By this ceremony, they become fit for the repetition of Gayatri. A Brahmin becomes a true Brahmin only after this ceremony.

It is said: *"Janmana Jayate Sudrah Karmana Jayate Dvijah*—By birth one is a Sudra; by Karma (*i.e.*, the investiture with the sacred thread) he becomes a Dvija or Brahmin." Upanayana or thread ceremony is the second birth; hence, the Brahmins are called Dvijas (Dvija means 'born twice').

The sacred thread or Yajnopavita consists of three threads. It denotes that one should be a Brahmachari in thought, word and deed. Each thread represents a Veda, *viz.*, the Rig, Yajur and Sama. It represents also Brahma, Vishnu and Shiva. The knot in the middle represents the formless Brahman, the Supreme Principle. The three threads represent also Sattva, Rajas and Tamas of the Trigunatmika Maya, and the knot represents the Isvara who controls Maya. Those who worship God at the three Sandhyas and repeat the Gayatri holding the Brahma knot of the sacred thread, derive immense strength and power. In days of yore, a Brahmana meditating upon the Gayatri holding the Brahma knot, had the power to bless and curse others.

The educated intelligentsia of the present day are quite ignorant of the power of the sacred thread and the performance of Sandhya. That is the reason why they have ignored it. The sacred thread is a great power for the Brahmin who leads a regulated life devoted to the worship of God. Kshatriyas and Vaishyas, too, acquire power, fame and wealth by the power of the sacred thread.

A householder wears, at the time of marriage, an additional sacred thread. A Brahmachari has only one. The additional thread at the time of marriage is intended for the well-being of the partner. The sacred thread should be on the body always. The custom of washing it after removing it from the body or sending it to the washerman, is a wrong procedure. Some people are ashamed to wear the thread when they go to the office and they leave it at home. How ignorant they are!

Yajnopavita, the Choti, caste-mark, etc., are the external symbols to show that one is a Hindu. Purity, self-restraint, non-violence, patience, love for one's fellow-beings—these are the internal marks of a Hindu.

### *Achamana and Prokshana*

Achamana is sipping water three times, repeating the Names of the Lord. Prokshana is sprinkling water over one's body for the sake of purity, when a bath is not possible. This is for internal as well as external purity. While sipping water, the following Mantras are repeated: "*Achyutaya Namah*—prostrations to the immutable Lord; *Anantaya Namah*—prostrations to the unlimited Lord; *Govindaya Namah*—prostrations to the Lord who is known by the Name of Govinda." Then the various Names of the Lord—Keshava, Narayana, Madhava, Govinda, Vishnu, Madhusudana, Trivikrama, Vamana, Sridhara, Hrishikesa, Padmanabha and Damodara—

are repeated, touching the various parts Of the body, *viz.*, the eyes, the ears, the face, the navel, the head, etc.

One becomes pure by doing Achamana after he answers calls of nature, after walking in the streets, just before taking food and after food, and after a bath. This reminds you of the Lord now and then. Every act, every ritual, every symbol has a deep philosophical importance. They help you in changing the mental substance from Rajas and Tamas to Sattva. They give you an opportunity to think of God frequently.

### *Offering Food to God, Guests and the Pancha-Pranas*

Before sitting for food, the place is purified, a seat is put and in a leaf the articles of food are served. Before taking the food, a little water is sprinkled making a line all round the leaf repeating some Vedic Mantras. This repetition purifies the food. Then a little water is sipped. According to science as well as medicine, a little water, if drunk before the food is taken, is highly beneficial.

Then the food is offered to the five Pranas and Brahman seated in the heart, by repeating *Om Pranaya Svaha, Apanaya Svaha, Vyanaya Svaha, Udanaya Svaha, Samanaya Svaha*, and lastly, *Brahmane Svaha*. Just mark the importance of this offering. The person who takes the food offers it to the deities who dwell in the body in the form of Prana, Apana, etc. He does not eat for himself. The physical body is not the eater. It is the Pancha Prana that takes the food. Thus, taking food also can be converted into an act of Yoga or sacrifice.

One should daily offer to the Lord the food that he has prepared, before he partakes of it. He should say: *"Tvadiyam Vastu Govinda Tubhyameva Samarpaye*—I offer to Thee, O Govinda, this (food) which belongs to Thee only." The custom of the Hindus is that they should feed the guest who comes to their house before they take food. The guest is a representative of the Lord. The Srutis say: *"Athhi Devo Bhava."*

### *Bells, Lights, Dhupa, Camphor and Sandal Paste*

Bells are rung in temples while doing Puja, to shut out the external sounds and to make the mind inward and concentrated.

Lights are waved before the Deity. This denotes that the Lord is Jyotis-Svarupa. He is all-light. The devotee says: "O Lord! Thou art the self-effulgent Light of the universe. Thou art the light in the sun, moon and fire. Remove the darkness in me by bestowing your divine light. May my intellect be illumined." This is the significance of waving lights.

Dhupa or scented sticks are burnt before the Deity. The smoke spreads the whole room. It acts as a disinfectant. Burning of Dhupa denotes that the Lord is all-pervading and that He fills the whole universe by His living presence. It is to remind this fact that Dhupa is burnt. The devotee prays: "O Lord! Let the Vasanas and Samskaras dormant in me vanish like the smoke of this Dhupa and become ashes. Let me become stainless." Burning of camphor denotes that the individual ego melts like the camphor and the Jivatman becomes one with the supreme Light of lights.

The sandal paste reminds the devotee that he should, in his difficulties, be as patient as the sandal. Sandal emanates sweet odour when it is rubbed on a hard surface and made into a paste. So also the devotee should not murmur when difficulties arise, but on the other hand, remain cheerful and happy and emanate sweetness and gentleness like the sandal. He should not hate even his enemy. This is another precept we learn from this. Though the sandalwood is crushed and made into a paste, it silently wears out emanating only very sweet odour. One should not wish evil even to his enemy.

### *Prasada—Its Sacredness and Glory*

Prasada is that which gives peace. Prasada is the sacred food offering of the Lord. During Kirtana, worship, Puja, Havan and Arati, the devotee offers sweet rice, fruits, jaggery, milk, coconut, plantain and such other articles to the Lord, according to his ability. After offering them to the Lord, they are shared between the members of the house or the Bhaktas in a temple.

Water, flowers, rice, etc., are offered to the Lord in worship. This denotes that the Lord is pleased with even the smallest offering. What is wanted is the heart of the devotee. The Lord says in the Gita: *"Patram Pushpam Phalam Toyam Yo Me*

*Bhaktya Prayacchati; Tadaham Bhaktyupahritamasnami Prayatatmanah*—Whoever offers a leaf, a flower, a fruit or even water, with devotion, that I accept, offered as it is with a loving heart."

It is not necessary that one should offer gold, silver and costly dress to the Lord. The devotee offers these according to his ability and position in life, thereby denoting that the whole wealth of the world belongs to the Lord. A rich man offers costly things to the Lord. He feeds the poor and serves the sick, seeing the Lord in his fellow-beings.

Puja is done with Bael leaves, flowers, Tulasi, Vibhuti and these are given as Prasada from the Lord. Vibhuti is the Prasada of Lord Shiva. It is to be applied on the forehead. A small portion can be taken in. Kumkuma is the Prasada of Sri Devi or Shakti. It is to be applied at the space between the eyebrows (Ajna or Bhrumadhya). Tulasi is the Prasada of Lord Vishnu, Rama or Krishna. It is to be taken in. They are charged with mysterious powers by the chanting of Mantras during Puja and Havan.

The mental Bhava of the devotee offering Bhog to the Lord has a very great effect. If an ardent devotee of the Lord offers anything to the Lord, that Prasada, if taken, would bring very great change even in the minds of atheists. The Grace of the Lord descends through Prasada. Go through the life of Narada. You will realise the greatness of the sacred leavings of the Lord as well as those of advanced Sadhakas and saints.

Namadeva offered rice, etc., to Panduranga Vitthala and He ate the food and shared it with Namadeva as well. If the food is offered with an yearning heart, sometimes, the Lord takes that food assuming a physical form. In other cases, the Lord enjoys the subtle essence of the food offered, and the food remains as it is in the shape of Prasada. While feeding Mahatmas and the poor people, that which is left behind is taken as Prasada. When a sacrifice is performed, the participants share the Prasada which bestows the blessings of the gods. When Dasaratha performed Putrakameshti (a sacrifice performed wishing for son), he got a vessel full of sweetened rice which he gave to his queens, by taking which they became pregnant.

Prasada is the most sacred object for a devotee. One should consider himself lucky to take the Prasada, and there is no restriction of any kind in taking Prasada. Time and place, and the condition in which one is placed—all these do not affect him in any way. Prasada is all-purifying.

The benefits of Prasada and Charanamrita are beyond description. They have the power to change entirely the outlook of a man's life. Prasada and Charanamrita have the power to cure diseases and even bring back to life dead persons.

There had been ever so many instances in the past in this holy land of ours which bear witness to the potency and efficacy of Prasada. Prasada destroys all pains and sins. It is an antidote for misery, pain and anxiety. Faith is the important factor in testing the accuracy of this statement. For faithless persons, it brings very little effect.

Those who are brought up in modern education and culture have forgotten all about the glory of Prasada. Many English-educated persons do not attach any importance to Prasada when they get it from Mahatmas. This is a serious mistake. Prasada is a great purifier. As they are brought up in the western style of living, they have imbibed the spirit of westerners and forgotten the spirit of the true children of Indian Rishis of yore. Live for a week in Vrindavana or Ayodhya or Varanasi or Pandharpur. You will realise the glory and the miraculous effects of Prasada.

Many incurable diseases are cured. Many sincere devotional aspirants get wonderful spiritual experiences from mere Prasada alone. Prasada is a panacea. Prasada is a spiritual elixir. Prasada is the Grace of the Lord. Prasada is a cure-all and an ideal pick-me-up. Prasada is an embodiment of Shakti. Prasada is Divinity in manifestation. Prasada energises, vivifies, invigorates and infuses devotion. It should be taken with great faith.

### *The Japa Mala*

***Significance of the Number of Beads*:** Generally, the rosary or Mala used for Japa contains 108 beads. A man breathes 21,600 times every day. If one does 200 Malas of Japa, it becomes 21,600; thereby, he does one Japa for every breath.

If he does 200 Malas of Japa every day, that amounts to remembrance of God throughout the day.

Malas may contain beads which form divisions of 108 also, so that the same calculation can be maintained. The Meru (the central bead in the Mala) denotes that you have done your Japa 108 times. This also denotes that every time you come to the Meru bead, you have gone one step further on the spiritual path and crossed over one obstacle. A portion of your ignorance is removed. A rosary or Mala is a whip to goad you to do Japa. Mohammedans also have a rosary (Tasbi) in their hands when they repeat their prayers. They roll the beads and repeat the name of Allah. Christians have their paternoster.

### *The Raksha Stotra*

Before sitting for Japa and meditation, the Raksha Stotra is generally repeated. It means: "May the Lord protect me, staying in every part of my body." Each part is separately named and a particular Name of the Lord is repeated for the protection of that part. Anganyasa and Karanyasa also have the same effect. They drive away the evil effects of evil spirits, if any. The obstacles that stand in the way of concentration and meditation are removed. Evil thoughts will not enter the mind. This is a prayer to remove obstacles in Japa and meditation.

### *The Ochre Cloth and the Shaven Head*

***Symbols of Renunciation*:** The ochre colour (Gerua) of the dress of a Sannyasin indicates that he is as pure as fire itself. He shines like the burnt gold, free from all impurities of desires and Vasanas. It denotes purity. It stands for purity. For an aspirant who has taken to the path of Nivritti Marga, it is a help. He will swerve and shrink from evil actions. This cloth will remind him that he is not entitled to worldly enjoyments. Gradually his nature will be moulded. This coloured cloth serves as an external symptom to show that one is a Sannyasin.

A Sannyasin shaves his head completely. This removes from him all beauty. He will not have to take care about dressing his hair with scented oils, etc. This shows that he has renounced all external beauties and that he dwells in the Self which is Beauty of beauties. This Mundana (shaving of head) indicates that he is no more of the world. He should not desire any sensual object. It is only an external symbol of the mental state of complete dispassion and turning away from the pleasures of the world.

He removes his Choti also at the time of Sannyasa to indicate that he is no more bound by the various Nitya and Naimittika Karmas and that they have been burnt in the fire of Vairagya. Further, this shaving of the head is suitable for a wandering life. The existence of long hairs will prevent him from taking bath whenever he likes. Shaving will relieve him of much worry, and the time he would have otherwise spent in drying, combing and dressing his hair he may spend in prayers and meditation.

### *Conclusion*

The Vedas and the Upanishads state that the ultimate truth in its pure and naked form, very unceremoniously. The Itihasas, Puranas and Agamas give this truth a homely, personal and symbolic touch through narration of history, legend and mythology. Do not neglect outward symbols. Make a research study of our Vedic customs and injunctions. You will find wonderful and precious gems in every one of them. Their utility and efficacy will be revealed in following them. May you all tread the path of Dharma and attain Kaivalya Moksha in this very birth.

# 5

# Serving God with Faith and Confidence

Regarding accepting initiation from the spiritual master, in the Eleventh Canto of Srimad-Bhagavatam, Seventeenth Chapter, verse 27, it is stated by Lord Krishna, "My dear Uddhava, the spiritual master must be accepted not only as My representative, but as My very self. He must never be considered on the same level with an ordinary human being. One should never be envious of the spiritual master, as one may be envious of an ordinary man. The spiritual master should always be seen as the representative of the Supreme Personality of Godhead, and by serving the spiritual master one is able to serve all the demigods."

### *Following in the Footsteps of Saintly Persons*

In the Skanda Purana it is advised that a devotee follow the past acaryas and saintly persons, because by such following one can achieve the desired results, with no chance of lamenting or being baffled in his progress.

The scripture known as Brahma-yamala states as follows: "If someone wants to pose himself as a great devotee without following the authorities of the revealed scriptures, then his activities will never help him to make progress in devotional service. Instead, he will simply create disturbances for the sincere students of devotional service." Those who do not strictly follow the principles of revealed scriptures are generally called sahajiyas—those who have imagined everything to be cheap, who have their own concocted ideas, and who do not follow the scriptural injunctions. Such persons are simply creating disturbances in the discharge of devotional service.

In this connection, an objection may be raised by those who are not in devotional service and who do not care for the revealed scriptures. An example of this is seen in Buddhist philosophy. Lord Buddha appeared in the family of a high-grade kshatriya king, but his philosophy was not in accord with the Vedic conclusions and therefore was rejected. Under the patronage of a Hindu king, Maharaja Ashoka, the Buddhist religion was spread all over India and the adjoining countries. However, after the appearance of the great stalwart teacher Shankaracarya, this Buddhism was driven out beyond the borders of India.

The Buddhists or other religionists who do not care for revealed scriptures sometimes say that there are many devotees of Lord Buddha who show devotional service to Lord Buddha, and who therefore should be considered devotees. In answer to this argument, Rupa Goswami says that the followers of Buddha cannot be accepted as devotees. Although Lord Buddha is accepted as an incarnation of Krishna, the followers of such incarnations are not very advanced in their knowledge of the Vedas. To study the Vedas means to come to the conclusion of the supremacy of the Personality of Godhead. Therefore any religious principle which denies the supremacy of the Personality of Godhead is not accepted and is called atheism. Atheism means defying the authority of the Vedas and decrying the great acaryas who teach Vedic scriptures for the benefit of the people in general.

Lord Buddha is accepted as an incarnation of Krishna in the Srimad-Bhagavatam, but in the same Srimad-Bhagavatam it is stated that Lord Buddha appeared in order to bewilder the atheistic class of men. Therefore his philosophy is meant for bewildering the atheists and should not be accepted. If someone asks, "Why should Krishna propagate atheistic principles?" The answer is that it was the desire of the Supreme Personality of Godhead to end the violence which was then being committed in the name of the Vedas. The so-called religionists were falsely using the Vedas to justify such violent acts as meat-eating, and

Lord Buddha came to lead the fallen people away from such a false interpretation of the Vedas. Also, for the atheists Lord Buddha preached atheism so that they would follow him and thus be tricked into devotional service to Lord Buddha, or Krishna.

***Inquiring about Eternal Religious Principles***

In the Naradiya Purana it is said, "If one is actually very serious about devotional service, then all of his purposes will be served without any delay."

Being Prepared to Give Up Everything Material for Krishna's Satisfaction. In the Padma Purana it is stated, "For one who has given up his material sense enjoyment and has accepted the principles of devotional service, the opulence of Vishnuloka [the kingdom of God] is awaiting."

***Residing in a Sacred Place***

In the Skanda Purana it is also said that for a person who has lived in Dwarka for six months, for one month, or even for one fortnight, there is awaiting elevation to the Vaikunthalokas and all the profits of sarupya-mukti (the privilege of having the same four-handed bodily features as Narayana).

In the Brahma Purana it is said, "The transcendental significance of Purushottama-kshetra, which is the eighty-square-mile field of Lord Jagannath, cannot be properly described. Even the demigods from higher planetary systems see the inhabitants of this Jagannath Puri as having exactly the same bodily features possessed by one in Vaikuntha. That is, the demigods see the inhabitants of Jagannath Puri as being four-handed."

When there was a meeting of great sages at Naimisharanya, Suta Goswami was reciting Srimad-Bhagavatam, and the importance of the Ganges was stated as follows: "The waters of the Ganges are always carrying the flavour of tulasi offered at the lotus feet of Sri Krishna, and as such the waters of the Ganges are ever flowing, spreading the glories of Lord Krishna. Wherever the waters of the Ganges are flowing, all will be sanctified, both externally and internally."

### *Accepting Only What is Necessary*

In the Naradiya Purana it is directed, "One should not accept more than necessary if he is serious about discharging devotional service."

The purport is that one should not neglect following the principles of devotional service, nor should one accept the rulings of devotional service which are more than what he can easily perform. For example, it may be said that one should chant the Hare Krishna mantra at least one hundred thousand times daily on his beads.

But if this is not possible, then one must minimize his chanting according to his own capacity. Generally, we recommend our disciples to chant at least sixteen rounds on their japa beads daily, and this should be completed. But if one is not even able to chant sixteen rounds, then he must make it up the next day. He must be sure to keep his vow. If he does not strictly follow this out, then he is sure to be negligent. That is offensive in the service of the Lord. If we encourage offences, we shall not be able to make progress in devotional service. It is better if one fixes up a regulative principle according to his own ability and then follows that vow without fail. That will make him advanced in spiritual life.

### *Observing Fasting on Ekadasi*

In the Brahma-vaivarta Purana it is said that one who observes fasting on Ekadasi day is freed from all kinds of reactions to sinful activities and advances in pious life. The basic principle is not just to fast, but to increase one's faith and love for Govinda, or Krishna. The real reason for observing fasting on Ekadasi is to minimize the demands of the body and to engage our time in the service of the Lord by chanting or performing similar service. The best thing to do on fasting days is to remember the pastimes of Govinda and to hear His holy name constantly.

### *Offering Respect to the Banyan Trees*

In the Skanda Purana it is directed that a devotee should offer water to the tulasi plant and amalaka trees. He should offer respect to the cows and to the brahmanas and should serve the Vaishnavas by offering them respectful obeisances and meditating upon them. All of these processes will help the devotee to diminish the reactions to his past sinful activities.

### *Giving Up the Company of Nondevotees*

Lord Chaitanya was once asked by one of His householder devotees what the general behaviour of a Vaishnava should be. In this connection, Lord Chaitanya replied that a Vaishnava should always give up the company of nondevotees. Then He explained that there are two kinds of nondevotees: one class is against the supremacy of Krishna, and another class is too materialistic. In other words, those who are after material enjoyment and those who are against the supremacy of the Lord are called avaishnava, and their company should be strictly avoided.

In the Katyayana-samhita it is stated that even if one is forced to live within a cage of iron or in the midst of a blazing fire, he should accept this position rather than live with nondevotees who are through and through against the supremacy of the Lord. Similarly, in the Vishnu-rahasya there is a statement to the effect that one should prefer to embrace a snake, a tiger or an alligator rather than associate with persons who are worshippers of various demigods and who are impelled by material desire.

In the scriptures it is instructed that one may worship a certain demigod if he is desirous of achieving some material gain. For example, one is advised to worship the sun-god if he is desirous of getting rid of a diseased condition. For a beautiful wife, one may worship Uma, the wife of Lord Shiva, and for advanced education one may worship Saraswati. Similarly, there is a list in the Srimad-Bhagavatam for worshippers of all demigods, according to different material desires.

But all of these worshippers, although they appear to be very good devotees of the demigods, are still considered to be nondevotees. They cannot be accepted as devotees. The Mayavadis (impersonalists) say that one may worship any form.

of the Lord and that it doesn't matter, because one reaches the same destination anyway.

But it is clearly stated in the Bhagwad Gita that those who are worshippers of the demigods will ultimately reach only the planets of those demigods, while those who are devotees of the Lord Himself will be promoted to the Lord's abode, the kingdom of God. So actually these persons who are worshippers of demigods have been condemned in the Gita. It is described that due to their lusty desires they have lost their intelligence and have therefore taken to worshipping the different demigods. So in the Vishnu-rahasya these demigod worshippers are forcefully condemned by the statement that it is better to live with the most dangerous animals than to associate with these persons.

### *Not Accepting Unfit Disciples, Constructing Many Temples or Reading Many Books*

Another stricture is that a person may have many disciples, but he should not act in such a way that he will be obliged to any of them for some particular action or some favour. And one should also not be very enthusiastic about constructing new temples, nor should one be enthusiastic about reading various types of books, save and except the ones which lead to the advancement of devotional service. Practically, if one very carefully reads Bhagwad Gita, Srimad-Bhagavatam, Teachings of Lord Chaitanya and this Nectar of Devotion, that will give him sufficient knowledge to understand the science of Krishna consciousness. One need not take the trouble of reading other books.

In the Seventh Canto of Srimad-Bhagavatam, Thirteenth Chapter, verse 8, Narada Muni, while discussing with Maharaja Yudhishthira the various functions of the different orders in society, especially mentions rules for the sannyasis, those persons who have renounced this material world. One who has accepted the sannyasa order of life is forbidden to accept as a disciple anyone who is not fit. A sannyasi should first of all examine whether a prospective student is sincerely seeking Krishna consciousness. If he is not, he should not be accepted. However, Lord Chaitanya's causeless mercy is such that He advised all bona fide spiritual masters to speak about Krishna consciousness everywhere. Therefore, in the line of Lord Chaitanya even the sannyasis can speak about Krishna consciousness everywhere, and if someone is seriously inclined to become a disciple, the sannyasi always accepts him.

The one point is that without increasing the number of disciples, there is no propagation of the cult of Krishna consciousness. Therefore, sometimes even at a risk, a sannyasi in the line of Chaitanya Mahaprabhu may accept even a person who is not thoroughly fit to become a disciple. Later on, by the mercy of such a bona fide spiritual master, the disciple is gradually elevated. However, if one increases the number of disciples simply for some prestige or false honour, he will surely fall down in the matter of executing Krishna consciousness.

Similarly, a bona fide spiritual master has no business reading many books simply to show his proficiency or to get popularity by lecturing in different places. One should avoid all these things. It is also stated that a sannyasi should not be enthusiastic about constructing temples. We can see in the lives of various acaryas in the line of Sri Chaitanya Mahaprabhu that they are not very enthusiastic about constructing temples. However, if somebody comes forward to offer some service, the same reluctant acaryas will encourage the building of costly temples by such servitors. For example, Rupa Goswami was offered a favour by Maharaja Mansingh, the commander-in-chief of Emperor Akbar, and Rupa Goswami instructed him to construct a large temple for Govindaji, which cost vast amounts of money.

So a bona fide spiritual master should not personally take any responsibility for constructing temples, but if someone has money and wants to spend it in the service of Krishna, an acharya like Rupa Goswami may utilize the devotee's money to construct a nice, costly temple for the service of the Lord. Unfortunately, it happens that someone who is not fit to become a spiritual master may approach wealthy persons to contribute for temple constructions. If such money is utilized by unqualified spiritual masters for living comfortably in costly temples without actually doing any preaching work, this is not acceptable. In other words, a spiritual master needn't be very enthusiastic for constructing temple buildings simply in the name of so-called spiritual advancement.

Rather, his first and foremost activity should be to preach. In this connection, Srila Bhaktisiddhanta Saraswati Goswami Maharaja recommended that a spiritual master print books. If one has money, instead of constructing costly temples, one should spend his money for the publication of authorized books in different languages for propagating the Krishna consciousness movement.

### *Straightforwardness in Ordinary Dealings and Equilibrium in Loss and Gain*

There is a statement in the Padma Purana: "Persons who are engaged in Krishna consciousness should never be disturbed by some material gain or loss. Even if there is some material loss, one should not be perturbed, but should always think of Krishna within himself." The purport is that every conditioned soul is always absorbed in thinking of materialistic activities; he has to free himself from such thoughts and transfer himself completely to Krishna consciousness. As we have already explained, the basic principle of Krishna consciousness is to always think of Krishna. One should not be disturbed in material loss, but, rather, should concentrate his mind upon the lotus feet of the Lord.

A devotee should not be subjected to lamentation or illusion. There is the following statement in the Padma Purana: "Within the heart of a person who is overpowered by lamentation or anger, there is no possibility of Krishna's being manifested."

### *The Demigods*

One should not neglect to offer due respect to the demigods. One may not be a devotee of demigods, but that does not mean that he should be disrespectful to them. For example, a Vaishnava is not a devotee of Lord Shiva or Lord Brahma, but he is duty-bound to offer all respects to such highly positioned demigods. According to Vaishnava philosophy, one should offer respect even to an ant, so then what is there to speak of such exalted persons as Lord Shiva and Lord Brahma?

In the Padma Purana it is said, "Krishna, or Hari, is the master of all demigods, and therefore He is always worshipable. But this does not mean that one should not offer respect to the demigods."

## Not Giving Pain to any Living Entity

This is the statement of Mahabharata: "A person who does not disturb or cause painful action in the mind of any living entity, who treats everyone just like a loving father does his children, whose heart is so pure, certainly very soon becomes favoured by the Supreme Personality of Godhead."

In so-called civilized society there is sometimes agitation against cruelty to animals, but at the same time regular slaughterhouses are always maintained. A Vaishnava is not like that. A Vaishnava can never support animal slaughter or even give pain to any living entity.

Other rules are that one should not offer foodstuff which is cooked by a non-Vaishnava, one should not worship the Deity before a nondevotee, and one should not engage himself in the worship of the Lord while seeing a nondevotee. One should begin the worship of the demigod Ganapati, who drives away all impediments in the execution of devotional service. In the Brahma-samhita it is stated that Ganapati worships the lotus feet of Lord Nrisimhadeva and in that way has become auspicious for the devotees in clearing out all impediments. Therefore, all devotees should worship Ganapati.

The Deities should not be bathed in water which has been touched by the nails or fingers. When a devotee is perspiring, he should not engage himself in worshipping the Deity. Similarly, there are many other prohibitions. For example, one should not cross or step over the flowers offered to the Deities, nor should one take a vow in the name of God. These are all different kinds of offences in the matter of executing devotional service, and one should be careful to avoid them. In the Padma Purana it is stated that even a person whose life is completely sinful will be completely protected by the Lord if he simply surrenders unto Him.

So it is accepted that one who surrenders unto the Supreme Personality of Godhead becomes free from all sinful reactions. And even when a person becomes an offender unto the Supreme Personality of Godhead Himself, he can still be delivered simply by taking shelter of the holy names of the Lord: Hare Krishna, Hare Krishna, Krishna Krishna, Hare Hare/ Hare Rama, Hare Rama, Rama Rama, Hare Hare. In other words, the chanting of Hare Krishna is beneficial for eradicating all sins, but if one becomes an offender to the holy names of the Lord, then he has no chance of being delivered.

The offences against the chanting of the holy name are as follows: (1) To blaspheme the devotees who have dedicated their lives for propagating the holy name of the Lord. (2) To consider the names of demigods like Lord Shiva or Lord Brahma to be equal to, or independent of, the name of Lord Vishnu. (Sometimes the atheistic class of men take it that any demigod is as good as the Supreme Personality of Godhead, Vishnu. But one who is a devotee knows that no demigod, however great he may be, is independently as good as the Supreme Personality of Godhead.

Therefore, if someone thinks that he can chant "Kali, Kali!" or "Durga, Durga!" and it is the same as Hare Krishna, that is the greatest offense.) (3) To disobey the orders of the spiritual master. (4) To blaspheme the Vedic literature or literature in pursuance of the Vedic version. (5) To consider the glories of chanting Hare Krishna to be imagination. (6) To give some interpretation on the holy name of the Lord. (7) To commit sinful activities on the strength of the holy name of the Lord. (It should not be taken that because by chanting the holy name of the Lord one can be freed from all kinds of sinful reaction, one may continue to act sinfully and after that chant Hare Krishna to neutralize his sins. Such a dangerous mentality is very offensive and should be avoided.) (8) To consider the chanting of Hare Krishna one of the auspicious ritualistic activities offered in the Vedas as fruitive activities (karma-kanda). (9) To instruct a faithless person about the glories of the holy name. (Anyone can take part in chanting the holy name of the Lord, but in the beginning one should not be instructed about the transcendental potency of the Lord. Those who are too sinful cannot appreciate the transcendental glories of the Lord, and therefore it is better not to instruct them in this matter.) (10) To not have complete faith in the chanting of the holy names and to maintain material attachments, even after understanding so many instructions on this matter.

Every devotee who claims to be a Vaishnava must guard against these offences in order to quickly achieve the desired success.

There are three ways of dealing with such insults. If someone is heard blaspheming by words, one should be so expert that he can defeat the opposing party by argument. If he is unable to defeat the opposing party, then the next step is that he should not just stand there meekly, but should give up his life. The third process is followed if he is unable to execute the above-mentioned two processes, and this is that one must leave the place and go away. If a devotee does not follow any of the above-mentioned three processes, he falls down from his position of devotion.

### *Tilaka and Tulasi Beads*

In the Padma Purana there is a statement describing how a Vaishnava should decorate his body with tilaka and beads: "Persons who put tulasi beads on the neck, who mark twelve places of their bodies as Vishnu temples with Vishnu's symbolic representations [the four items held in the four hands of Lord Vishnu—conch, mace, disc and lotus], and who have vishnu-tilaka on their foreheads, are to be understood as the devotees of Lord Vishnu in this world. Their presence makes the world purified, and anywhere they remain, they make that place as good as Vaikuntha."

A similar statement is in the Skanda Purana, which says, "Persons who are decorated with tilaka or gopi-chandana [a kind of clay resembling fuller's earth which is produced in certain quarters of Vrindavana], and who mark their bodies all over with the holy names of the Lord, and on whose necks and breasts there are tulasi beads, are never approached by the Yamadutas." The Yamadutas are the constables of King Yama (the lord of death), who punishes all sinful men. Vaishnavas are never called for by such constables of Yamaraja. In the Srimad-Bhagavatam, in the narration of Ajamila's deliverance, it is said that Yamaraja gave clear instructions to his assistants not to approach the Vaishnavas. Vaishnavas are beyond the jurisdiction of Yamaraja's activities.

The Padma Purana also mentions, "A person whose body is decorated with the pulp of sandalwood, with paintings of the holy name of the Lord, is delivered from all sinful reactions, and after his death he goes directly to Krishnaloka to live in association with the Supreme Personality of Godhead."

### *Accepting Flower Garlands*

The next instruction is that one should put on flower garlands which are offered to the Deity. In this connection, in the Eleventh Canto, Sixth Chapter, verse 46, of Srimad-Bhagavatam, Uddhava says to Krishna, "My dear Krishna, I have taken things which You have used and enjoyed, such as garlands of flowers, saintly articles, garments and ornaments, and I eat only the remnants of Your foodstuff, because I am Your menial servant.

So, therefore, I am sure that I shall not be attacked by the spell of material energy." The purport of this verse is that for any person who simply follows these rules and regulations of decorating the body with the marks of tilaka of gopi-chandana or sandalwood pulp, and who puts on the garlands which were offered to Krishna, there is no question of being conquered by the spell of material energy.

At the time of death, there is no question of such a person's being called by the constables of Yamaraja. Even if one does not accept all the Vaishnava principles, but still takes the remnants of foodstuff offered to Krishna, or krishna-prasada, he will gradually become qualified to rise to the platform of a Vaishnava.

Similarly, in the Skanda Purana Lord Brahma tells Narada, "My dear Narada, anyone who puts on his neck the flower garland which was formerly used by Krishna becomes relieved from all disease and reactions to sinful activities, and gradually he is liberated from the contamination of matter."

### *Dancing Before the Deity*

In the Dwarka-mahatmya the importance of dancing before the Deity is stated by Lord Krishna as follows: "A person who is in a jubilant spirit, who feels profound devotional ecstasy while dancing before Me, and who manifests different features of bodily expression can burn away all the accumulated sinful reactions he has stocked up for many, many thousands of years."

In the same book there is a statement by Narada wherein he asserts, "From the body of any person who claps and dances before the Deity, showing manifestations of ecstasy, all the birds of sinful activities fly away upward." Just as by clapping the hands one can cause many birds to fly away, similarly the birds of all sinful activities which are sitting on the body can be made to fly away simply by dancing and clapping before the Deity of Krishna.

### *Bowing Down in Honour of the Deity*

In the Naradiya Purana there is a statement about bowing down and offering respect to the Deity. It is said there, "A person who has performed a great ritualistic sacrifice and a person who has simply offered his respectful obeisances by bowing down before the Lord cannot be held as equals." The person who has executed many great sacrifices will attain the result of his pious activities, but when such results are finished, he has to take birth again on the earthly planet; however, the person who has once offered respects, bowing down before the Deity, will not come back to this world, because he will go directly to the abode of Krishna.

### *Standing Up to Receive the Lord*

In the Brahmanda Purana it is said, "A person who sees the Lord's Ratha-yatra car festival and then stands up to receive the Lord can purge all kinds of sinful results from his body."

***Following the Deity***

A similar statement is there in the Bhavishya Purana, in which it is said, "Even if born of a lowly family, a person who follows the Ratha-yatra car when the Deities pass in front or from behind will surely be elevated to the position of achieving equal opulence with Vishnu."

***Going to the Temple of Vishnu or to Places of Pilgrimage***

It is stated in the Puranas, "Persons who attempt to visit the holy places of pilgrimage, like Vrindavana, Mathura or Dwarka, are actually glorified. By such travelling activities, they can pass over the desert of material existence."

In the Hari-bhakti-sudhodaya there is a statement about the benefit of visiting the temples of Lord Krishna. As we have explained previously, in Vrindavana, Mathura and Dwarka the system is that all the devotees take advantage of visiting various temples situated in those holy places. It is stated in the Hari-bhakti-sudhodaya, "Persons who are impelled by pure devotional service in Krishna consciousness and who therefore go to see the Deities of Vishnu in the temple will surely get relief from entering again into the prison house of a mother's womb." The conditioned soul forgets the trouble of living within the mother's womb during birth, but it is a very painful and terrible experience. In order to make an escape from this material condition, one is advised to visit a temple of Vishnu with devotional consciousness. Then one can very easily get out of the miserable condition of material birth.

## Circumambulating the Temple of Vishnu

It is said in the Hari-bhakti-sudhodaya, "A person who is circumambulating the Deity of Vishnu can counteract the circumambulation of repeated birth and death in this material world." The conditioned soul is circumambulating through repeated births and deaths on account of his material existence, and this can be counteracted simply by circumambulating the Deity in the temple.

The Chaturmasya ceremony is observed during the four months of the rainy season in India (approximately July, August,

September and October), beginning from Sravana. During these four months, saintly persons who are accustomed to travel from one place to another to propagate Krishna consciousness remain at one place, usually a holy place of pilgrimage. During these times, there are certain special rules and regulations which are strictly followed.

It is stated in the Skanda Purana that during this period, if someone circumambulates the temple of Vishnu at least four times, it is understood that he has travelled all over the universe. By such circumambulation, one is understood to have seen all the holy places where the Ganges water is flowing, and by following the regulative principles of Chaturmasya one can very quickly be raised to the platform of devotional service.

***Archana***

Archana means worship of the Deity in the temple. By executing this process one confirms himself to be not the body but spirit soul. In the Tenth Canto, Eighty-first Chapter, verse 19, of Srimad-Bhagavatam, it is told how Sudama, an intimate friend of Krishna's, while going to the house of a brahmana, murmured to himself, "Simply by worshipping Krishna one can easily achieve all the results of heavenly opulence, liberation, supremacy over the planetary systems of the universe, all the opulences of this material world, and the mystic power of performing the yoga system.

The events leading to Sudama's murmuring this statement are as follows. Sri Krishna had ordered His friend Sudama to go to a brahmana's house and ask for some food. The brahmanas were performing a great sacrifice, and Sri Krishna told Sudama to plead with them that He and Balram were feeling hungry and needed some food. When Sudama went there, the brahmanas refused to offer anything, but the wives of the brahmanas, upon hearing that Sri Krishna wanted some foodstuff, immediately took many palatable dishes and went to offer them to Sri Krishna. In the Vishnu-rahasya, also, it is stated, "Any person within this world who is engaged in the worship of Vishnu can very easily achieve the ever-blissful kingdom of God, known as Vaikunthaloka."

***Rendering Service to the Lord***

It is stated in the Vishnu-rahasya, "Any person who can arrange for service to the Lord in the same way that a king is given service by his attendants is surely elevated to the abode of Krishna after death." Actually, in India the temples are just like royal palaces. They are not ordinary buildings, because the worship of Krishna should be performed in just the way that a king is worshipped in his palace. So in Vrindavana there are many hundreds of temples wherein the Deity is worshipped exactly like a king. In the Naradiya Purana it is stated, "H a person stays in the Lord's temple even for a few moments, he can surely achieve the transcendental kingdom of God."

The conclusion is that those who are rich men in society should construct beautiful temples and arrange for the worship of Vishnu, so that people may be attracted to visit such temples and thereby be offered the opportunity of dancing before the Lord or chanting the holy name of the Lord, or else of hearing the holy name of the Lord. In this way, everyone will be given the chance to elevate himself to the kingdom of God. In other words, even a common man, simply by visiting such a temple, will be able to attain the highest benedictions, not to mention the devotees who are constantly engaged in the service of the Lord in full Krishna consciousness.

In this connection, there is a statement in the Fourth Canto, Twenty-first Chapter, verse 31, of the Srimad-Bhagavatam, wherein King Prithu says to his subjects, "My dear citizens, please note that the Supreme Personality of Godhead, Hari, is actually the deliverer of all fallen, conditioned souls. No demigod can perform this act of delivering the conditioned souls, because the demigods themselves are conditioned. A conditioned soul cannot deliver another conditioned soul. Only Krishna or His bona fide representative can deliver him. The Ganges water which is flowing down from the toe of Lord Vishnu falls upon the earthly planet and other planets and thereby delivers all the conditioned sinful living entities. So what need is there to speak of the deliverance of persons who are always engaged in the service of the Lord?

There is no doubt about their liberation, even if they have stocks of sinful activities from many, many births." In other words, a person who is engaged in the worship of the Deities can minimize his stock of sinful reactions coming from many, many previous births. This process of worshipping the Deity has already been described, and one should try to follow these rules and regulations seriously.

### *Singing*

In the Linga Purana there is a statement about glorifying and singing about the Lord. It is said there, "A brahmana who is constantly engaged in singing the glories of the Lord is surely elevated to the same planet as the Supreme Personality of Godhead. Lord Krishna appreciates this singing even more than the prayers offered by Lord Shiva."

### *Sankirtana*

When a person loudly chants the glories of the Lord's activities, qualities, form, etc., his chanting is called sankirtana. Sankirtana also refers to the congregational chanting of the holy name of the Lord.

In the Vishnu-dharma there is a statement glorifying this process of congregational chanting: "My dear King, this word Krishna is so auspicious that anyone who chants this holy name immediately gets rid of the resultant actions of sinful activities from many, many births." That is a fact. There is the following statement in Chaitanya-charitamrita: "A person who chants the holy name of Krishna once can counteract the resultant actions of more sinful activities than he is able to perform." A sinful man can perform many, many sinful activities, but he is unable to perform so many that they cannot be wiped out by one single uttering of Krishna.

In the Seventh Canto, Ninth Chapter, verse 18, of Srimad-Bhagavatam, Maharaja Prahlada offers the following prayers to the Lord: "My dear Lord Nrisimha, if I can be elevated to the position of Your servant, then it will be possible for me to hear about Your activities. You are the supreme friend, the supreme worshipable Deity. Your pastimes are transcendental, and simply by hearing of them one can counteract all his sinful activities. Therefore, I shall not care for all those sinful activities, because simply by hearing about Your pastimes I shall get out of all the contamination of material attachment."

There are many songs about the Lord's activities. For example, there is the Brahma-samhita, sung by Lord Brahma; Narada-Pancharatra, sung by Narada Muni; and Srimad-Bhagavatam, sung by Sukhdeva Goswami. If these songs are heard by any person, he can easily get out of the clutches of material contamination. There should be no difficulty in hearing these songs of God. They are coming down from many, many millions of years ago, and people are still taking advantage of them. So why, at this time, should one not take full advantage and thus become liberated?

In the First Canto, Fifth Chapter, verse 22, of Srimad-Bhagavatam, Narada Muni tells his disciple Vyasadeva, "My dear Vyasa, you should know that persons who are engaged in executing austerities and penances, studying the Vedas, performing big sacrifices, chanting the hymns of the Vedas, speculating on transcendental knowledge and performing charitable functions have for all their auspicious activities simply to gain a place in the association of devotees and chant the glories of the Lord." It is indicated here that chanting about and glorifying the Lord is the ultimate activity of the living entity.

## Japa

Chanting a mantra or hymn softly and slowly is called japa, and chanting the same mantra loudly is called kirtana. For example, uttering the maha-mantra (Hare Krishna, Hare Krishna, Krishna Krishna, Hare Hare/ Hare Rama, Hare Rama, Rama Rama, Hare Hare) very softly, only for one's own hearing, is called japa. Chanting the same mantra loudly for being heard by all others is called kirtana.

The maha-mantra can be used for japa and kirtana also. When japa is practiced it is for the personal benefit of the chanter, but when kirtana is performed it is for the benefit of all others who may hear.

In the Padma Purana there is a statement: "For any person who is chanting the holy name either softly or loudly, the paths to liberation and even heavenly happiness are at once open."

***Submission***

In the Skanda Purana there is a statement about submission unto the lotus feet of the Lord. It is said there that those who are sober devotees can offer their submission to Krishna in the following three ways: (1) samprarthanatmika, very feelingly offering prayers; (2) dainyavodhika, humbly submitting oneself; (3) lalasamayi, desiring some perfectional stage. This desiring some perfectional stage in spiritual life is not sense gratification. When one realizes something of his constitutional relationship with the Supreme Personality of Godhead, he understands his original position and wants to be reinstated in this position, either as friend, servant, parent or conjugal lover of Krishna.

That is called lalasamayi, or very eagerly desiring to go to one's natural position. This lalasamayi stage of submission comes in the stage of perfect liberation, which is technically called svarupa-siddhi, when the living entity understands, by perfect spiritual advancement and revelation, his original relationship with the Lord.

In the Padma Purana there is a statement of submission in feeling by devotees praying to the Lord: "My Lord, I know that young girls have natural affection for young boys, and that young boys have natural affection for young girls. I am praying at Your lotus feet that my mind may become attracted unto You in the same spontaneous way." The example is very appropriate. When a young boy or girl sees a member of the opposite sex there is a natural attraction, without the need for any introduction.

Without any training there is a natural attraction due to the sex impulse. This is a material example, but the devotee is praying that he may develop a similar spontaneous attachment for the Supreme Lord, free from any desire for profit and without any other cause. This natural attraction for the Lord is the perfectional stage of self-realization.

In the same Padma Purana there is a statement about submission in humbleness. It is stated there, "My dear Lord, there is no sinful living entity who is more of a sinner than myself. Nor is there a greater offender than myself. I am so greatly sinful and offensive that when I come to confess my sinful activities before You, I am ashamed." This is a natural position for a devotee.

As far as the conditioned soul is concerned, there is no wonder that he has some sinful activities in his past life, and this should be admitted and confessed before the Lord. As soon as this is done, the Lord excuses the sincere devotee. But that does not mean that one should take advantage of the Lord's causeless mercy and expect to be excused over and over again, while he commits the same sinful activities. Such a mentality is only for shameless persons. Here it is clearly said, "When I come to confess my sinful activities I become ashamed."

So if a person is not ashamed of his sinful activities and continues to commit the same sinful activities with the knowledge that the Lord will excuse him, that is a most nonsensical proposition. Such an idea is not accepted in any part of the Vedic literature. It is a fact that by chanting the holy name of the Lord one becomes washed clean of all sinful activities from his past life.

But that does not mean that after being washed off, one should again begin sinful activities and expect to be washed again. These are nonsensical propositions and are not admitted in devotional service. Someone may think, "For a whole week I may commit sinful activities, and for one day I will go to the temple or church and admit my sinful activities so that I can become washed off and again begin my sinning." This is most nonsensical and offensive and is not acceptable to the author of Bhakti-rasamrita-sindhu.

In the Narada-Pancharatra there is a statement of submission accompanied by the desire for perfection. The devotee says, "My dear Lord, when shall that day come when You will ask me to fan Your body, and according to Your pleasure, You will say, 'You just fan Me in this way'?" The idea in this verse is that the devotee is desiring to personally fan the body of the

Supreme Personality of Godhead. That means that he is desiring to become the personal associate of the Supreme Lord. Of course, any devotee in any capacity, either as servant, friend or conjugal lover, always has direct association with the Lord. But according to his different individual taste, a person desires for just one of these relationships.

Here the devotee is desiring to become a servant of the Lord and desires to fan the Lord, as does His internal energy, Lakshmi, the goddess of fortune. He also wishes that the Personality of Godhead will be pleased to give him directions as to how to fan. This submission with transcendental desire, or lalasamayi vijnapti, is the highest perfectional stage of spiritual realization.

In the same Narada-Pancharatra, there is another expression of submission, wherein the devotee says, "My dear Lord, O lotus-eyed one, when will that day come when on the bank of the Yamuna I shall become just like a madman and continue to chant Your holy name while incessant tears flow from my eyes?"

This is another perfectional stage. Lord Chaitanya also desired that "a moment will appear unto me as twelve years of time, and the whole world will appear to me as vacant on account of not seeing You, my dear Lord." One should feelingly pray and become eager to render his particular type of service to the Lord. This is the teaching of all great devotees, especially Lord Chaitanya.

In other words, one should learn how to cry for the Lord. One should learn this small technique, and he should be very eager and actually cry to become engaged in some particular type of service. This is called laulyam, and such tears are the price for the highest perfection.

If one develops this laulyam, or excessive eagerness for meeting and serving the Lord in a particular way, that is the price to enter into the kingdom of God. Otherwise, there is no material calculation for the value of the ticket by which one can enter the kingdom of God. The only price for such entrance is this laulyam lalasamayi, or desire and great eagerness.

***Reciting Notable Prayers***

According to great learned scholars, the whole Bhagwad Gita contains many authorized prayers, especially in the Eleventh Chapter, where Arjuna prays to the universal form of the Lord. Similarly, in the Gautamiya-tantra all the verses are called prayers. Again, in Srimad-Bhagavatam there are hundreds of prayers to the Lord. So a devotee should select some of these prayers for his recitation. In Skanda Purana the glories of these prayers are stated as follows: "Devotees whose tongues are decorated always with prayers to Lord Krishna are always given respect even by the great saintly persons and sages, and such devotees are actually worshipable by the demigods."

Those who are less intelligent want to worship different demigods for some material gain rather than worship Krishna. But here it is stated that a devotee who is always engaged in offering prayers to the Lord is worshipable even by the demigods themselves. The pure devotees have nothing to ask from any demigod; rather, the demigods are anxious to offer prayers to the pure devotees.

In the Nrisimha Purana it is stated, "Any person who comes before the Deity of Lord Krishna and begins to chant different prayers is immediately relieved from all the reactions of sinful activities and becomes eligible, without any doubt, to enter into the Vaikunthaloka."

***Partaking of Prasada***

There is this specific statement in the Padma Purana: "A person who honours the prasada and regularly eats it, not exactly in front of the Deity, along with charanamrita [the water offered to the lotus feet of the Lord, which is mixed with seeds of the tulasi tree], immediately can achieve the results of pious activities which are obtained through ten thousand performances of sacrificial rites."

***Drinking Charanamrita***

Charanamrita is obtained in the morning while the Lord is being washed before dressing. Scented with perfumes and flowers, the water comes gliding down through His lotus feet and is collected and mixed with yogurt. In this way this charanamrita not only becomes very tastefully flavoured, but also has tremendous spiritual value.

As described in the Padma Purana, even a person who has never been able to give in charity, who has never been able to perform a great sacrifice, who has never been able to study the Vedas, who has never been able to worship the Lord—or, in other words, even one who has never done any pious activities—will become eligible to enter into the kingdom of God if he simply drinks the charanamrita which is kept in the temple. In the temple it is the custom that the charanamrita be kept in a big pot. The devotees who come to visit and offer respects to the Deity take three drops of charanamrita very submissively and feel themselves happy in transcendental bliss.

### *Smelling the Incense and Flowers Offered to the Deity*

In the Hari-bhakti-sudhodaya there is a statement about the incense which is offered in the temple: "When the devotees smell the good flavor of the incense which is offered to the Deity, they thus become cured of the poisonous effects of material contamination, as much as one becomes cured of a snakebite by smelling the prescribed medicinal herbs." The explanation of this verse is that there is an herb found in the jungles which expert persons know how to use to revive the consciousness of one who is bitten by a snake. Simply by smelling that herb one becomes immediately relieved of the poisonous effects of the snakebite. The same example is applicable: when a person comes to visit the temple and smells the incense offered to the Deity, he is cured at that time from all his material contamination.

Any devotee coming into the temple should always offer something to the Deity—fruit, flowers, incense, etc. If one cannot offer anything in cash, something else must be offered. In India the system is that all the ladies and gentlemen who come in the morning to visit the temple bring so many things. Even one morsel of rice or one morsel of flour can be offered. It is a regulative principle that one should not go to see a saintly person or the Deity in the temple without any offering. The offering may be very humble, or it may be priceless. Even a flower, a little fruit, a little water—whatever is possible—must be offered. So when a devotee comes to offer something to the Deity in the morning, he is sure to smell the good flavour of the incense, and then at once he will become cleansed of the poisonous effect of material existence.

It is stated in the Tantra-shastra, "If the smell of the garland which was offered to the Deity in the temple enters into a person's nostrils, immediately his bondage to sinful activities becomes cleared. And even if one has no sinful activities, still, by smelling such remnants of flowers, one can advance from Mayavadi [impersonalist] to devotee." There are several instances of this, a prime one being the advancement of the four Kumaras. They were impersonalist Mayavadis, but after smelling the remnants of flowers and incense in the temple, they turned to become devotees. From the above verse it appears that the Mayavadis, or impersonalists, are more or less contaminated. They are not pure.

It is confirmed in Srimad-Bhagavatam, "One who has not washed off all reactions of sinful activities cannot be a pure devotee. A pure devotee has no more doubts about the supremacy of the Personality of Godhead, and thus he engages himself in Krishna consciousness and devotional service." A similar statement is in the Agastya-samhita: just to purify the impurities of our nostrils, we should try to smell the remnants of flowers offered to Krishna in the temple.

### *Touching the Deity*

In the Vishnu-dharmottara there is a statement about touching the lotus feet of the Lord. It is said, "Only a person who is initiated as a Vaishnava and is executing devotional service in Krishna consciousness has the right to touch the body of the Deity." In India there was agitation during Gandhi's political movement because the lowborn classes of men like street sweepers and chandalas are prohibited, according to the Vedic system, from entering the temple. Due to their unclean habits they are prohibited, but at the same time they are given other facilities so they may be elevated to the highest grade of devotional service by association with pure devotees. A man born in any family is not barred, but he must be cleansed. That cleansing process must be adopted. Gandhi wanted to make them clean simply by stamping them with a fictitious name, harijana ("children of God"), and so there was a great tug-of-war between the temple owners and Gandhi's followers.

But anyway, the present law is the law of all scripture—that if anyone is purified he can enter into the temple. Actually, that is the position. Only one who is properly initiated, who is properly following the rules and regulations, can enter, and touch the Deity—not all. And one who touches the body of the Deity, following such regulative principles, is immediately delivered from the contamination of material sins, and all of his desires become fulfilled without delay.

***Seeing the Deity***

In the Varaha Purana there is a statement praising the seeing of the Deity of Sri Krishna in the temple. A devotee says there, "My dear Vasundhara, any person who goes to Vrindavana and sees the Deity of Govindadeva is free from the courthouse of Yamaraja and is allowed to enter into the highest planetary system, in which reside the demigods." This means that even an ordinary person who goes to Vrindavana out of inquisitiveness and by chance sees the temple, especially that of Govindadeva, even if he is not elevated to the spiritual kingdom, is still assured promotion to the higher planetary systems. This means that simply by visiting the Deity of Govinda in Vrindavana one becomes highly elevated in pious life.

***Observing Arati and Celebrations of the Lord***

In the Skanda Purana there is the following description of the result of seeing arati (worship) of the Deity: "If someone sees the face of the Lord while arati is going on, he can be relieved of all sinful reactions coming from many, many thousands and millions of years past. He is even excused from the killing of a brahmana or similar prohibited activities.

As we have already explained, there are different ceremonies to be observed, such as the birthday of Krishna, the birthday of Lord Ramachandra, the birthday of some prominent Vaishnavas, the ceremony of Jhulana-yatra with the Lord sitting on a swing, and Dola-yatra (the Lord's activities in the month of March). In all festivals the Lord is seated on a car, and the car moves through different streets of the city so that people may take advantage of visiting the Lord. In the Bhavishya Purana it is said, "In such a ceremony, if even a candala [dog-eater], simply out of curiosity, sees the Lord on the cart, he becomes counted as one of the associates of Vishnu."

In the Agni Purana it is stated, "Any person who in gladness sees the worship of the Deity in the temple will obtain the results of kriya-yoga which are described in the Pancharatra scripture." Kriya-yoga is a system of practice much like practical devotional service, but it is especially meant for the mystic yogis. In other words, by this gradual process the mystic yogis are eventually elevated to the devotional service of the Lord.

In the Fourth Canto of Srimad-Bhagavatam, Twenty-ninth Chapter, verse 40, the importance of hearing of the pastimes of the Lord is stated by Sukhdeva Goswami to Maharaja Parikshit: "My dear King, one should stay at a place where the great acaryas [holy teachers] speak about the transcendental activities of the Lord, and one should give aural reception to the nectarean river flowing from the moonlike faces of such great personalities. If someone eagerly continues to hear such transcendental sounds, then certainly he will become freed from all material hunger, thirst, fear and lamentation, as well as all illusions of material existence."

Sri Chaitanya Mahaprabhu also recommended this process of hearing as a means of self-realization in the present age of Kali. In this age it is very difficult to follow thoroughly the regulative principles and studies of the Vedas which were formerly recommended. However, if one gives aural reception to the sound vibrated by great devotees and acaryas, that alone will give him relief from all material contamination. Therefore it is the recommendation of Chaitanya Mahaprabhu that one should simply hear from authorities who are actually devotees of the Lord. Hearing from professional men will not help. If we hear from those who are actually self-realized, then the nectarean rivers, like those which are flowing on the moon planet, will flow into our ears. This is the metaphor used in the above verse.

As stated in Bhagwad Gita, "A materialistic person can give up his material hankerings only by becoming situated in Krishna consciousness." Unless one finds a superior engagement, he will not be able to give up his inferior engagement. In the material world everyone is engaged in the illusory activities of the inferior energy, but when one is given the opportunity to relish the activities of the superior energy performed by Krishna, then he forgets all his lesser pleasures. When Krishna speaks on the Battlefield of Kurukshetra, to the materialistic person it appears that this is simply talk between two friends, but actually it is a river of nectar flowing down from the mouth of Sri Krishna. Arjuna gave aural reception to such vibrations, and thus he became freed from all the illusions of material problems. In the Twelfth Canto of Srimad-Bhagavatam, Third Chapter, verse 15, it is stated, "A person who desires unalloyed devotional service to Lord Krishna, who is praised by transcendental sound vibrations, should always hear about His glorification and transcendental qualities. This will surely kill all kinds of inauspiciousness in the heart."

***Expecting the Lord's Mercy***

In the Tenth Canto, Fourteenth Chapter, verse 8, it is said, "My dear Lord, any person who is constantly awaiting Your causeless mercy to be bestowed upon him, and who goes on suffering the resultant actions of his past misdeeds, offering You respectful obeisances from the core of his heart, is surely eligible to become liberated, for it has become his rightful claim." This statement of Srimad-Bhagavaṭam should be the guide of all devotees. A devotee should not expect immediate relief from the reactions of his past misdeeds. No conditioned soul is free from such reactionary experiences, because material existence means continued suffering or enjoying of past activities. If one has finished his material activities then there is no more birth. This is possible only when one begins Krishna conscious activities, because such activities do not produce reaction. Therefore, as soon as one becomes perfect in Krishna conscious activities, he is not going to take birth again in this material world. A devotee who is not perfectly freed from the resultant actions should therefore continue to act in Krishna consciousness seriously, even though there may be so many impediments.

When such impediments arise he should simply think of Krishna and expect His mercy. That is the only solace. If the devotee passes his days in that spirit, it is certain that he is going to be promoted to the abode of the Lord. By such activities, he earns his claim to enter into the kingdom of God. The exact word used in this verse is daya-bhak. Daya-bhak refers to a son's becoming the lawful inheritor of the property of the father. In a similar way, a pure devotee who is prepared to undergo all kinds of tribulations in executing Krishna conscious duties becomes lawfully qualified to enter into the transcendental abode.

### *Remembrance*

Some way or other, if someone establishes in his mind his continuous relationship with Krishna, this relationship is called remembrance. About this remembrance there is a nice statement in the Vishnu Purana, where it is said, "Simply by remembering the Supreme Personality of Godhead all living entities become eligible for all kinds of auspiciousness. Therefore let me always remember the Lord, who is unborn and eternal." In the Padma Purana the same remembrance is explained as follows: "Let me offer my respectful obeisances unto the Supreme Lord Krishna, because if someone remembers Him, either at the time of death or during his span of life, he becomes freed from all sinful reactions."

### *Meditation*

To meditate means to engage the mind in thinking of the form of the Lord, the qualities of the Lord, the activities of the Lord and the service of the Lord. Meditation does not mean anything impersonal or void. According to Vedic literature, meditation is always on the form of Vishnu. In the Nrisimha Purana there is a statement about meditation on the form of the Lord. It is said there, "Meditation focusing on the lotus feet of the Supreme Personality of Godhead has been accepted as transcendental and beyond the experience of material pain and pleasure. By such meditation, even one who is grossly miscreant can be delivered from the sinful reactions of his life."

In the Vishnu-dharma there is a statement about meditation on the transcendental qualities of the Lord. It is said, "Persons who are constantly engaged in Krishna consciousness, and who remember the transcendental qualities of the Lord, become free from all reactions to sinful activities, and after being so cleansed they become fit to enter into the kingdom of God." In other words, no one can enter into the kingdom of God without being freed from all sinful reactions. One can avoid sinful reactions simply by remembering the Lord's form, qualities, pastimes, etc. In the Padma Purana there is a statement about remembering the activities of the Lord: "A person who is always engaged in meditation on the sweet pastimes and wonderful activities of the Lord surely becomes freed from all material contamination."

In some of the Puranas the evidence is given that if someone is simply meditating on devotional activities, he has achieved the desired result and has seen face to face the Supreme Personality of Godhead. In this connection, there is a story in the Brahma-vaivarta Purana that in the city of Pratishthanapura in South India there was once a brahmana who was not very well-to-do, but who was nevertheless satisfied in himself, thinking that it was because of his past misdeeds and by the desire of Krishna that he did not get sufficient money and opulence.

So he was not at all sorry for his poor material position, and he used to live very peacefully. He was very openhearted, and sometimes he went to hear some lectures delivered by great realized souls. At one such meeting, while he was very faithfully hearing about Vaishnava activities, he was informed that these activities can be performed even by meditation. In other words, if a person is unable to actually perform Vaishnava activities physically, he can meditate upon the Vaishnava activities and thereby acquire all of the same results. Because the brahmana was not very well-to-do financially, he decided that he would simply meditate on grand, royal devotional activities, and he began this business thus:

> *Sometimes he would take his bath in the River Godavari. After taking his bath he would sit in a secluded place on the bank of the river, and by practicing the yoga exercises of pranayama, the usual breathing exercises, he would concentrate his mind. These breathing exercises are meant to mechanically fix the mind upon a particular subject. That is the result of the breathing exercises and also of the different sitting postures of yoga. Formerly, even quite ordinary persons used to know how to fix the mind upon the remembrance of the Lord, and so the brahmana was doing this. When he had fixed the form of the Lord in his mind, he began to imagine in his meditations that he was dressing the Lord very nicely in costly clothing, with ornaments, helmets and other paraphernalia. Then he offered his respectful obeisances by bowing down before the Lord. After finishing the dressing, he began to imagine that he was cleaning the temple very nicely. After cleansing the temple, he imagined that he had many water jugs made of gold and silver, and he took all those jugs to the river and filled them with the holy water.*
>
> *Not only did he collect water from the Godavari, but he collected from the Ganges, Yamuna, Narmada and Kaveri. Generally a Vaishnava, while worshipping the Lord, collects water from all these rivers by mantra chanting. This brahmana, instead of chanting some mantra, imagined that he was physically securing water from all these rivers in golden and silver waterpots. Then he collected all kinds of paraphernalia for worship—flowers, fruits, incense and sandalwood pulp. He collected everything to place before the Deity. All these waters, flowers and scented articles were then very nicely offered to the Deities to Their satisfaction. Then he offered arati, and with the regulative principles he finished all these activities in the correct worshipping method.*

He would daily execute similar performances as his routine work, and he continued to do so for many, many years. Then one day the brahmana imagined in his meditations that he had prepared some sweet rice with milk and sugar and offered the preparation to the Deity. However, he was not very satisfied with the offering because the sweet rice had been prepared recently and it was still very hot. (This preparation, sweet rice, should not be taken hot.

The cooler the sweet rice, the better its taste.) So because the sweet rice had been prepared by the brahmana very recently, he wanted to touch it so that he could know whether it was fit for eating by the Lord. As soon as he touched the sweet rice pot with his finger, he immediately was burnt by the heat of the pot. In this way, his meditation broke. Now, when he looked at his finger, he saw that it was burnt, and he was wondering in astonishment how this could have happened. Because he was simply meditating on touching the hot sweet rice, he never thought that his finger would actually become burnt.

While he was thinking like this, in Vaikuntha Lord Narayana, seated with the goddess of fortune, Lakshmi, began to smile humorously. On seeing this smiling of the Lord, all the goddesses of fortune attending the Lord became very curious and asked Lord Narayana why He was smiling. The Lord, however, did not reply to their inquisitiveness, but instead immediately sent for the brahmana. An airplane sent from Vaikuntha immediately brought the brahmana into Lord Narayana's presence.

When the brahmana was thus present before the Lord and the goddesses of fortune, the Lord explained the whole story. The brahmana was then fortunate enough to get an eternal place in Vaikuntha in the association of the Lord and His Lakshmis. This shows how the Lord is all-pervading, in spite of His being locally situated in His abode. Although the Lord was present in Vaikuntha, He was present also in the heart of the brahmana when he was meditating on the worshipping process. Thus, we can understand that things offered by the devotees even in meditation are accepted by the Lord, and they help one achieve the desired result.

In the Naradiya Purana there is a statement of how this servitorship is transcendental. It is said there that a person who is constantly engaged in devotional service by his body, mind and words, or even a person who is not practically engaged but is simply desiring to be so, is considered to be liberated.

***Devotional Service in Friendship:*** Devotional service in friendship can be divided into two categories: the first is to act as the confidential servant of the Lord, and the other is to act as the well-wisher of the Lord. The devotee who has confidence in devotional service to the Lord systematically follows the rules and regulations, with the faith that lie will achieve the platform of transcendental life. The second type of devotional friendship is to become a well-wisher of the Supreme Personality of Godhead. In Bhagwad Gita it is said that the Lord accepts a preacher as the most dear servant. Anyone who is preaching the confidential message of the Gita to the people in general is so dear to Krishna that no one can be equal to him in human society. In the Mahabharata, Draupadi says, "My dear Govinda, Your promise is that Your devotee can never be vanquished. I believe in that statement, and therefore in all kinds of tribulations I simply remember Your promise, and thus I live." The purport is that Draupadi and her five husbands, the Pandavas, were put into severe tribulations by their cousin-brother Duryodhana, as well as by others.

The tribulations were so severe that even Bhishmadeva, who was both a lifelong brahmachari and a great warrior, would sometimes shed tears thinking of them. He was always surprised that although the Pandavas were so righteous and Draupadi was practically the goddess of fortune, and although Krishna was their friend, still they had to undergo such severe tribulations. Though their tribulations were not ordinary, Draupadi was not discouraged. She knew that because Krishna was their friend, ultimately they would be saved. A similar statement is there in the Eleventh Canto of Srimad-Bhagavatam, Second Chapter, verse 53, where Havi, the son of King Rishabha, addresses Maharaja Nimi: "My dear King, a person who never deviates even for a moment from engagement in service at the lotus feet of the Supreme Person (engagement which is sought even by great demigods like Indra), with firm conviction that there is nothing more worshipable or desirable than this, is called the first-class devotee."

Sri Rupa Goswami says that a neophyte devotee who has simply developed a slight love of Godhead is certainly a prospective candidate for devotional service. When he becomes firmly fixed in such devotional service, that assured status becomes a confidential part of his devotional service. Sometimes it is found that a pure devotee lies down in the temple of the Lord in order to serve Him as a confidential friend. Such friendly behaviour of a devotee may be accepted as raganuga, or spontaneous. Although, according to regulative principles, no one can lie down in the temple of the Supreme Personality of Godhead, this spontaneous love of Godhead may be grouped under devotional service in friendship.

## Surrendering Everything to the Lord

Regarding complete self-surrender, there is a nice description in the Eleventh Canto of Srimad-Bhagavatam, Twenty-ninth Chapter, verse 34, where the Lord says, "A person who has completely surrendered unto Me and has completely given up all other activities is protected by Me personally, both in this life and in the next. In other words, I wish to help him become more and more advanced in spiritual life. Such a person is to be understood as having already achieved sarshti [having equal opulences with the Supreme]." It is also confirmed in Bhagwad Gita that as soon as a person surrenders unto the lotus feet of Krishna, Krishna takes charge of him and gives him a guarantee of protection from all sinful reactions. He also instructs from within, so that the devotee may very quickly make advancement toward spiritual perfection.

This self-surrender is called atma-nivedana. According to different authorities, self is differently defined. Self is sometimes considered to refer to the spirit self, or soul, and self is sometimes considered to refer to the mind or to the body. Full self-surrender, therefore, means not only surrendering one's self as spirit soul, but also surrendering one's mind and body to the service of the

Lord. Srila Bhaktivinoda Thakura has sung a nice song in this connection. While offering himself as a fully surrendered soul, he said, "My mind, my household affairs, my body, whatever is in my possession, my dear Lord, I offer to You for Your service. Now You can do with them as You like. You are the supreme possessor of everything, so if You like You can kill me, or if You like You can give me protection.

All authority belongs to You. I have nothing to claim as my own." Sri Yamunacharya, in his prayers to the Lord, has expressed a similar idea in the following words: "My dear Lord, I may be living within some body as a human being or as a demigod, but whatever mode of life, I do not mind, because these bodies are simply by-products of the three modes of material nature, and I, who am in possession of these bodies, am surrendering myself unto You." In the Hari-bhakti-viveka, there is a statement regarding how one can offer his body in self-surrender. There the devotee says, "My dear Lord, as a sold animal has no need to think about his maintenance and sustenance, so, because I have given up my body and soul unto You, I am no longer concerned with my maintenance and sustenance." In other words, one should not bother about his personal or family maintenance or sustenance. If one is actually surrendered in body and soul, he should always remember that his only concern is to be engaged in the service of the Lord.

Srila Rupa Goswami says that devotional service in friendship and devotional service in self-surrender are two difficult processes. Therefore such relationships with the Lord can very rarely be seen. Only for the advanced devotees are these two processes easily executed. The purport is that it is very rare to see surrender which is mixed with sincere ecstatic devotion. One must give himself completely to the will of the Lord.

### *Offering a Favourite Article*

In the Eleventh Canto of Srimad-Bhagavatam, Eleventh Chapter, verse 41, Lord Krishna tells Uddhava, "My dear friend, if someone offers Me the best thing in his possession, or anything which is very pleasing to him, he will be eternally benefited."

# 6

# Important Symbolism and Themes in Hinduism

Hinduism, a religious tradition of Indian origin, comprising the beliefs and practices of Hindus. The word *Hindu* is derived from the river Sindhu, or Indus. *Hindu* was primarily a geographical term that referred to India or to a region of India (near the Sindhu) as long ago as the 6th century BC. The word *Hinduism* is an English word of more recent origin. *Hinduism* entered the English language in the early 19th century to describe the beliefs and practices of those residents of India who had not converted to Islam or Christianity and did not practice Judaism or Zoroastrianism.

In the case of most religions, beliefs and practices come first, and those who subscribe to them are acknowledged as followers. In the case of the Hindu tradition, however, the acknowledgment of Hindus came first, and their beliefs and practices constitute the contents of the religion.

Hindus themselves prefer to use the Sanskrit term *sanatana dharma* for their religious tradition. *Sanatana dharma* is often translated into English as "eternal tradition" or "eternal religion" but the translation of *dharma* as "tradition" or "religion" gives an extremely limited, even mistaken, sense of the word. *Dharma* has many meanings in Sanskrit, the sacred language of Hindu scripture, including "moral order," "duty," and "right action."

The Hindu tradition encourages Hindus to seek spiritual and moral truth wherever it might be found, while acknowledging that no creed can contain such truth in its fullness and that each individual must realize this truth through his or her own systematic effort. Our experience, our reason, and our dialogue with others—especially with enlightened individuals—provide various means of testing our understanding of spiritual and moral truth. And Hindu scripture, based on the insights of Hindu sages and seers, serves primarily as a guidebook. But ultimately truth comes to us through direct consciousness of the divine or the ultimate reality. In other religions this ultimate reality is known as God. Hindus refer to it by many names, but the most common name is Brahman.

In many religions truth is delivered or revealed from a divine source and enters the world through a single agent: for example, Abraham in Judaism, Jesus in Christianity, and Muhammad in Islam. These truths are then recorded in scriptures that serve as a source of knowledge of divine wisdom: the Hebrew Bible, the New Testament, and the Qur'an. In the Hindu tradition, by contrast, there is no single revelation or *orthodoxy* (established doctrine) by which people may achieve knowledge of the divine or lead a life backed by religious law. The Hindu tradition acknowledges that there are many paths by which people may seek and experience religious understanding and direction. It also claims that every individual has the potential to achieve enlightenment.

The Hindu community today is found primarily in India and neighbouring Nepal and in Bali in the Indonesian archipelago. Substantial Hindu communities are present in Sri Lanka and Bangladesh, Mauritius, Fiji, the West Indies, East Africa, and South Africa. Scattered Hindu communities are found in most parts of the Western world. Hindus today number nearly 900 million, including about 20 million who live outside India, making them the third largest religious community in the world, after Christians and Muslims.

Since ancient times, Hindu thought has transcended geographical boundaries and influenced religious and philosophical ideas throughout the world. Persian, ancient Greek, and ancient Roman thought may well have been influenced by Hinduism. Three other religions that originated in India are closely related to Hinduism: Buddhism, Jainism, and Sikhism. In the 19th century German philosopher Arthur Schopenhauer read both Hindu and Buddhist scriptures and based much of his thinking on them.

In the United States, 19th-century writers such as Ralph Waldo Emerson and Henry David Thoreau drew on Hinduism and its scriptures in developing their philosophy of transcendentalism. More recently, civil-rights leader Martin Luther King, Jr., studied the teachings of Hindu leader Mohandas Gandhi on nonviolent protest. In the sphere of popular culture, rock musician George Harrison embraced Hinduism during the 1960s, and some members of the United States counterculture explored Hinduism and Buddhism, as did the Beat poets (Beat Generation). Millions of Westerners today practice meditation or yoga to achieve relief from stress or physical fitness, indicating Western receptiveness to Hindu practices.

***What is Hinduism?:*** An encyclopedia article should have a definition at the outset, but this requirement presents unique difficulties in the case of Hinduism. This difficulty arises from Hinduism's universal world-view and its willingness to accept and celebrate diverse philosophies, deities, symbols, and practices. A religion that emphasizes similarities and shared characteristics rather than differences has a difficult time setting itself apart—unless this very quality is considered its defining feature.

This is not to say that there are no beliefs and practices that may be identified as Hindu, but rather that the Hindu tradition has concerned itself largely with the human situation rather than the Hindu situation. Instead of basing its identity on separating Hindu from non-Hindu or believer from nonbeliever, Hinduism has sought to recognize principles and practices that would lead any individual to become a better human being and understand and live in harmony with dharma.

The distinction of dharma from the Western sense of religion is crucial to understanding Hindu religious identity. To the extent that *Hinduism* carries with it the Western meaning of being a religion the words distort Indian reality. In the West a religion is understood to be conclusive—that is, it is the one and only true religion.

Second, a religion is generally exclusionary—that is, those who do not follow it are excluded from salvation. Finally, a religion is separative—that is, to belong to it, one must not belong to another. Dharma, however, does not necessarily imply any of these.

## Ahimsa and Veganism

A note of the element of ahimsa in Hinduism is vital to understanding the society that has arisen around some of its principles. The term first appears in the Upanishads. A large section of Hindus embraced vegetarianism in a bid to respect higher forms of life, restricting their diet to plants and vegetables. About 30% of today's Hindu population, especially in orthodox communities in South India, in certain northerly states like Gujarat, and in many Brahmin enclaves around the subcontinent, is vegetarian. While vegetarianism is not dogma, it is recommended as a sattwic (purifying) lifestyle in Yoga.

## Sacred Status of Cow

Some of the Hindus who do eat meat even avoid the use of leather products. This is most likely because the largely pastoral Vedic people and subsequent generations of Hindus throughout the centuries relied so heavily on the cow for all sorts of dairy products, tilling of fields and fuel for fertilizer that its status as a willing 'caretaker' of humanity grew to identifying it as an almost maternal figure (so the term gau mata). Thus, while scriptural injunctions against eating beef arose long after the Vedas had been written, the cow still holds an honoured place in Hindu society. It is said that Krishna is both Govinda (herder of cows) and Gopala (protector of cows), and Shiva's attendant is Nandi, the bull.

## Hindu Symbolism

Among the most revered symbols in Hinduism, two are quintessentially a part of its culture and representative of its general ethos:

*Aum is the standard sign of Hinduism, and is prefixed and sometimes suffixed to all Hindu mantras and prayers. It contains an enormous and diverse amount of symbolism; Hindus consider its sound and vibration to be the divine representation of existence, encompassing all of manifold nature into the One eternal truth. The swastika (PS) is an Arya, or noble symbol. It stands for satya, truth, and stability within the power of Brahma or, alternatively, of Surya, the sun. Its rotation in four directions has been used to represent many ideas, but primarily describes the four directions and their harmonious whole. It has been used in Hinduism since the early Vedic culture and is still widespread in the Indian subcontinent.*

## Forms of Worship: Murtis and Mantras

Contrary to popular belief, practiced Hinduism is neither polytheistic nor exclusive monotheistic. Contemporary Hinduism, at is practiced today, more strongly adheres to a Smarta model, which is a form of inclusive monotheism. The various gods and avatars that are worshipped by Hindus are understood as different forms of One truth, sometimes seen as beyond a mere God and as a formless Divine Ground (Brahman), akin but not limited to monism, or as one monotheistic principle like Vishnu or Shiva as the exclusive monotheistic faiths of Vaishnavism and Shaivism adhere to.

Whether believing in the One source as formless (nirguna Brahman, without attributes) or as a personal God (saguna Brahman, with attributes), Hindus understand that the one truth may be seen as different to different people. Hinduism encourages devotees to describe and develop a personal relationship with their chosen deity (ishta devata) in the form of a God or Goddess.

Worship of lesser deities is often done through the aid of pictures or icons (murti) which are said not to be God themselves but conduits for the devotee's consciousness, markers for the human soul that signify the ineffable and illimitable nature of the love and grandeur of God. They are symbols of the greater principle, representing and are never presumed to be the concept or entity itself. Thus, Hindu image worship is a form of iconolatry, in which the symbols are venerated as putative sigils of divinity.

***Mantra***

Reciting mantras is a fundamental practice in Hinduism. Much of mantra yoga, as it is called, is done through japa (repetition). Mantras are said, through their meaning, sound, and chanting style, to help meditational focus for the sadhaka (practitioner). They can also be used to aid in expression of love for the deity, another facet of Bhakti yoga akin to the understanding of the murti. They often give courage in exigent times and serve to help 'invoke' one's inner spiritual strength.

The most revered mantra in Hinduism is the famed Gayatri Mantra (see Sanskrit for pronunciation):

*Transliteration: OM bhur bhuva sva* |
*tat savitur varenyam* |
*bhargo devasya dhimahi* |
*dhiyo yo na pra-codayat* |

***Translation:*** "May we attain that excellent glory of Savitar the God/so May he stimulate our prayers."

It is considered one of the most universal of all Hindu mantras, invoking the universal Brahman as the principle of knowledge and the illumination of the primordial Sun. Many Hindus to this day, in a tradition that has continued unbroken for at least 3,000 years, perform morning ablutions at the bank of a sacred river. Known as a universal mantra, it is revered as being the most condensed form of Divine Knowledge (Veda). Its presiding principle, Ma (Mother) Gayatri, is also known as Veda Mata (Mother of the Vedas) and is strongly associated with the Goddess of Learning and Illumination, Saraswati.

The chief aim of the Vedic religion is to achieve moksha, or liberation, through constant dedication to Satya (Truth) and eventual realisation of the atman (Universal Soul), held to be achievable by all, whether through meditation or pure love. The great rishis (Hindu sages) have termed the samsaric (one who lives in samsara, *i.e.* the temporal or earthly plane) who succeeds in living an honest, loving and dharmic life a jivanmukta (living free soul). Hinduism's fundamental truth is best expressed in the Upanishadic dictum, Tat Twam Asi (Thou Art That), and the ultimate aspiration as follows:

*OM Asato ma sad gamaya, tamaso ma jyotir gamaya, mrityor ma aamritaam gamaya*
*"OM Lead me from ignorance to truth, from darkness to light, from death to immortality."*

***Hindu Sacred Texts:*** The overwhelming majority of Hindu sacred texts are composed in the Sanskrit language. The texts are divided into two categories: Shruti-that which is heard (*i.e.*, revelation) and Smriti-that which is remembered (*i.e.* tradition, not revelation).

### *Shruti*

The Vedas are considered as shruti (inspired) by all Hindus. While the overwhelming majority of Hindus may never read the Vedas, the reverence for the more abstract notion of eternal knowledge (Veda means knowledge) is etched deep into the hearts of all those who follow Veda Dharma. The four Vedas (the Rig, Yajur, Sama and Atharva Vedas) were preserved by various shakhas or schools. Depending on the school, various commentaries and instructions are associated with each Veda. The oldest of these are the Brahmanas. The Shrautasutras and Grhyasutras form a younger stratum dealing with domestic ritual. The Aranyakas and the Upanishads were originally esoteric, mystical teachings related in secrecy.

While the Vedas and their early commentaries on one hand centre on ritual and sacrifice, the late Vedantic (End of Vedas) texts emphasize mystic insight and express abhorrence for ritual practiced at the expense of spiritual insight, claiming to streamline the excessive litany of praise to Vedic gods and to capture the essence of the Rig Vedic dictum "Truth Is One." They set Hindu philosophy apart with its embrace of a single transcendent and yet immanent force that is native to each man's soul, an identification of micro-and macrocosm as One. It can be said that while early Hinduism is most reliant on the four Vedas, Classical Hinduism, from the Yoga and Vedanta to Tantra and Bhakti streams, was moulded around the Upanishads.

***Bhagwad Gita***

The Bhagwad Gita occupies a special position in the hearts of most Hindus as a keystone yoga Upanishad whose eternal words perhaps are the most representative of all Hindu thought. The text documents a conversation between Arjuna, a warrior, and Lord Krishna immediately prior to the major battle described in the epic Mahabharata. While technically it is considered Smriti, it has singularly achieved nearly unquestioned status as Shruti, or revealed, and is thus the most definitive single Hindu text.

***Smriti***

The post-Vedic Hindu scriptures form the latter category, the most notable of which are the Mahabharata and the Ramayana, major epics considered scripture by most followers. Other texts considered important by today's Hindus include the Yoga Sutras, a key meditative yoga text of Shri Patanjali. There are also a number of revered Hindu Tantras and Sutras that command the respect of various Hindu sects of different persuasion, some including the Mahanirvana Tantra, Tirumantiram and Shiva Sutras. Other important scriptures are the sectarian Hindu Agamas which are texts dedicated to Vishnu, Shiva and Devi.

## The Dharmic Tradition

Dharma is an all-important concept for Hindus. In addition to tradition and moral order, it also signifies the path of knowledge and correct action. Because of Hinduism's emphasis on living in accordance with dharma, anyone who is striving for spiritual knowledge and seeking the right course of ethical action is, in the broadest sense, a follower of sanatana dharma.

Buddhism, Jainism, and Sikhism share with Hinduism the concept of dharma along with other key concepts, and the four religions may be said to belong to the dharmic tradition. At one level *Hinduism* can refer to the beliefs or practices of followers of any of the dharmic traditions. The word Hinduism retains this sense in some usages in the Indian Constitution of 1950. In the field of religious studies, however, Hinduism is used in a narrower sense to distinguish it from the other religions of Indian origin.

A Hindu is thus identified by a dual exclusion. A Hindu is someone who does not subscribe to a religion of non-Indian origin, and who does not claim to belong exclusively to another religion of Indian origin—Buddhism, Jainism, or Sikhism. This effort at definition produces a rather artificial distinction between Hinduism and other dharmic traditions, which stems from an attempt to limit a system that sees itself as universal to an identity that is strictly religious. In many ways, labelling the other dharmic traditions as non-Hindu has a basis that derives more from politics than from philosophy. Indeed, greater differences of belief and practices lie within the broad family labelled as Hinduism than distinguish Hinduism from other dharmic systems.

Indian historian Irfan Habib makes this point when he quotes an early Persian source that Hindus are those who have been debating with each other within a common framework for centuries. If they recognize another as somebody whom they can either support or oppose intelligibly, then both are Hindus. Despite the fact that Jains reject many Hindu beliefs, Jains and Hindus can still debate and thus Jains are Hindus. But such discourse does not take place between Hindus and Muslims because they do not share any basic terms.

### *Sanatana Dharma*

Evidence from inscriptions indicates that Hindus had begun to use the word *dharma* for their religion by the 7th century. After other religions of Indian origin also began to use this term, Hindus then adopted the expression *sanatana dharma* to distinguish their dharma from others. The word *sanatana,* meaning immemorial as well as eternal, emphasized the unbroken continuity of the Hindu tradition in contrast to the other dharmas. The Buddhist, Jaina, and Sikh dharmas possess distinct starting points, whereas Hinduism has no historical founder.

The Hindu tradition might be said to begin in the 4th century BC when the growth and separation of Buddhism and Jainism provided it with a distinctive sense of identity as sanatana dharma. Some scholars prefer to date its beginnings to about 1500 BC, the period when its earliest sacred texts originated, although recent evidence suggests these texts may be even older. Certain beliefs and practices that can clearly be identified as Hindu—such as the worship of sacred trees and the mother goddess—go back to a culture known as Harappan, which flourished around 3000 BC. Other Hindu practices are even older. For example, belief in the religious significance of the new and full moon can be traced to the distant proto-Australoid period, before 3000 BC. It is with good reason that Hinduism perceives itself as sanatana dharma or a cumulative tradition. Its origins are shrouded in the mist of antiquity, and it has continued without a break.

## A Comprehensive and Universal Tradition

The Hindu tradition aims at comprehensiveness so far as religious beliefs and practices are concerned. First, it wishes to make the riches of Hinduism available to the Hindu and to any genuine seeker of truth and knowledge. But it does not limit Hindus to their tradition. Instead, it encourages them to explore all avenues that would lead to a realization of the divine, and it provides a system with many paths for such realization.

Second, in the manner of science, Hinduism is constantly experimenting with and assimilating new ideas. Also like science, it is far less concerned with the origin or history of ideas than with their truth as demonstrated through direct experience. Hinduism's openness to new ideas, teachers, and practices, and its desire for universality rather than exclusivity, set it apart from religions that distinguish their followers by their belief in particular historical events, people, or revelations.

Two events in the life of Mohandas Gandhi exemplify aspects of the Hindu tradition. First, Gandhi entitled his autobiography *The Story of My Experiments with Truth* (1929). In doing so, he was practicing the Hindu willingness to experiment continually as a means of discovering truth and to record the results of such experiments. Although Gandhi was seeking spiritual truth, he approached it in the spirit of science. Second, when asked, "What is your religion?" in 1936, Gandhi answered, "My religion is Hinduism, which for me is the Religion of humanity and includes the best of all religions known to me." Saintly figures such as Gandhi have periodically renewed Hinduism throughout its history and kept it abreast of the times. Because Hinduism has no central orthodoxy, and no belief in the need for one, renewal of its tradition has invariably come from sages in every age who base their knowledge on experience of the divine.

***Hindu Teachings:*** *What Do Hindus Believe?:* Because defining Hinduism is so difficult and because we have called it the sum of the belief and practices of Hindus, it is best to approach Hinduism through its teachings.

Within Hinduism there are various schools of thought, which Hindu scholars have systematized in different ways. All of these schools have enriched Hinduism with their individual emphases: *Nyaya* on rigorous logic, *Vaiseshika* on atoms and the structure of matter, *Sankhya* on numbers and categories, Yoga on meditation techniques, *Mimamsa* on the analysis of sacred texts, and *Vedanta* on the nature and experience of spirituality. Their teachings are usually summarized in texts called sutras or aphorisms. These sutras can be memorized easily and recited as a means of gaining spiritual focus.

## Brahman: The Ultimate Reality

Various schools have contributed to Hindu thought, each school with a different emphasis. The school known as Vedanta has been the standard form of intellectual Hinduism. According to Vedanta, the highest aim of existence is the realization of the identity or union of the individual's innermost self (*atman*) with the ultimate reality. Although Vedanta states that this ultimate reality is beyond name, the word *Brahman* is used to refer to it.

Whether this ultimate reality is itself ultimately without distinguishing attributes (*nirguna*) or with personal attributes (*saguna*) has been a subject of extensive debate among Hindu scholars. To be ultimate Brahman must *transcend* (exist above and beyond) all limiting attributes, such as name, gender, form, and features. But how can the human mind, with its limitations, conceive of this transcendent reality? Human comprehension requires a more personal reality, with attributes.

Saguna Brahman is also called Ishvara, a name best translated as "Lord." A quotation attributed to 8th-century Hindu scholar Shankara illustrates the subtlety of these ideas: "Ishvara, forgive these three sins of mine: that although you are everywhere I have gone on a pilgrimage, although you are beyond the mind I have tried to think of you; and although you are ineffable [indescribable] I offer this hymn in praise of you."

***Brahma, Vishnu, and Shiva: Aspects of Brahman***

Saguna Brahman—that is, Brahman with attributes—generally takes the form of one of three main Hindu deities: Brahma, Vishnu, or Shiva. These personified forms of Brahman correspond to three stages in the cycle of the universe. Brahma corresponds to the creative spirit from which the universe arises. Vishnu corresponds to the force of order that sustains the universe. Shiva corresponds to the force that brings a cycle to an end—destruction acting as a prelude to transformation, leaving pure consciousness from which the universe is reborn after destruction. Other forms of Ishvara widely worshipped by Hindus are Shakti, the female aspect of divinity, and Ganesha, the elephant-headed deity associated with the removal of obstacles.

Brahman also may choose to take birth in a knowable form, or *avatar* (incarnation), to uphold dharma and restore balance to the world. Krishna, a well-known avatar of Vishnu, appears at times to save the world. Rama, another well-known avatar of Vishnu, is the subject of the Hindu epic Ramayana (Way of Rama). Whether nirguna or saguna, Brahman represents the ultimate reality (*sat*), ultimate consciousness (*sit*), and ultimate bliss (*ananda*).

Vishnu has ten major avatars, which are described in Hindu texts called the Puranas. These incarnations and their Hindu names are: fish (*matsya*), tortoise (*kurma*), boar (*varaha*), man lion (*narasimha*), dwarf (*vamana*), axe-wielding human (Parashurama), ideal person (Rama of the Ramayana), all-attractive perfect person (Krishna), the enlightened (Buddha), and a future incarnation (Kalki).

The majority of Hindus choose a personal deity, a saguna form of Brahman with whom they can feel a direct personal connection. Devotion to this deity can take a number of forms, including prayer, ceremonial worship, chanting of the deity's name, and pilgrimage to sites sacred to the deity.

### *Brahmanda: The Universe*

The relationship of the universe, which Hindus call brahmanda, to the ultimate reality poses a deep philosophical problem: Whereas Brahman represents a permanent reality, the universe is constantly changing. The universe is also eternal, but it is eternally changing, whereas Brahman is eternal in another sense in that it is beyond change. According to Vedanta, Brahman alone is real. Such reality as the universe possesses is derived from Brahman, just as the light of the Moon really belongs to the Sun.

All of creation arises from Brahman, according to Hindu teaching. Brahman is both the efficient cause of the universe (creator) as well as the material cause (substance of which the universe is created). For this reason, all of creation is divine and deserving of our respect.

Time in the Hindu universe moves in endlessly recurring cycles, much like the motion of a wheel. The duration of the various phases of the universe's existence are calculated in units of mind-boggling astronomical duration organized around such terms as *yugas, mahayugas, manvantaras,* and *kalpas*.

### *Atman: The Innermost Self*

We as individuals are also a part of this changing universe. Our bodies are constantly undergoing change, while our minds, formed of thoughts and feelings, are also in a state of flux. According to Vedanta, however, our self consists of more than mind and body.

At its core lies the unchanging *atman,* our innermost, transcendental self, as opposed to the material self (our body, thoughts, and feelings) that is part of the universe. The atman is our true self. But we lose sight of it because of our passionate involvement with our material self and its search for happiness in this universe. The universe can never provide perfect and permanent happiness, however, because it, like our material self, is in a state of constant flux. We attain true happiness only through an awareness of our atman and the discovery of its true relationship with Brahman.

By achieving awareness of our atman and its unity with Brahman, we attain not only happiness, but also *moksha,* or liberation. But liberation from what? At one level, the liberation is from unhappiness, but the answer provided by Vedanta Hinduism goes deeper: Moksha is liberation from a chain of lives.

### *Samsara: The Chain of Lives*

We normally think of ourselves as coming into being when we are born of our parents and as perishing when we die. According to Hinduism, however, this current life is merely one link in a chain of lives that extends far into the past and projects far into the future. The point of origin of this chain cannot be determined. The process of our involvement in the universe—the chain of births and deaths—is called samsara.

Samsara is caused by a lack of knowledge of our true self and our resultant desire for fulfilment outside ourselves. We continue to embody ourselves, or be reborn, in this infinite and eternal universe as a result of these unfulfilled desires. The chain of births lets us resume the pursuit. The law that governs samsara is called karma. Each birth and death we undergo is determined by the balance sheet of our karma—that is, in accordance with the actions performed and the dispositions acquired in the past.

## Karma: Action and its Consequences

Karma is a crucial Hindu concept. According to the doctrine of karma, our present condition in life is the consequence of the actions of our previous lives. The choices we have made in the past directly affect our condition in this life, and the choices we make today and thereafter will have consequences for our future lives in samsara. An understanding of this interconnection, according to Hindu teachings, can lead an individual toward right choices, deeds, thoughts, and desires, without the need for an external set of commandments.

The principle of karma provides the basic framework for Hindu ethics. The word *karma* is sometimes translated into English as "destiny," but karma does not imply the absence of free will or freedom of action that destiny does. Under the doctrine of karma, the ability to make choices remains with the individual. We are subject to the "law" of karma just as our physical movements on earth are subject to the law of gravitation. But just as the law of gravitation does not take away our freedom to move about, the doctrine of karma does not leave us unfree to act. It merely describes the moral law under which we function, just as the law of gravitation is a physical law governing our being..

When we cause pain or injury, we add to the karmic debt we carry into our future lives. When we give to others in a genuine way, we lighten our karmic load. In the Bhagwad-Gita, an important Hindu text, Krishna states that the best way to be free of debt is by selfless action, or by dedicating every action as an offering to Krishna himself. In addition, human beings can purify themselves of karmic debt through different *yogas* (disciplines), *krïyas* (purification processes), and *bhakti* (devotions).

## Purusharthas: Goals of Human Life

Hinduism takes a comprehensive view of our human condition and has classified all the things we seek in the world and beyond into four broad categories: *kama*, *artha, dharma,* and *moksha*. Kama includes the pleasure of the senses, both *aesthetic* (refined artistic) pleasures and sensual and sexual pleasure. Artha includes the pursuit of material well-being, wealth, and power. Dharma includes our striving for righteousness and virtue. Moksha describes our desire for liberation from the chain of lives. The first three goals pertain to the world we know, whereas moksha involves freedom from the world and from desires for kama, artha, and dharma. Attaining moksha is an extraordinary goal, which only some people specifically seek. In preparing for it, the prior pursuit of dharma can be a great help. Dharma, in the sense of duty or desire to do right, occupies a central role in regulating artha and kama and promoting moksha. On account of dharma's centrality, the goals of human life are often listed in the following order: dharma, artha, kama and moksha.

Hinduism accepts all four purusharthas as valid goals of human endeavour. It does not look down upon kama or artha, as indicated by the *Kamasutra*, a work on sexuality from about the 4th century AD, and by the *Arthashastra*. The latter text by Kautilya, a minister to a king of the 4th century BC, discusses how a king should wield political and economic power.

However, the ultimate aim of human life is moksha, liberation from sorrow and desire and realization of the union with the Ultimate Reality. In our future lives we may not always enter the world in human form. Thus, Hindus consider that birth as a human being is a unique and valuable opportunity for seeking moksha, an opportunity that should not be wasted. To guide us along the way, the system of Vedanta and the yogas provide a good road map for the journey.

### *Jiva: The Individual*

Our personality has a strong influence on the goal we seek. According to one Hindu scheme a human being consists of not one but three bodies. There is the gross physical body; a subtle body of thought and feelings; and an even subtler body, known as the causal body, where our primal ignorance of our true nature is located, along with the knowledge of that ignorance. The physical body disintegrates after our death; only the subtle and causal bodies travel from one life to the next.

Another Hindu system envisions the human being as consisting of five layers or sheaths, called koshas, that cover up the true self or atman. Beginning with the outermost, these layers are constituted by food or the physical body (*annamaya*), energy (*pranamaya*), mind (*manomaya*), consciousness (*vijnanamaya*), and bliss (*anandamaya*). Identification with one or more of these koshas—for example, imagining, "I am my physical body"—limits people and prevents knowledge of their true nature. Other Hindu concepts of personality employ other schemes. One popular concept visualizes a person's dormant energy residing at the bottom of the spine like a coiled serpent (*kundalini*). Upon awakening, it confers liberation when it reaches the head after piercing nodal points, called chakras, along the spine. Hinduism offers spiritual and physical exercises for awakening and liberating all these aspects of the personality.

### *Yogas: Paths to Brahman*

How do we proceed if we wish to rise toward Brahman? Hindu thought takes the personality of the seeker as the starting point. It divides human personalities into types dominated by physicality, activity, emotionality, or intellectuality. The composition of our personality intuitively predisposes us to a type of *yoga*—that is, a path we might follow to achieve union with Brahman. Although many people associate the word *yoga* with a physical discipline, in its original Hindu meaning *yoga* refers to any technique that unites the seeker with the ultimate reality.

While physical fitness buffs may seek such a union by practicing *hatha yoga*, people with different personality traits have other choices. For the action-oriented person there is *karma yoga,* the yoga of action, which calls for a life of selfless deeds and actions appropriate to the person's station in life. For the person of feeling, *bhakti yoga,* the yoga of devotion, calls for unconditional love for a personal divinity. For the person of thought, *jnana yoga,* the yoga of knowledge, calls for spiritual and physical discipline intended to bring direct insight into ultimate reality. The yogas do not represent tightly sealed compartments, merely convenient classifications. A well-balanced personality might well employ all four. These yogas are sometimes called margas (paths), suggesting that the same destination can be approached by more than one route, and indeed by more than one mode of travel.

***Varna: Social Organization***

The individual stands in relationship not only to Brahman but also to the society in which he or she lives. Two Hindu concepts—*varna* and *ashrama*—address this social dimension of human existence.

Every society distinguishes among occupations on the basis of power, wealth, education, or other factors. Hindu thought has long recognized four major occupational groupings. In the first group are priests, teachers, scholars, and others who represent knowledge and spirituality. People in this group are called brahmanas, or Brahmans. Those in the second group, called ksatriyas, are represented by kings, warriors, government bureaucrats, and others who represent power. Those in the third group, called vaishyas, are represented by farmers, traders, merchants, and other skilled workers. Those in the fourth group, called shudras, are represented by unskilled workers. A group sometimes known as untouchables has at times constituted a subcategory within the shudra class, sometimes referred to as a fifth group.

Hindu thinkers visualized these groups as constituting the four limbs of society conceived as a body. This hierarchical system, with Brahmans as the first category and shudras as the last, is known as the varna system. The system also indicates the different roles and responsibilities of each group within society and the relationship of the groups within a harmonious whole. The varna system was never intended as a permanent assignment of hereditary roles, and it once possessed considerable flexibility even though people tended to inherit the family profession, as in many other traditional societies.

The process of establishing the varna system was completed by the 4th century BC. By that time Hindu social organization accommodated thousands of subgroups called jatis, which were based upon marriage and other associations as well as on occupational specialization in crafts. Hindu law books from the 4th century BC onward bear witness to the blending of the varna and jati systems. In this process each jati became loosely linked with a varna. Yet the standing of jatis altered with changes in wealth, education, and political power. Over time, especially during the long period of Islamic rule, the groupings hardened into what became known as the caste system. The British census in the late 19th century helped formalize this system by mapping each jati to a specific varna.

## Ashrama: Stages of Life

Much as the varna system provides the organizing principle of Hindu society, the *ashrama* system provides the organizing principle of an individual's life. According to the ashrama system, human life is divided into four stages, each succeeding the other. Ashrama provides a road map for the journey through these stages and provides a clear sense of purpose for each stage, including old age. Hindus consider the last stage of life highly meaningful. Ashrama also addresses the four goals that constitute a fulfilling life: dharma, artha, kama, and moksha.

The first stage is the life of a celibate student, a time when an individual acquires the values of dharma—that is, preparation and training for leading a proper life. It is followed by that of the householder, during which the individual seeks artha and kama by marrying, working, and raising a family as an active member of society. During this second stage, Hindu householders are expected to carry out their responsibilities in accordance with dharma and free themselves of debts owed to the gods, the sages, and their ancestors.

After the years of enjoyment and responsibility, the third stage of life begins. Around age 50, when the children are grown, the individual gradually begins to give up acquisitions and worldly ties and to take up spiritual contemplation in preparation for the next stage. The fourth and final stage involves renunciation of the world to seek liberation in sublime isolation. Renunciation allows the individual to be free of external responsibilities and to concentrate on an inner search. The life of the *sanyasi* (renunciant) focuses on achieving realization of the innermost self (atman) and union with the divine (moksha).

The ashrama system recognizes the division between active participation in life (*pravrtti*) and ascetic withdrawal from life (*nivrtti*). Although this division has applied to all Hindus, regardless of gender or caste, men of the three higher varnas (Brahmans, ksatriyas, and vaishyas) have been more likely to enact it through the ashrama system. Some Hindus choose to devote their entire lives to the quest for moksha. They become renunciants and are free from the obligations of varna and ashrama. Such people are called sannyasis. A sanyasi who joins a monastic order takes the title swami.

In addition to the duties belonging to each stage of life, Hinduism also emphasizes duties belonging to all human beings, especially cultivation of truth and nonviolence. Many Hindus choose not to eat meat because of their cultivation of nonviolence.

***Hindu Rituals—What Do Hindus Do?:*** Hindus consider all of creation worthy of worship, and thus religious activity in Hinduism takes many forms. Rituals may be performed by the individual, the family, the village, the community or region; at home or in a temple; and frequently or infrequently. The prevalence and persistence of Hindu ritual may well provide the stabilizing factor in a tradition that is so flexible in doctrine. Ritual might even be considered the glue that holds Hindus and Hinduism together.

Many rites and observances that Hindus practice daily have come down from ancient times. Others grew up around the lives and teachings of Hindu saints and sages. While details of rituals may differ from region to region and jati to jati, their meaning and central practices have remained consistent over vast distances of time and space.

Virtually all rituals in Hinduism possess multiple meanings, including symbolic interpretations. Even the way Hindus regularly greet each other may be regarded as symbolically bowing to the divine. The Hindu greeting involves pressing the palms of the hands together, which symbolizes the meeting of two people; placing the hands over the heart where Brahman dwells, indicating that one meets the self in the other; bowing the head in recognition of this meeting; and saying *namaste,* a Sanskrit word that means "I bow to you" and signifies "I bow to the divine in you." Bindi, the red dot that many Hindu women wear on the forehead, is an auspicious mark and symbol of good fortune. Once worn only by married women, bindi can be seen today on girls and women of all ages. Its location, over a chakra (energy point), is intended to help focus concentration during meditation.

### *Categories of Ritual*

The school of Hindu philosophy called Mimamsa, which is specially concerned with ritual, divides all religious activities in Hinduism into three types: (1) actions that are performed daily, called nitya; (2) actions performed on specific occasions, called naimittika; and (3) actions performed voluntarily according to personal desire, called kamya.

Hindus fulfil all three religious activities—nitya, naimittika, and kamya—through three types of ritual. These rituals are *yajna,* (involving a sacrificial fire); *puja* (devotional offerings, usually flowers); and *dhyana* (meditation). Yajnas are performed on major occasions, such as marriage and housewarming, when sacred substances are offered into the sacrificial fire. Puja may be performed publicly or privately. Public puja, usually performed in a temple, consists of anointing a statue of a deity and offering flowers, incense, and carefully prepared food to the deity. Chanting and devotional singing follow, accompanied by the waving of a small, camphor-burning lamp that illuminates the image of the deity. Most ceremonies have clearly marked opportunities for dhyana, or meditation.

### *Household Worship*

Hindu religious activities also can be divided into those that take place at home and those that take place in public. Many rituals are performed at home, either by individual family members or by the head of the household. Some of these household rituals involve a deity or a sacred fire; other rituals commemorate important passages in life.

## Puja: Devotion

Many Hindus worship daily the deity they have personally chosen. This personal deity is known as the *ishta-devata.*

Household puja usually consists of worshipping the *ishta-devata* with prayer and offerings of food, accompanied by chanting and the waving of a lamp or light. The offering of food acknowledges that all food has a divine source. After the offering, the food is ready to be shared by the worshippers. Household puja generally takes place in front of an image or statue of the *ishta-devata*, which may be set up as a domestic shrine. Hindus who are more deeply involved in ritual may also tend a domestic fire.

Puja possesses a markedly personal character and is more often performed privately by individuals and families than publicly at temples. The private nature of puja may arise from the extremely personal relationship that Hinduism nurtures with the divinity, as parent, friend, or other supportive person. It also could have evolved from Hindu historical experience under foreign occupation, during which expression of Hindu identity in public was frowned upon and even dangerous.

### *Samskaras: Sacraments to Mark Passages*

Sacraments called *samskaras* punctuate the life cycle of the individual and have greater religious significance than puja. A standard list cites 16 samskaras, but in other sources samskaras range in number from a maximum of about 40 to a minimum of 2, marriage and death. The number varies with varna and gender. The samskaras cluster in the early phases of life, including the prenatal phase. Four samskaras occur between birth and the beginning of studies at about age five. At birth a simple ceremony welcomes and blesses the newborn. The naming of the child, a significant event, occurs shortly after birth. Then come the taking of the first solid food and the first ritual shaving of the head. When the child is ready to study the Vedas (sacred Hindu scriptures), the major *samskara* of *upanayana* occurs.

In the course of it, the child receives a sacred thread and chants a mantra whispered into the child's ear: "Let us meditate on the glorious splendour of enlivening Sun-god. May he inspire our minds." In early times, a Hindu boy traditionally moved to the home of a *guru* (teacher) to study the Vedas after the upanayana samskara. After completing study of the Vedas, the student shaved the hair and was ready for marriage. A Hindu wedding consists of ceremonies performed over several days, culminating in the joining of the bride and groom. As part of the marriage samskara, a knot is tied to join the bride's and the groom's garments, after which they walk around a sacred fire seven times.

The sacred fire serves as a witness to the vows exchanged between the bride and the bridegroom. They then take seven steps together, symbolizing friendship and emphasizing the idea of companionship in marriage. To strengthen the union, the bride and groom place their right hands on each other's heart; the groom then recites a prayer from the Vedas, "I give you my heart. May our minds be as one." At the end of this ritual the pair become man and wife. Additional rites before and after the main Hindu marriage ritual vary from region to region.

The sacrament of death calls for *cremation* (burning of the dead body), at the end of which the ashes are collected and deposited, usually by the side of or in a river. For ten days after cremation, family members offer rice balls to the person who has departed. This offering provides a good example of the persistence of ritual in Hindu tradition: The rice symbolizes growth and is meant to provide the person with a body in which to dwell in the world of the ancestors. The alternative, while waiting for the next birth, is the less pleasant prospect of wandering in the world of ghosts. These actions are required only of the Hindu householder and do not apply to the renunciate.

### *Other Domestic Rituals*

Some Hindu rituals are performed to obtain a specific reward, according to instructions in the Vedas. Such rewards include securing a suitable life partner, conceiving a child, or attaining wealth, as well as warding off negative outcomes.

### *Communal Worship*

Household religious activities involve the family or an individual member of the family. Other Hindu religious activities involve a larger community. A cluster of families may have a shrine where they worship periodically. Beyond the family and the cluster of families lies the village. At the village level, worship of the favoured deity of the village dominates. From the village level, worship moves to public rituals, which may be performed at temples and other sacred sites or at sacred times.

## Temple Worship

Rituals performed at temples, like household rituals, may be described as those that take place daily, *nitya*; those performed on specific occasions, *naimitikka;* and those performed voluntarily, *kamya*. Hindu temples are dedicated to a deity or several deities who are believed to preside over the temple. Hindus visit temples to worship the temple deity or to worship another deity of their choosing by means of these three types of rituals. As at household shrines, they worship sculptures or painted images of the presiding deity and make offerings.

Basic rituals performed daily at most Hindu temples include rousing the deity from sleep at dawn, making the deity available for worship and offerings by visitors at midday, and putting the deity to bed at dusk. At some temples, the additional rituals of bathing and feeding the deity take place between dawn and midday. These rituals express the personal nature of Hindu love of and devotion to their deities.

Naimittika at temples is an occasion for carrying about the image of the temple deity. For example, a festival at the temple of Jagannath in the town of Puri celebrates the god Jagannath's annual visit to his birthplace, the temple site, in his chariot. More than 4,000 celebrants pull the god's wooden chariot, which stands about 14 m (45 ft.) high.

The English word *juggernaut* comes from Jagannath. Public processions and festivals at the temples of Rama and Krishna mark the birthdays of these avatars of Vishnu. *Kamya puja* is typically performed at temples to gain a specific end. A visitor to a temple might request the performance of puja, or daily prayers, at the temple and make a donation for that purpose.

***Sacred Sites***

Hindus consider the entire Earth, as well as the Indian land mass known as mother India (*Bharata Mata*), to be sacred. This view once found expression in such practices as visiting the four corners of India as represented by the pilgrimage sites of Badrinath to the north, Puri to the east, Rameshvaram to the south, and Dwarka to the west. Hindus make pilgrimages to sacred sites in the hope of cleansing themselves of sins and lessening their karmic debt.

Certain parts of India are held in special veneration. For example, Hindu tradition regards seven cities as holy: Ayodhya (the birthplace of Rama); Mathura (where Krishna grew up); Haridwar (where the Ganges River widens onto a plain); Kasi (sacred to Shiva); Kanci (associated with the Hindu philosopher Shankara); Avanti or Ujjain (site of the temple of Mahakala); and Puri (associated with the later life of Krishna).

Other sacred Hindu locations involve rivers and events in Hindu epics. Particular regions also have their own sacred locations. Certain sites in India are sacred because of their association with the Great Goddess, Devi, who takes many forms. In the form of Devi Sati, according to legend, her dismembered body parts fell on 51 locations that became sacred to worshippers of Shakti (the female aspect of the divine). The Jvala Mukhi Temple near Jullundur, for example, is said to represent her tongue. Worshippers visit the Kamakshya Temple in Assam to partake of her cosmic energy.

***Sacred Times***

Religious festivals dot the Hindu calendar. A number of them commemorate events in the great Sanskrit epic Ramayana (Way of Rama) or in the life of Krishna. The timing of these festivals is related to the movements of the Sun and the Moon.

An important festival known as the Dusshera marks the victory of Prince Rama over the demon king Ravana in a struggle between good and evil that is related in the Ramayana. Dusshera takes place in September or October and is followed by Diwali (also known as Deepavali), the festival of lights. Diwali commemorates events that restored truth and light in early times: the victorious return of Rama with his bride Sita to Ayodhya in the north and the victory of Krishna over the monster Narakasura in the south.

The festival of Holi celebrates the arrival of spring in February or March. During this festival people spray each other with coloured powders and coloured water, forget the cares of winter, and rejoice in the onset of spring. A popular family festival, Raksabandhana, occurs in July or August and renews the bonds of affection between brothers and sisters. Sisters tie lucky threads around the wrists of brothers and are rewarded with gifts. Other important festivals are Shivaratri, the night sacred to Shiva when worshippers recite prayers to be freed of sins, and Ganesha-Chaturthi, dedicated to the elephant god Ganesha, when worshippers recite prayers to remove obstacles in their lives. Shivaratri falls in the winter months, and Ganesha-Cahturthi in August or September. Among the major regional festivals are the Dolayatra, a spring festival in the eastern state of Orissa; Pongal, a winter festival in southern India; and Onam, a harvest festival in the southwestern state of Kerala.

## Satsanga: Fellowship

A popular form of participation in religious life is the *Satsanga*, which literally means keeping company with *sat* (truth and goodness). The Satsanga may consist of Hindus who gather for discussions of Hindu scripture or of a circle of devotees who have formed around a saintly figure. A saint ("sant" in Sanskrit) in Hinduism in someone who has realized the truth and attained recognition from the community for doing so. Other forms of worship that occur at satsangas are chanting or singing, especially devotional songs called bhajans. On religious occasions the chanting the *Om* sound is considered particularly holy.

### *Om: Sacred Symbol and Sacred Sound*

The sacred syllable *Om* or *aum* functions at many levels. Hindus chant it as a means of meditating on the ultimate reality and connecting with the innermost self (atman) and

Brahman. At one level, om possesses a vibrational aspect apart from its conceptual significance. If pronounced correctly, its vibrations resonate through the body and penetrate the atman. At another level, the three sounds that constitute the syllable—*a, u,* and *m*—have been associated with the states of waking, dreaming, and deep sleep, states to which all life can be reduced.

Thus, by repeating the syllable the chanter passes through all three states. Other associations of the three sounds are with the three states of the cosmos—manifestation, maintenance, and dissolution—and with the three aspects of Ishvara who preside over these cosmic states: Brahma, Vishnu, and Shiva. Om thus functions at a practical level as a mantra and at a cosmic level as signifying the trinity.

### *Guru: Teacher*

Spiritual authority in Hinduism flows from enlightened sages called gurus. The guru is someone who has attained realization and acts as a guide for other human beings. He or she guides the individual seeker of truth and self-realization to the appropriate deity, practice, or yoga within Hinduism. The disciple's goal is to transcend the need for a guru through direct experience of the divine and self-awareness. Having a guide is considered critical for traversing the complexities of spiritual practice and self-discovery. The guru thus constitutes an important centre of spiritual activity in Hinduism. Numerous Hindu hymns express adoration for the guru.

***Sacred Literature—What Do Hindus Read?:*** Although Hindu tradition maintains that the ultimate reality lies beyond all scriptures, it is equally convinced that the scriptures help people orient their minds and lives towards Brahman. This attitude has given rise to a body of sacred literature so vast that by one calculation it would take 70 lifetimes of devoted study to read all of it.

### *The Vedas*

The four Vedas constitute the most important body of sacred Hindu literature, at least in theory. Other sacred literature, especially the Hindu epics, may be more popular with readers, but the Vedas, written in the ancient Sanskrit language, are the oldest and most respected scriptures. They are separately titled the Rig-Veda, Yajur-Veda, Sama-Veda, and Atharva-Veda, and collectively referred to as the Veda.

Each of the Vedas can be divided into four types of texts, which are roughly chronological in order: *mantra* or *samhita*, *brahmana*, *aranyaka*, and *upanishad*. The mantra or samhita portion largely consists of hymns addressed to the various deities. The brahmana texts gather the authoritative utterances of Brahmans (those with knowledge of Brahman, the ultimate reality) and describe the rituals, chiefly sacrificial offerings, in which the hymns are employed. The third section consists of aranyakas, or forest texts, presumably composed by sages who sought seclusion in the forests. The last section consists of the Upanishads, philosophical texts that have an air of mystery and secrecy about them.

Scholars have suggested that the four types of texts represent four different stages in the spiritual evolution of the Aryans, the peoples of the Vedas. During the earliest stage in their religious life, the Aryans may have recited simple hymns of praise for the divinities they felt dwelt around them. In the next stage ritual evolved out of the early worship and became increasingly elaborate, until people were driven to ask what it was all about. Sages then retired to the forests to reflect on the meaning of sacrifice and the person who makes the sacrifice. This reflection opened the floodgates of philosophical speculation found in the Upanishads.

Hindus traditionally have viewed the four types of texts as dating from the same period but serving different purposes. The first three texts deal with the realm of action and are concerned with dharma, artha, and kama, whereas the last text concerns knowledge of the self and moksha. In this view, following dharma while experiencing the ups and downs of life produces a devout and mature mind that is then able to fully grasp what the Upanishads have to say.

The Upanishads are also called Vedanta (meaning "end of the Vedas") because they represent the final essence of the

Vedas. The Vedanta marks the culmination as well as the conclusion of the Vedas, although the Vedic canon was never formally closed.

## Shruti and Smriti: Eternal Truth and Tradition

Hindu scriptures can be classified into two types: *shruti* and *smriti*. Shruti, meaning "heard," may be thought of as revelation or eternal truth, whereas smriti, meaning "remembered," is comparable to tradition. By distinguishing that which is eternally true from that which holds true for a specific time and culture, the categories of shruti and smriti enable Hindus to reform outdated practices while remaining faithful to Hinduism's essence. Where there is a conflict between the two, shruti takes precedence over smriti. The Vedas constitute shruti, whereas there are many different smriti texts.

The Vedas correspond, among the Hindus, to the Bible among Christians and the Qur'an among Muslims. However, unlike the revealed texts of Christianity and Islam, whose source is considered to be God speaking through the son or the prophet, the Vedas have no author. According to Vedanta, shruti is revelation without a revealer. Because in Hinduism the universe is without beginning or end, the Vedas appear along with creation at the beginning of each cycle of time. Then Brahma, who presides over the remanifestation of the universe, recites the Vedas and sages hear them anew. These divinely heard scriptures are then transmitted orally from master to disciple.

The Vedas as also called *shruti* because they are divinely "heard" by the sages at the beginning of a cycle; and also because they are transmitted orally from master to disciple thus once again justifying the meaning of *shruti* as audition.

The word *smriti* is applied to a vast category of literature in Hinduism. Unlike shruti, Sanskrit scripture without an author, smriti is considered to have an author and may even be written in one of the regional languages of India.

One category of smriti consists of more than 20 law books that lay down in detail the rules to follow in life, especially the rules that pertain to *varna* (social order) and *ashrama* (stages of life). Another category includes texts called Puranas, which deal with the lives of the gods and celestial beings. There are 18 Puranas, and they can be classified according to which of the three gods of the Hindu trinity they focus on—Brahma, Vishnu, or Shiva.

The most famous of these is the Bhagavata Purana, which deals with the life of Krishna, an avatar of Vishnu, in the pastoral surroundings of Vrndavana. A third category of smriti consists of two texts of legendary history: the Ramayana and the Mahabharata. These are the two well-known epics of Hinduism. Scholars believe the Ramayana assumed its present form between 300 BC and AD 200, while the Mahabharata evolved over a period extending from about 400 BC to about AD 400.

## Religion and the Epics

### *Ramayana*

The Ramayana of Valmiki consists of about 24,000 verses and describes the life of Prince Rama, an incarnation of Vishnu. The author, Valmiki, according to later tradition, belonged to the shudra varna and made his living by robbing travellers. After an encounter with the sage Narada, Valmiki turned his life around and became a poet and scholar. Classical Hinduism recognizes him as a brahman and as India's first poet. Rama and his wife Sita embody virtue and righteousness, and their lives demonstrate dharma in various spheres of activity. Their life stories contain lessons for Hindus on ideal behaviour in various roles, such as son, brother, wife, king, and married couple. Rama's reign ushers in a golden age, and the expression *Rama-rajya* (rule of Rama) describes the best of times in which the divine presence rules on Earth.

### *Mahabharata*

The Mahabharata, an epic story of 100,000 verses, is attributed to a sage named Vyasa and considered to be the longest poem in the world. It traces the descendants of two sets of cousins, the Kauravas and the Pandavas, whose disputes eventually lead to the Mahabharata war. Krishna, an avatar of Vishnu, is central to the story. Like the Ramayana, the Mahabharata addresses many questions related to dharma and the actions of individuals and society. These discourses have provided inspiration for Hindus in many areas of life.

### *Bhagwad-Gita*

One part of the Mahabharata, the Bhagwad-Gita, functions virtually as a text on its own in Hinduism. On the eve of the Mahabharata war, the hero Arjuna suddenly develops a disinclination to fight. Arjuna's decision leads to a prolonged dialogue with Krishna during which Krishna tries to resolve Arjuna's moral and metaphysical dilemmas in 700 verses. The way in which Krishna seeks to guide Arjuna has endeared the text to the Hindus as a guide to their faith.

In the Bhagwad-Gita Hinduism comes closest to possessing a universal scripture. Since the Gupta period (AD 320 to 550; *see* Gupta Dynasty) it has inspired a stream of commentaries, summaries, and translations, all of which attest to its wide popularity. The process shows no signs of letting up. The Bhagwad-Gita's doctrine of *svadharma* (understanding one's own role and responsibility) implies a cosmic mirroring of the essential nature of reality (Brahman) in the reality of the individual's essential nature (atman). This implication has proved spiritually intriguing for practitioner, believer, and scholar alike.

The Mahabharata and the Bhagwad-Gita carry meaning on multiple levels. In one interpretation, the Pandavas and Kauravas represent the forces of good and evil that exist within each person, and the contest between them represents the perpetual battle between these tendencies. The Bhagwad-Gita describes the techniques and paths by which the individual can attain realization of the Ultimate Reality with Krishna as the guide. As part of the Mahabharata, the Bhagwad-Gita technically falls in the category of smriti rather than shruti. However, it virtual enjoys the status of shruti by representing the words of the divinity, incarnated as Krishna and addressed to human beings through Arjuna.

### *Tantric Literature*

*Tantra* represents another vast body of Hindu literature. After centuries of neglect, it has gradually begun to receive fuller recognition. The word *tantra* has two meanings. In one sense it refers to sacred literature which appeared from the 5th century onward and focused not only on Vishnu and Shiva, but also on the cults of earlier deities: Ganapati (another name for the elephant-headed god, Ganesha), Kumara (a son of Brahma), Surya (sun) and Shakti (the goddess). The second sense restricts *tantra* to texts that deal with the worship of Shakti.

After the Gupta age ended in the 6th century the Tantric tradition heavily influenced Hinduism, Buddhism, and Jainism. If elite or intellectual Hinduism is Vedic in nature, then mainstream Hinduism is Tantric in orientation. Some accounts consider both traditions equally revelatory. Tantric literature largely eliminates caste distinctions in terms of religious practices. It also holds women in high regard. It thus provides a useful corrective to the negative stereotypes of Hinduism as '*patriarchal* (male-controlled). Although smriti literature can be described as male oriented, Tantric literature is female oriented.

Consider these statements from Tantric literature. The *Gautamiya Tantra* clearly states that tantra is open to women and members of all castes. The *Mahanirvana Tantra* requires a man to fast for a day for talking rudely to a woman. The *Kubjikamata Tantra* states that all houses of women should be worshipped as holy shrines. In the *Shakta* model of Hinduism, which focuses worship on the Great Goddess, all women are regarded as gurus and may initiate others by reading out the mantra from an authoritative text. Men have no authority to do so. In addition, the Devi (goddess) is worshipped in her own right, rather than in relation to a male god.

Hindu gods are regularly displayed with their female counterparts. When they are invoked together, the female partner is named first, as in Sita-Rama and Radha-Krishna. In the case of Shiva and Shakti the relationship gets so close that they are represented as inhabiting a single body in the *Ardhanrishvara* (Lord-who-is-half-female) form. Tantra at times involves the balancing of these two aspects—Shiva (representing consciousness) and Shakti (representing energy)—in a manner reminiscent of *yin and yang* in Daoism.

### *Literature in Regional Languages*

Most Hindus first encounter Hinduism through their regional languages, despite the special significance of Sanskrit. Almost every regional language in India has produced its own version of the Ramayana and the Mahabharata, sharing in the religious admiration given to the original versions.

Deservedly famous translations of the Ramayana include one in the Tamil language by the 9th-century Hindu scholar Kamban and one in Hindi and by the 16th-century poet and saint Tulsidas. A wave of literature in Tamil appeared in the 7th to 9th centuries as the result of a surge of devotion of Vishnu and Shiva. Most of the influential works of modern Hinduism were originally composed in English. Masters who have realized Brahman continually renew the Hindu tradition and express themselves in a language appropriate to their time and place.

The utilization of these various bodies of literature provides insight into how Hinduism tries to sanctify what it touches. Thus the title of Veda came to be conferred on any worthwhile body of knowledge, including writings on architecture, on music, and even on military science. Highly esteemed sacred texts that came after the Vedas have come to be described as the fifth Veda.

### *History of Hinduism*

Hinduism does not attach the same religious significance to historical events that Judaism, Christianity, and Islam do. Some have compared Hinduism's indifference to the history of a religious idea or practice to a scientist's indifference to the history of science. What is of value to both is the idea or practice as such.

The history of Hinduism thus becomes a history of its quest to incorporate the various developments it has encountered or generated, rather than a history of conquest of or triumph over these historical developments. The contrast is apparent in the Biblical injunction to believe in one God who is the only God and the Vedic perception that "Truth is one, sages call it variously."

Considerable controversy remains over Hinduism's historical origins. At one time scholars believed that the arrival of the Aryan people in India about 1500 BC represented a critical moment in the history of Hinduism. The Aryans replaced the earlier Harappan culture in the Indus valley, and they are the people described in the Vedas, the earliest sacred literature of Hinduism.

Although linguistic evidence tends to support the notion of an Aryan migration, most scholars now believe this view awaits confirmation by archaeology, especially because it has been challenged by the discovery of extensive sites in northwestern and western India. So far there is no clear-cut answer to the key question: Did Hinduism as described in the Vedas originate in India or did it arise as a result of migrations from outside? What is clear is that the Hinduism of the Vedas goes back at least to 1200 BC in India and perhaps much earlier.

### *Vedic Hinduism*

The beginnings of Vedic Hinduism, no later than 1200 BC, trace back to the Rig-Veda, which contains hymns of praise to various deities called devas. *Agni* (deva of fire) and *Indra* (king of devas and deva of the atmosphere, storms, rain, and battle) were prominent, judging by the number of hymns addressed to them. Fire was the deity of the domestic hearth as well as of public ritual. The Rig-Veda calls the deity "smoke-bannered" as it carries the offering made into it toward the gods. Indra was a martial leader in the Rig-Veda who carried his followers to victory in battle and also battled drought as a rain-god. An entire book of the Rig-Veda is devoted to soma, a plant whose juice produced ecstatic experiences. It is already clear in the Rig-Veda that all these devas were aspects of one underlying reality.

By the 4th century BC Vedic Hinduism had appeared in virtually all of India and had assimilated and absorbed various local religious beliefs and practices. The resulting mixture is what we refer to comprehensively as Vedic Hinduism.

### *Classical Hinduism*

The period from the 3rd century BC to the late 7th century AD is known as classical Hinduism. Even as Vedic Hinduism flourished throughout India, various aspects of its world-view had come under challenge by the 6th century BC. This challenge came from Upanishadic thinkers and from the rise of new sects including the Jains and the Buddhists.

The Upanishadic thinkers considered themselves in the line of descent from Vedic seers, while the followers of Buddhism and Jainism tended to question Vedic authority, although they retained many concepts from the Vedas. All were concerned about release from eternal rebirth and generally agreed that release was obtained not by sacrifice but by meditation and contemplation.

Buddhism and Jainism gradually gained strength in India during the centuries just before and just after the beginning of the first millennium. Buddhism benefited in the 3rd century BC from the patronage extended to it by King Ashoka, who ruled almost all of India. Jainism similarly benefited from royal patrons. By the start of the Gupta period, which lasted from about AD 320 to 550, Hinduism resurged, having integrated a variety of Buddhist and Jain beliefs and practices. These included the doctrine of *ahimsa* (nonviolence) and an emphasis on vegetarianism. The Gupta period is celebrated as a glorious epoch of classical Hindu culture.

During this classical Gupta period, Hindu thought and its systematization flourished. By then many *shastras* (classical works) of Hindu philosophy had been compiled. These shastras include the *Arthashastra* (principles of statecraft), *Nayashastra* (aesthetics of performing arts), poetry and dramatic works by writers such as Kalidasa and Bhavabhuti, grammars by Panini and Patanjali, works on human sexuality such as the *Kamasutra,* and the medical compendia of Charak and Susruta. In addition, the major epics—the Ramayana and Mahabharata—received their present form. Also during this period, rules were developed for representations of the deities and for building structures to house these statues and images.

### *Medieval Hinduism*

As a vigorous and multifaceted Hinduism unfolded in India during the 7th century, a new religion made its appearance in Arabia: Islam. Within a century, Islam's dominions extended from Spain to Sindh (now part of Pakistan). By the 10th and 11th centuries the followers of Islam consolidated their hold on northwestern India. By 1200 Islamic rule was established in the city of Delhi in northern India, and it then spread in two waves over nearly the whole of India. The first wave of expansion occurred under the Delhi Sultanate, which ruled from 1206 to 1526. During the second wave, under the Mughal Empire (1526-1858), Islamic rule achieved its maximum extension.

This encounter between Hinduism and Islam lasted more than 800 years. During most of this time, Islam had the upper hand politically, a fact that had enormous consequences for Hinduism and that presented challenges for both Hinduism and Islam which continue to this day. Islam's military victories outside India were followed by the conversion of the masses to Islam, with the possible exceptions of Spain and the Balkans. In India, however, Islam succeeded in converting barely a quarter of the population to Islam by 1900. Although Hinduism had successfully incorporated all previous invaders and political conquerors within the Hindu religious system—from the Persians in 6th century BC to the Huns in the 6th century AD—its powers of assimilation failed in the face of Islam.

One response of Hinduism to the presence of Islam was political. It included the emergence of the Hindu Vijayanagar kingdom, which held power in southern India from about 1336 to 1565, and the Hindu Maratha state in western India during the 17th and 18th centuries. The rise of Sikhism and the Sikh Empire (1767-1846) in the Punjab can also be considered part of this response. Willing to use violence in self-defense, Sikhs took a militant stance toward the conquerors.

The Islamic presence evoked a paradoxical Hindu religious response that blended hostile rejection and active emulation.

Mainstream Hinduism retreated into a defensive position under the protective cover of *orthodoxy* (conformity to rule), judging by the number of Hindu religious codes produced during this period. At the theological level, however, Hinduism witnessed the rise and flowering of the *bhakti* (devotion) movement.

This movement of ecstatic devotion to Vishnu or Shiva had gained a firm foothold in the south by the 9th century, and it swept over the rest of the country by the 17th century. Devotion to the divine *(bhakti)*, rather than knowledge of the divine *(jnana)*, became the dominant form of Hinduism, perhaps reflecting the historical circumstances. Bhakti poetry expressed love for the divine, often in the forms of Krishna and Rama. Among the mystical bhakti poets were Chaitanya, Tulsidas, Mirabai, and Kabir.

The bhakti movement also provided a point of contact with a mystical movement in Islam known as Sufism. Sufis were religious figures known for their piety and love of God. As they carried out their work in India, the two traditions of Hinduism and Islam came together in their love of God. This coming together, however, never crossed over from communion to union, but the rise of Sikhism points to a possible crossover. Sikhism rejects image worship and ritualism in keeping with Islam, while retaining many aspects of the Hindu world-view.

### Modern Hinduism

Following the decline of the Mughal Empire during the late 17th century, the British gradually succeeded in establishing themselves as the paramount power in India during the next century. The process began with a British victory in the Battle of Plassey in 1757, followed by the defeat of the Marathas in 1818. British victory over the Sikhs in 1846 completed the process. By this time the British had made two decisions of far-reaching importance for the future of Hinduism: to allow Christian missionaries to operate within the British dominions, in 1813; and to introduce English as the language of public instruction, in 1835.

These decisions forced Hinduism to confront Christianity and Western modernity. At the same time, the Western world was exposed to Hindu scriptures translated into European languages.

***Movements for Reform***

One response to the encounter with Europe was reform. The Bengali scholar Ram Mohan Roy set the tone for reform in the early 19th century. Roy campaigned against medieval or regional Hindu practices that were objectionable in the modern world. He advocated allowing widows to remarry and abolition of the relatively rare practice of *sati* (self-immolation of a wife after her husband's death; *see* suttee). In 1828 Mohan Roy founded the Brahmo Samaj (Society of Brahma) to spread his ideas.

Another movement kept India from moving too far toward imitation of the modern Christian West. The movement was named after Ramakrishna, a Hindu spiritual leader who served as a priest at the Dakshineshwar Temple in the city of Kolkata (Calcutta). His reputation as a mystic drew many to him, including Swami Vivekananda, who founded the Ramakrishna movement after Ramakrishna's death in 1886.

Vivekananda, a representative Hindu product of India's new English-language education system, became a devotee of Ramakrishna and renounced the world after the priest's death. His message was a return to the timeless wisdom of the Vedas. As an unknown swami, he turned up uninvited at the Parliament of World Religions in Chicago in 1893 to present Ramakrishna's teachings. He won instant celebrity and was hailed as a hero in India for his vigorous advocacy of Hinduism. In 1895 he founded the Vedanta Society in New York City to promote Hindu ideas.

Vivekananda primarily used English in his work of reforming Hinduism and stressing the inclusive aspects of Hindu spirituality over ritual and rules. Another reform-minded leader of the 19th century, Dayananda Saraswati, used Hindi in responding to the challenges of Christianity and modernity. Saraswati founded the Arya Samaj, a movement also dedicated to modernizing Hindu practices and asserting the universality of the Hindu tradition. These movements helped revitalize

Hinduism. Another issue that engaged Hindu reformers was the plight of the lowest social class, the panchama jatis who are also known as untouchables. Local movements, such as one led by Sri Narayana Guru in Kerala, were most successful at reform. Narayana, who was born in 1856, believed that education and greater self-esteem, rather than confrontation and blame, would elevate the untouchables. He established temples where all castes could pray together.

# 7

# Popular Systems of Hindu Religious Thought

Hindu religious thought embodies a variety of ideas, principles and practices, giving rise to various religious schools (*sampradayas*). Each school venerates the Supreme Deity, which represents a particular aspect of the Ultimate Reality (*Brahman*). Each school has temples, *guru* lineages, religious leaders, pilgrimage centres, monastic communities and sacred literature.

Some of these schools hold such divergent views that each appears to be a complete religion in itself. Yet, they all believe in the central doctrines of Hindu religion, such as *karma, dharma*, reincarnation, divinity of the *atman*, sacraments, deity worship, *guru-shishya* (teacher-disciple) tradition and the scriptural authority of the Vedas. None of these schools is in any way superior or inferior to the others. They simply represent different ways of approach to the same goal and are meant for various classes of people having different tastes, aptitudes, temperaments, and exhibiting various levels of spiritual development.

## Vedanta

The science of Vedanta is enshrined in the original spiritual texts of India. It is founded on the authority of the Upanishads, the *Bhagwad Gita* and the *Brahmasutram* of Badrayana Vyasa. Vedanta brings out the mystical, ethical and metaphysical aspects of philosophy. The abiding knowledge of Vedanta rests in the vision of the One Reality, a vision that transcends race, class, creed, gender and nationality. Vedanta is the one principle of truth encompassing all religions.

There are three different philosophies on this concept. *Advaita* (non-duality) implies that there is an identity of Brahman and *Jiva atman* while *Dvaita* (duality) differs from *Advaita* and maintains an ultimate diversity between Brahman and *Jiva atman*. *Vishistadvaita* (qualified non-duality) maintains a crucial differentiation as well as a fundamental identity.

Advaita is the oldest extant school of Vedanta founded by Adi Shankaracharya. Advaita asserts that the real, essential identity of the *jiva*, the individual self, is nothing other than *Brahman* itself.

It asserts that Brahman, the 'impersonal' God and the universal soul, is the Absolute Truth. Brahman has multiple roles to play: the creator, the maintainer, and the destroyer all in one. The teaching follows from the statements of the Upanishads (*Mahavakyas*) like *tat tvam asi* and *aham brahmasmi*. It is in this cardinal doctrine that *Advaita* differs from all other schools of Vedanta.

The *Vishishtadvaita* philosophy was expounded by Sri Ramanuja. According to this desirable qualities *viz.*, *satyam, jnanam* and *anandam.* The main exponent of the *Dvaita* philosophy was Sri Madhava (Purnaprajna). It says that the supreme goal of life is service of god.

Other systems which are not quite popular as the above mentioned philosophies include *Dvaitadvaita* (dual-non-dual doctrine), *Suddhadvaita* (pure non-dualism) and *Acinntyaa bhedabheda* (oneness and difference) were expounded by Nimbarka, Vallabha and Vidyabhusana respectively. All the above philosophers have written commentaries on the *Prasthana-traya* (triple canon) of the *Vedanta*, which are the *Upanishads*, *Brahma sutra* and the *Bhagwad Gita*.

The Hindu religious systems have been classified by Adi Shankaracharya into six major paths, called *Shad-maths*. These are *Shaivism*, *Vaishnavism*, *Shaktism*, *Ganapathyam*, *Kaumaram*, and *Sauram* or *Jyotiam*.

## Shaivism

The followers of Shaivism venerate the Ultimate Reality as Lord Shiva. This tradition has been traced back by scholars to the Indus Valley Civilization. The archeologists have discovered the so-called proto-*Pasupathy* seals of this civilization, which depict Shiva as Lord *Pasupathy*, seated in a yogic pose. There are many schools of Shaivism, of which the six major systems are *Shaiva Siddhanta*, *Pashupata Shaivism,* Kashmir *Shaivism*, *Vira Shaivism*, *Siddha Siddhanta* and *Shiva Advaita*. These systems differ somewhat in their doctrines pertaining to the relationship between Shiva, the *Atman* and the world.

Most Hindus worship Lord Shiva as a member of the Hindu Trinity. However, the followers of Shaivism, called *Shaivas* or *Shaivites*, worship Him as the Ultimate Reality. The predominant philosophy of Shaivism is monistic-theism. According to this doctrine, Lord Shiva is both personal and impersonal. In the personal aspect, Shiva creates, controls and pervades all that exists. In this aspect, Shiva is what other religions call God. Shaivism declares that there is nothing outside Shiva and, thus, recognizes the oneness of *Pati-pau-pasa* (God-*Atman*-World). In the impersonal aspect, Shiva transcends all existence and in the liberated state the *Atman* is one with Shiva.

The main objects of Shiva worship are *shivalinga* and images of Shiva. The *linga* symbolizes both the creative and destructive power of the Lord and great sanctity is attached to it by the devotees. The *banalingas* are very sacred objects of worship to the followers of Shaivism. These are the elliptical stones of a special kind found in the bed of the river Narmada, one of the seven sacred rivers in India. Fresh flowers, pure water, young sprouts of *Kusha* (a holy grass) and *durva* (called bent or panic grass), fruit, *bilva* leaves and sun-dried rice are used in the ritual part of the Shiva worship.

According to tradition, offering leaves of the *bilva* tree (wood-apple) is considered very auspicious for the worship of Lord Shiva. *Mahashivaratri* (the great night of Shiva) is an annual festival that falls on the fourteenth day of the dark fortnight of *Phalguna* (February-March), and is dedicated to the worship of Lord Shiva. In mythology, Shiva is the husband of Parvati, the daughter of the Himalayas. They have two sons, Ganesha and Karttikeya and a daughter Jyoti. Their residence is the snow-clad mountain Kailash. The mythology depicts Shiva both as God of terror as well as benevolence. His five powers are revealment (offering grace to the devotees), concealment (obscuring by His power of *maya*), creation, preservation and dissolution. The major scriptures of Shaivism are Vedas, Shaiva Agamas and Shaiva Puranas.

## Vaishnavism

Vaishnavism venerates the Ultimate Reality as Lord Vishnu. This tradition began during the Vedic period when its earliest schools *Pancharatra* and *Bhagavata* became popular around 300 BC. Modern day Vaishnavism includes five popular schools founded by Ramanuja, Madhva, Nimbarka, Vallabha and Chaitanya. Most Hindus worship Lord Vishnu as a member of the Hindu Trinity. However, the followers of Vaishnavism, called *Vaishnavas* or *Vaishnavites*, worship Lord Vishnu as the Ultimate Reality.

Although the philosophy of Vaishnavism includes dualism of Madhva, qualified dualism of Ramanuja, and nearly monistic views of Vallabha, the predominant philosophy of Vaishnavism is dualism. According to this doctrine, there are two categories of the Ultimate Reality. Lord Vishnu as personal God is the Absolute Reality, and the *Atmans* (individuals souls) are the relative realities, eternally distinct from each other and Lord Vishnu, but dependent on Him. The doctrine of incarnation (*avatara*) is fundamental to all Hindus, especially to Vaishnavas. Lord Vishnu assumed each *avatara* for a particular end and as the situation demanded. The number of *avataras* of Lord Vishnu is generally accepted to be ten, with Rama and Krishna being the two most popular among Hindus.

Vaishnavism stresses on complete surrender (*prapatti*) to Lord Vishnu and His incarnations and advocates devotion (*bhakti*) as the highest spiritual discipline. The objects of worship are the images of Lord Vishnu and His incarnations, and *salagramas*, small stones of different colours (predominantly black) recovered from the bed of the river Gandaki, one of the tributaries of the Ganges river in India. Fresh flowers, water, fruits and leaves of the *tulasi* plant are used in the ritual part of the worship of Lord Vishnu and His incarnations. One of the unique features of the Vaishnava worship is *kirtana*, which consists of choral singing of the names and deeds of Lord Vishnu and His incarnations, accompanied by drums and cymbals and synchronized with rhythmic bodily movements. The major scriptures of Vaishnavism are Vedas, Agamas, Puranas, Ramayana, Mahabharata and Bhagwad Gita.

## Shaktism

*Shakti* means "creative energy," and *Shaktism* means "Doctrine of the Creative Energy." Shaktism venerates the Ultimate Reality as the Divine Mother-*Shakti* or *Devi*-of the universe.

Archeologists have recovered thousands of female statuettes at the Mehrgarh village in India, which indicate that Shakti worship existed in India as far back as 5500 BC. There are references to the female deities in the Rig Veda, including a popular Hymn to the Divine Mother, which holds special sanctity to Hindus in general and *Shaktas* (the followers of Shaktism) in particular. Shaktism visualises the Ultimate Reality as having two aspects, transcendent and immanent. Shiva is the transcendent aspect, the supreme cosmic consciousness, and Shakti is the supreme creative energy. Shiva and Shakti are God and God's creative energy, which are inseparably connected. Metaphorically, Shiva and Shakti is an inseparable divine couple, representing the male and female principles in creation.

Shaktism greatly resembles Shaivism, but Shiva is considered solely transcendent and is not worshipped. Like Shaivism, the goal of Shaktism is to unite with Shiva. Such unity is possible only with the grace of the Divine Mother, who unfolds as *iccha shakti* (the power of desire, will and love), *kriya shakti* (the power of action), and *jnana shakti* (the power of knowledge and wisdom). Within Shaktism, Shiva is the unmanifest Absolute and Shakti is the Divine Mother of the manifest creation. The Divine Mother is worshipped in both the fierce and benign forms. The fierce forms of Goddess include Kali, Durga, Chandi, Chamundi, Bhadrakali and Bhairavi. The benign forms of Goddess include Uma, Gauri, Ambika, Parvati, Maheshvari, Lalita, Lakshmi, Saraswata and Annapurna. The major scriptures of Shaktism are *Vedas*, *Shakta agamas* and *Puranas*.

### *Ganapathyam*

Ganesha, the elephant-headed deity, represents that aspect of the Ultimate Reality which removes obstacles. Hindus, therefore, invoke Lord Ganesha at the beginning of all undertakings, whether religious, spiritual or worldly, for Lord Ganesha removes obstacles and brings success to the enterprise. Ganesha is also called *Vighneshvara*, meaning "the Lord presiding over the obstacles." In the Rig Veda, Ganesha is the name of *Brihapati*, the Lord of prayer (the Holy Word). In mythology Ganesha is the first son of the divine couple Shiva and Parvati.

*Ganapatyas*, followers of Ganapathyam, venerate Lord Ganesha exclusively as the form of the Ultimate Reality (*Brahman*) that is accessible to the mind, senses and (through devotional practices) the heart. Ganapatyas regard Moraya Gosavi (1651 AD), the famous devotee of Ganesha, as their spiritual progenitor. Tradition holds that Moraya experienced a series of visions of Ganesha at a shrine at Moragaon, near Pune. An annual ten-day festival, *Ganesha Chaturthi*, is held in August-September to celebrate the birth of Ganesha. The major scriptures of this tradition are Vedas, Skanda Purana, and Mudgala Purana.

### *Kaumaram*

The followers of this tradition venerate Lord Karttikeya, also called by other names such as Murugan, Kumara, Skanda, Subramanya and Shanmukhanatha, as their *Ishta Devata* (personal-God). Lord Karttikeya represents the power of the Ultimate Reality (Brahman) that destroys ignorance, bestows divine knowledge, upholds dharma (righteousness), removes worries and strengthens human will. In popular pictures and images, Karttikeya is shown holding a spear, which symbolizes his divine power to destroy ignorance and unrighteousness. On the day of Vaikasi Vishakham in May-June, elaborate *pujas* and special ceremonies (*abhishekam*) are conducted in homes and temples in the honour of Lord Karttikeya. His protection and grace are specially invoked on the day of *Skanda Shashthi*, which falls on the sixth day after the new moon in October-November. In January-February, another holy festival (*Tai Pusam*) is celebrated in his honour. Special *pujas* are performed in honour of Lord Karttikeya every month on *Krittika nakshatra* and *Shashthi*, the sixth day after the new moon.

***Sauram***

The power of the sun to dispel darkness, illuminate the world and nourish mankind is recognized by Hindus as an aspect of the infinite power of the Ultimate Reality (Brahman). The worship of this triple power of the Divine, symbolized by the Vedic deity Surya, the Sun-god, is called Sauram. Surya is worshipped by Hindus as an object of meditation during many physical exercises. Devout Hindus recite sacred verses selected from the epic and Puranic literature daily early in the morning before commencing the day's work. The best known of the hymns to the sun is one from Ramayana that was imparted to Rama during his battle with Ravana.

Hindus in general worship the sun every year on the seventh day after the new moon in the month that corresponds to January-February. Sacred mantras are recited for the special worship of the sun, especially on Sundays, birthdays and at other special functions. Prostrations are made to the sun after each tenth mantra until one hundred and thirty-two prostrations have been completed. These prostrations are called *Surya-Namaskara*.

The following most sacred Rigvedic prayer, named after its meter, is called *Gayatri*, meaning "the saviour of the singer." It is considered to be the mantra of all mantras, the most potent mantra, repeated as many times as possible by Hindus daily in *puja* and personal chanting to venerate the sun as the Creator (*Savitar*). The mystic power of this mantra is so high that it is called *Vedamatri*, meaning "Mother of the Vedas." *Gayatri Mantra* is imparted to a young boy for initiation into Vedic tradition.

### *Yamas & Niyamas—The Moral and Ethical Ideals of Hindus*

Ethics can be described as the science of morality, and morality as the living of a virtuous life. Hindus place greater emphasis on the attitude of the mind rather than on postulation of the elaborate theories of what is right and what is wrong. Accordingly, the Hindu vision of morality and ethics is characterized by the following considerations: *Ahimsa* (non-injury), *Satya* (truthfulness), *Asteya* (non-stealing), *Brahmacharya* (controlling sex), *Kshama* (forgiveness), *Dhriti* (firmness), *Daya* (compassion), *Arjava* (honesty), *Mitahara* (Refrain from consuming meat), *Shaucha* (purity), *Hri* (remorse), *Santosha* (contentment), *Dana* (tithing), *Astikya* (faith), *Pujana* (worship), *Shravana* (hearing of scriptures), *Mati* (cognition), *Vrata* (sacred vows), *Japa* (chanting) and *Tapas* (austerity).

# 8

# Lord Brahma–The Creator

Brahma is the Hindu god (deva) of creation and one of the Trimurti, the others being Vishnu and Shiva. He is not to be confused with the Supreme Cosmic Spirit in Hindu Vedanta philosophy known as Brahman. Also, in Sanskrit Grammer, Brahman is Nominative Singular of generic word Brahman, as Aatma is Nominative Singular for Aatman. Brahaman and Aatman are same in Vedanta Philospthy, the Para-Aatma (Supersoul) and Jeeva Aatma (Individual Soul) are Brahman. His consort is Saraswati, the goddess of learning. Brahma is often identified with Prajapati, a Vedic deity.

Brahma, the infinite, the source of all space, time, causation, names and forms, has many interesting and instructive designations. Theologically, he is the single letter (eka aksharam) Om and the uncreated creator (svayambhu), the self-born first person. Philosophically, he is the first manifestation of one's existence (ahankara). Cosmologically, he is hiranya garbha (golden embryo), the ball of fire, from which the universe develops. He is Prajapati, since all creatures are his progeny. He is pitamaha (patriarch), vidhi (ordinator), Iokesha (master of the universe), dhatru (sustainer) and Viswakarma (architect of the world).

Mythology describes Brahma as springing from Kamala (lotus), from the nabhi (navel) of Vishnu. Hence, his names Nabhija (navel born), Kanja (water born). His consort Saraswati manifested out of him and all creatures of the world resulted from their union.

### *Brahma and Saraswati*

Brahma and his consort Saraswati, represent the vedas, their spirit and meaning. They form the subject of many tales in Hindu literature. All knowledge, religious and secular emanate from them. The name Narayana (one dwelling in the causal water, the abode of man) was applied to him first and later to Vishnu. The Avataras (incarnations) of fish (matsya) and tortoise (koorma) (later called the avataras of Vishnu), the boar (varaha) to raise the earth from under the waters and created the world, the sages, and prajapatis were all attributed to Brahma originally and shifted to Vishnu later. Brahma, created all knowledge, sciences, arts, music, dance and drama. He also officiated over the wedding of Shiva and Parvati.

### *Origin of Brahma*

Accounts of creation differ in many respects. As per Hindu mythology, Brahma was born from a (kamala) lotus springing from Vishnu's navel and created the world through his daughter SaraswatL According to Manu Smriti, the self-existent Lord manifested to dispel the darkness enveloping universe. He created the waters and deposited a seed that became a golden egg from which he was born as Brahma. He divided the egg into two parts to construct the heaven and earth, and created the ten Prajapatis, mind-born sons, who completed the work of creation.

By a third account, the Lord separated himself into two parts, the male and the female after dividing the golden egg. From him sprang Viraja and from him Manu. Ramayana states that Brahma sprang from the ether and that sages Marichi, Atri, Angiras, Narada, Sanaka, Sanandana, Sanatkumara, Sanasujata and others are his manasa putras (mentally conceived sons). From Marichi sprang Kashyapa from whom sprang Vishwavata who created Manu, the procreator of all human beings. Thus, Manu is Brahma's great grandson.

### *Demise of Brahma Concept*

Despite the fact that Brahma is one of the trimurthis, there are no temples dedicated to his worship, except the place of pilgrimage, Pushkar in Ajmer. Puranas give crude reasons for this. Some scholars believe that Brahma cult existed in pre-Vedic Hinduism and was superseded by Shiva-Vishnu cult later. The Shakti concept, in which both Shiva and Vishnu have their consort and creation proceeds from the combination of the god and his shakti, has made the Brahma concept redundant.

***Representations of Brahma***

Mythology has it that Brahma originally had five heads. One of them was cut down by Shiva in his rage. Now, Brahma's icon has four heads (chatur mukha brahma) facing the four quartem. They represent the four Vedas (Rig, Yajur, Sama, Atharva), the four yugas (krita, treta, dwapara, kali) (epochs of time), the four varnas (brahmana, kshatriya, vaisya, sudra). The faces have beards with eyes closed in meditation.

There are four arms holding up different objects, akshamala (rosary), kurcha (kusha grass), sruk (ladle), sruva (spoon), kamandala (water pot) and pustaka (book) and in different poses representing the four quartem. Their combination and arrangement vary with the image. Akshamala symbolizes time; Kamandala, the waters of all creation. The implements kusha, sruk and sruva, denote the system of sacrifices used by creatures to sustain each other. The book represents religious and secular knowledge. Hand postures (mudras) are abhaya (protector) and varada (giver of boons). The icon may be in standing posture on a lotus or in sitting posture on a hamsa (swan). Hamsa stands for wisdom and discrimination.

Brahma is also shown riding a chariot drawn by seven swans, representing the seven worlds. Temples dedicated to Brahma show his Viswakarma aspect with four heads, the four arms holding the rosary, the book, kusha and kamandala and riding his swan. Temples of Shiva or Vishnu have a niche in the northern wall for Brahma as a parivara devata and his image receives daily worship.

***Creation***

According to the Puranas, Brahma is self-born (without mother) in the lotus flower which grew from the navel of

Vishnu at the beginning of the universe. This explains his name *Nabhija* (born from the navel). Another legend says that Brahma was born in water.

In this he deposited a seed that later became the golden egg. From this golden egg, Brahma the creator was born, as *Hiranyagarbha*. The remaining materials of this golden egg expanded into the Brahm-anda or Universe. Being born in water, Brahma is also called *Kanja* (born in water). Brahma is said also to be the son of the Supreme Being, *Brahman* and the female energy known as Prakrti or Maya.

### *Attributes*

At the beginning of the process of creation, Brahma created eleven *Prajapatis* (used in another sense), who are believed to be the fathers of the human race. The *Manusmriti* enumerates them as *Marichi*, *Atri*, *Angirasa*, *Pulastya*, *Pulaha*, *Kratu*, *Vasishtha*, *Prachetas* or *Daksha*, *Bhrigu*, and *Narada*. He is also said to have created the seven great sages or the *Saptarishi* to help him create the universe. However since all these sons of his were born out of his mind rather than body, they are called *Manas Putras* or mind-sons.

Within Vedic and Puranic scripture Brahma is described as only occasionally interfering in the affairs of the other devas (gods), and even more rarely in mortal affairs. He did force Soma to give Tara back to her husband, Brihaspati. He is considered the father of Dharma and Atri.

### *Lack of Brahma Worship in India*

India today has but three temples dedicated to Brahmdev alone as opposed to the thousands of temples dedicated to the other deities in the Trimurti: Shiva and Vishnu. The more famous one being at Pushkar in Rajasthan state. There are various stories in Hindu mythology that talks of the curse that has prevented Brahma from being worshipped on Earth.

At the beginning of time in Cosmos, Vishnu and Brahma approached a huge Shiva linga and set out to find it's beginning and end. Vishnu was appointed the end, and Brahma the beginning. Each took their journey, Vishnu took the form of a boar and began digging downwards into the earth while Brahma took on the shape of a swan began flying upwards. But neither could find their appointed destination.

Vishnu, satisfied, came up to Shiva and bowed down to him as a swarupa of Brahman. Brahma did not give up so easily. As he was going up, he saw a kaitha flower, dear to Shiva. His ego forced him to ask the flower to bear false witness of Brahma's finding Shiva's beginning. When Brahma told his tale, Shiva, the all-knowing, was angered by the former's ego. Shiva thus cursed him that no being in the three worlds will worship him.

According to another legend, Brahma is not being worshipped due to a curse by the great sage Brahmarishi Bhrigu. Once a great fire-sacrifice (yajna) was being organised on Earth with Bhrigu being the high priest. It was decided that the greatest among all Gods would be made the presiding deity. Bhrigu then set off to find the greatest among the Trinity. When he went to Brahma, he was so immersed in the music played by Saraswati that he could hardly hear Bhrigu's calls. The enraged Bhrigu then cursed Brahma that no person on Earth would ever invoke him or worship him again.

According to Brahma Purana and Hindu cosmology, Brahma is the creator but not necessarily regarded as God in Hinduism. He is mostly regarded as a creation of God/Brahman. The lifespan of Brahma is 100 Brahma years or 311 trillion human years. At the end of his lifespan, there is a gap of 100 Brahma years after which another Brahma or creator begins anew and the process is repeated forever. For this reason, Brahma might be considered only as a creator who is the executor of the order from the Supreme being-The Brahman.

***Appearance***

Brahma is traditionally depicted with four heads and four faces and four arms. With each head he continually recites one of the four Vedas. He is often depicted with a white beard (especially in North India), indicating the near eternal nature of his existence. He is shown as having four arms, with none holding a weapon, unlike most other Hindu Gods. One of his hands is shown holding a scepter in the form of a spoon, which is associated with the pouring of holy ghee or oil into a sacrificial pyre-indicating the fact that Brahma is the lord of sacrifices. Another of his hands holds a water-pot (sometimes depicted as a coconut shell containing water).

The significance of the water is that it is the initial, all-encompassing ether in which the first element of creation evolved. Brahma also holds a string of rosary beads that he uses to keep track of the Universe's time. He also is shown holding the Vedas, and sometimes, a lotus flower.

Another story in connection with Brahma's four heads is that when Brahma was creating the universe, he made a female deity known as Shatarupa (one with a hundred beautiful forms). Brahma became immediately infatuated. Shatarupa moved in various directions to avoid the gaze of Brahma. But wherever she went, Brahma developed a head. Thus, Brahma developed five heads, one on each side and one above the others.

In order to control Brahma, Shiva cut off the top head. Also, Shiva felt that Shatarupa was Brahma's daughter/son, being created by him. Therefore, Shiva determined, it was wrong for Brahma to become obsessed with her. He directed that there be no proper worship in India for the "unholy" Brahma. Thus, only Vishnu and Shiva continue to be worshipped, while Brahma is almost totally ignored. Ever since the incident, Brahma has been reciting the four Vedas in his attempt at repentance.

The Bhagavata Purana includes a story wherein the Brahma of our universe is called by Krishna to meet with the Brahmas of other worlds, some of which have many more than four heads, counting into the many thousands in some instances for Brahma's in control of universes much larger than our own.

### *Vehicle*

Brahma's vehicle is a divine Swan. This divine bird is bestowed with a virtue called Neera-Ksheera Viveka or the ability to separate milk and water from a mixture of the two. The significance of this is that justice should be dispensed to all creatures, however entwined it might be in a situation. Also, this virtue indicates that one should learn to separate the good from the evil and then accept that which is valuable and discard that which is worthless or evil.

***Temples***

Although Brahma is prayed to in almost all Hindu religious rites, there are very few temples dedicated to him in India, the more prominent of which is at Pushkar, close to Ajmer. Once a year, on the full moon night of the Hindu lunar month of Kartika (October-November), a religious festival is held in Brahma's honour. Thousands of pilgrims come to bathe in the holy lake adjacent to the temple.

There are also temples in Goa, (in the small, remote village of Carambolim in the Sattari taluka in the northeast region of the state); in the temple town of Kumbakonam, (Thanjavur District) in Tamil Nadu; and in Thirunavaya in Kerela. Regular pujas are held for Brahma and during Navrathris, this temple comes to life with colourful festivities.

There is also a shrine for Brahma within the Bramha-pureeshwarar temple in Thirupattur, near Trichy and a famous murti of Brahma at Mangalwedha, 52 km from Solapur district in Maharashtra, the largest of which is in Angkor Wat in Cambodia. In State of Gujarat, town name Khedbrhama has one of *Stand* of Statue of "Brahma".

***The Creative Principles***

The creative principle of the universe is called Brahma in Sanskrit. Brahma, who is depicted as emerging from the ṇavel lotus of Narayana, is a metaphor for all of creation: its laws, its inherent intelligence, and its consciously manifested potencies which operate as sages, saints, rishis, devas, celestials, and divine beings of all kinds of nature, temperament and description.

Narayana is the Sanskrit name given in the Upaniṣhads to that which is the sum and substance of all the manifested and unmanifested realms. Narayana is that which is neither created nor destroyed but transcends the creation, life and destruction of the universe. Brahma creates, operates in the form of this universe for trillions of years, then dissolves back into Narayana. Narayana, however, is neither created nor destroyed. Later, another Brahma appears to begin the process again.

Since the term "Brahma" does not appear in the Vedas, its creation stems from the Sanskrit work "Brih" which means "'to grow" or "to expand." In this way, it became synonymous with Hiranyagharba:

> *The Golden Egg of Creation. Growing from the Navel Lotus of Narayana, Brahma is the name for the principle which creates all of the manifest realms.*

Since the Vedas proclaim in the Purusha Suktam that "three quarters of this universe are in indestructible realms above," then clearly Brahma, with his finite duration, is connected to the realms of the universe which we inhabit which are subject to creation and dissolution.

Brahma was endowed with his "spouse" (Saraswati) and consciousness at the time of creation. Brahma made certain "beings" solely by the power of his mind and thought. These beings are called the mind-born sons of Brahma.

The state of their consciousness is summarized by the title Brahma Rishi: Seer with the Understanding of Brahma. Brahma Rishis, in turn, can confer this state of consciousness upon others who prove themselves capable and worthy. For an example of the conferring of the state of Brahma Rishi upon one being by another, see the Story of Vishwamitra in the Chapter on the Gayatri Mantra.

To further understand the concept of Brahma and his relation to the universe as we know it, it is helpful to view the cosmos through the lens of the Vedic descriptions of the life of the universe as interpreted in human years. Here are cycles of time as recorded in the Vedas and Upanishads.

Small Yuga: 2,000 years. The axis of the earth spends 2,000 years in an astrological sign and the moves on to the next sign, going backwards through the signs of the zodiac. Since we are finishing the Pisceaen cycle, we are ready to enter the Aquarian cycle for the next 2,000 years. We commonly refer to entering Aquarius as the "dawning of the age of Aquarius."

Complete Cycle of Small Yugas: 24,000 years. This is the amount of time needed for the earth to spend 2,000 years in each sign of the zodiac.

***The Great Cycle***

In addition to the earth's axis moving in an arc as it travels through the signs of the zodiac, there is another cycle. This is a cycle which involves the revolution of the entire solar system around the Central Sun of the Galaxy. The orbit is elliptical rather than circular. To make the elliptical movement of the solar system around a great central point more understandable, the analogy of "seasons" is used. This is a useful analogy because changes in overall states of consciousness are represented as "seasons" through which the solar system passes on its journey.

When consciousness is in a high state, it is summer. At this time, 90% of the inhabitants of the earth are enlightened. This is called Satya Yuga, or the Age of Truth. When Fall or Spring are in full swing, the numbers of enlightened beings drops to less than 10%. When Winter comes, far less than 1% of the people on earth are enlightened. However, there are trade offs.

First, it is easier to make progress in the "'winter of consciousness." The analogy is often used that if one tries to row one's boat in air, very little progress will be achieved. But when the oars are placed in water, much more rapid progress can be made.

This is because compared to air, the resistance of water is much higher enabling the work of the oars to bear fruit. It is the resistance itself which provides a route to rapid progress. Similarly, in spiritual winter our efforts to achieve spiritual growth produce much faster results than they would in any other age of consciousness because of the great general resistance to things spiritual.

There is no disagreement among all the sages, pundits, gurus and swamis that Kali Yuga, the present spiritual winter, affords an opportunity for more rapid spiritual progress than any other age. Further, the medium for rapid growth is almost universally prescribed by these same classes of spiritual teachers as divine sound through the medium of mantra. Here are the various seasons and ages of the universe as measured in human years.

Winter (Kali Yuga):* 432,000 years.

*The year 1998 is 5,090 years from the beginning of Kali Yuga of the long cycle. For the short cycle, winter is ending with the entrance of the planetary axis into Aquarius, which begins the season of Spring for the shorter, 24,000 year cycle:

*Spring (Treta Yuga) 1,296,000 years*

*Summer (Satya or Krita Yuga) 1,728,000 years*

*Autumn (Dwapara Yuga) 864,000 years*

*Total Time for One Cycle or Manvantara: 4,320,000,000 years*

*This is called "A Day of Brahma" and is followed by a night of equal length.*

*One complete day and night of Brahma: 8,640,000,000 years*

*360 of these days is called "One Year of Brahma": 3,110,400,000,000 years*

*100 of these years constitute the life of Brahma called a Maha Kalpa: 311,040,000,000,000 years*

At the end of a "Maha. Kalpa" or cycle of creation, Shiva manifests his destructive influence and the universe is dissolved. [Actually the entire universe becomes spiritualized, see the chapter on Shiva for discussion of this point.] The ancient texts call this the cosmic dissolution. All the levels of the manifest universe disappear. After a great cosmic rest cycle, another creative cycle begins as a new Brahma emerges out of the navel of Narayana and the universe is created anew.

Another item of importance is that one who has achieved the highest level of conscious realization is said to realize and become one with Brahman. At this point, all individuality as we know it disappears. The individual Jiva, Soul or Atman retums to its source from which it will not return of its own volition. However, for reasons known only to itself, certain souls may return for reasons understood only by Narayana.

***Story About Brahma and Ego***

There is a story in which Brahma and Vishnu were touring the Universe one day and found a pillar of light which extended farther than they could perceive in two directions. They were curious and decided to split up to see if one of them could find an end. Vishnu went in one direction and Brahma the other, After some time, they returned to their staring place. Vishnu said that he was unable to find the beginning, no matter how far he traveled.

Brahma said that he found a beginning. He lied. Thereupon, the Pillar of light immediately changed into a form of Shiva who called Brahma a liar and sentenced him to be little observed in the divine ceremonies. This is why you will not find many pujas to him.

The lesson of the story is that the ego always wishes to perpetuate itself. And the act of creation (Brahma is the Great Creator) takes ego even divine ego to accomplish things. There is a mantra to achieve understanding of the mysteries of the form of this creation. The secrets of the universe become unraveled. Many traditional gurus give this mantra to their advanced students.

***Brahma Mantra***

Sat Chid Ekam Brahma

***Surface Meaning***

Sat = Truth

Chid = Spiritual mind stuff

Ekam = one, without a second

Brahma = This entire cosmos, with all of its contents

***Brahma Mantra with Bijas***

Here is a longer version of the "Sat Chid Ekam Brahma" mantra.

Om Eim Hrim Shrim Klim Sauh Sat Chid Ekam Brahma

Om is a prefix to many mantras. It represents the energy at the Ajna chakra at the brow center, where the feminine and masculine currents become joined and consciousness becomes unitary and wholistic. Eim (aim) is a seed sound for the feminine principle known as Saraswati. This principle governs spiritual knowledge as well as the material pursuits of education, science, art, music, and spiritual discipline.

Hrim is a seed sound for "mahamaya" or the veil of creation. It is said that meditation on this seed sound will result in the meditator ultimately being shown the universe "as it is" and not as we see it currently. That is because reality as we see it is really an "agreement" among all of us which is passed on from generation to generation. Babies, if they could talk, would speak of the universe in quite a different way. They ultimately learn what humanity's "agreement" is and start to function in the world. For more about the Hrim bija, see the chapter on Narayana.

Shrim is the seed sound for the principle of abundance. This covers the abundance of food, friends, family, health and a myriad other things. Prosperity is, of course, included. Klim is a seed with several meanings. In the present context, it is the principle of attraction. In this mantra, it is attracting the fruit of the other principles to speed the process of mantra meditation. Sauh is a couple of things. It is a spiritual principle which operates through one of the petals in the Ajna chakra. It is also a shakti activating sound.

*Sat:* Truth

*Chid:* Spiritual mind stuff

*Ekam:* One, without a second

***Brahma:*** This entire cosmos, with all of its contents, sometimes also called Brahman, the state of conscious existence which is one with everything.

***Longer Brahma Mantra***

*Om Namo Rajo Jushei Sristau*
*Sthithou Sattwa Mayayacha*
*Tamo Mayaya Samharinei*
*Vishwarupayavedhasei*
*Om Brahmanyei Namaha*

"Om is the name of He who created this cosmos with its three gunas (qualities of nature: positive, negative and quiescent) who brought all things to form and who is universal. He is Brahma whom I salute."

## The God without and the God Within

When the doctrine of Evolution received an impetus with the work of Darwin, two great deductions were made which affected profoundly our conception of man. The first was the doctrine of the survival of the fittest. This presumed a struggle for existence in nature, and since that struggle is obvious to all, the doctrine of survival was easily accepted. The law of competition seemed absolute everywhere in nature; in plant and in animal, it is that individual who adapts himself best to his environment who survives. It appeared therefore logical that only the individual who struggles every moment of time to adapt himself to his environment survives, and so proves himself to be the fittest.

But the idea that the individual must spend all his energies in a perpetual watchfulness to crush his competitors was modified by a second deduction from the same facts regarding evolution. It was pointed out by Herbert Spencer that Nature does not spend all her energies only on a fierce competition to survive; she spends some of her energies in modes which appear to have no relation to survival. The two instincts to find food and to satisfy sexual cravings are very prominent in all animals, and certainly they are primary activities in the struggle for existence. But no less prominent is a third instinct, which is for play. When the appetites for food and for sex are satisfied, Nature still has a residuum of energy, and this she expresses in play.

There are then three instincts-for food, for sex, and for play-which characterise animals. They characterise men also, though their manifestations undergo subtle transformations. As human societies organise themselves for communal life, the brutalities of the perpetual struggle for existence become softened bit by bit; not all the hours of the day are necessary to find food, because, by a pooling of labour, energy is saved, and so there is time free for other purposes. Similarly, the violent forms of the sex instinct are curbed in civilisation, and a sense for propriety modifies the natural instincts of the brute.

It is when communities are highly organised, that is, when they use less and less energy to find food, and when they steadily refine the expressions of the sex instinct, that an increasing amount of their energy is devoted to play.

This play too undergoes transformation. Two children playing are not different from two puppies playing; the same energy of Nature manifests through them. But this energy has undergone a transformation when a spectator looks at a play. A play of his mind replaces the play of muscle and limb; but fundamentally it is the same instinct in Nature to play. So everything which is creative in civilisation, like poetry, music, sculpture, the dance, are but sublimations of the primordial instinct for play.

Sometimes this instinct for play undergoes a degeneration, as in gambling, whether with cards or dice, or with stocks and shares; it is also the play instinct which manifests in such degenerate forms as society chatter and spiteful gossip. Perhaps it is more true that it is not the play instinct which manifests as criticism or gossip, but rather the instinct to kill a rival; as Kipling remarks, there is little difference between the men of the Neolithic age and men of to-day; they killed with the spear, we try to stab with the tongue or the pen.

I have taken you into the field of Biology in order to draw attention to three fundamental modes of the natural energies which operate in man—to satisfy the craving for food, the craving for sex expression and the craving for play. But there is a fourth mode of expression of which evolutionary science has so far taken no account, though that mode is basic in the understanding of man both in Hinduism and Buddhism. This is the craving in man to *understand*. It is that fundamental instinct in men, to understand what they are and what is their environment, which is implied in the term Moksha. You are well aware that Moksha is the third in the triplicity of Artha, Raga, and Moksha. Artha is the desire for possessions, and he who possesses wealth need never starve; Raga is desire in every form, from that fiercely sexual to that of mere personal vanity. Moksha means Liberation, and an innate desire in man for Liberation is postulated both in Hinduism and Buddhism, as residing at the root of human nature.

Such a conception, that man is not merely the brute, whose savageries are slowly being refined by social organisation, but also the angel, a Divine Spark, imbedded and imprisoned in matter, but ever seeking his release, is utterly foreign to the Darwinian theories of evolution. Nevertheless, that conception is absolutely necessary, as I hope to show, if we are to profess a theory of life which is not only in accord with Nature's facts, but is also full of inspiration for our daily lives.

It is obvious that all men are not bothering their heads about understanding what life is; the vast majority take life as it comes, and it is only a small number who ask questions. Yet the fact that the desire to understand is deeply rooted in us all is evinced by the existence of religions. Even the savage has a religion. Today we can prove that his religion is based on an ignorance of Nature's facts and laws. But this does not annul the fact that the savage with his religion tries to understand, and therewith to state a solution. Certainly, when we look around us, the many do not feel that they are surrounded by puzzles and mysteries; the few of us here present today are indeed only a few. But why are we only a few?

Perhaps the reason is that the vast majority of mankind are still being pushed hither and thither, as pawns in a game, by Nature's primary forces which underlie the instincts of survival and of play. It is only a few at a time who throw off the thralldom to these two instincts; then it is that the third instinct, that for Liberation, begins to affect them. Sometimes, a calamity of some kind is necessary to make us sensitive to the voice within which bids us enquire and understand; sometimes, our awareness begins only when old age begins, and the clamours of the body die down. Undoubtedly it is only the few who respond to the call, "Arise, awake, seek out the Great Ones, and get understanding";but those few are nevertheless as "the first fruits of them that slept". Some day, as evolution advances, the many too will arise and awake and get understanding, as the few do today. When the man who desires to understand himself and his environment looks about him for explanations, he finds solutions offered to him in religion, philosophy and science.

Those of religion are offered to him as revelations; they are authoritative, and each religion declares that its solution is the final. The philosophers too pronounce their solutions as final, though they do not invest them as do the religions with divine sanctions. Science offers her solutions too, but the critical scientist knows that every solution offered by science is only tentative. From among these contradictory solutions, the seeker has to find truth, and the problem is not an easy one.

Theosophy here enters on the scene to help the inquirer. There has always existed in the world, if not openly then in secret gatherings, a tradition as to truth. Distinct and apart from the orthodox revelation of religion, each religion has had, at some time or other, a secret tradition, which attempts to formulate other truths than those proclaimed to the masses. Theosophy is a compilation of these hidden truths, and the study of them gives to many a clearer understanding of life's problems, and therefore a more intimate realisation where the final solution is to be found.

When we analyse the various solutions offered, especially in religions, those solutions fall into two groups. One group asserts that the key to the whole problem is God. Man must discover the supreme fact that God exists, the Author of all things, and their final Abode. Exoteric Hinduism, Zoroastrianism, Christianity and Mohammedanism all proclaim the existence of a Creator; they assert that all human problems can be solved only with the recognition that man depends upon God. Until the soul discovers that he is dependent upon God, until he turns to his Maker in humility and adoration, not only can there be no peace, there is also no real understanding. "The fear of the Lord is the beginning of Wisdom",says Christianity, and in one form or another this same thought appears in all the theistic religions. In some, it is less the fear of the Lord and more the love of the Lord; but all of them asseverate that no problem of man can be understood, unless man starts with the recognition that he is dependent upon a Godhead external to him, and whom he must worship and serve. "Seek the God without" is the message of those religions which teach the existence of a Creator.

But there is another group of solutions which equally offer to teach man the one true way to peace and understanding. These solutions are found in esoteric Hinduism, in Buddhism, and in Confucianism and Taoism. In the Upanishads, especially in the older ones, their principal doctrine of Atman proclaims the existence of God, but He is not a Personal God whose nature is in some manner different from that of man. The most vital of all truths in esoteric Hinduism is that God and man are one and not two. "THAT art thou, 0 Shvetaketu", is the ever insistent teaching of the Upanishads. It is only in the discovery of the God within that the way is found to solve ail problems; this is the clear teaching of esoteric Hinduism.

When we approach Buddhism, it is once again the path to the God within which is its characteristic, though the Buddha never proclaimed the existence of God. Neither did He deny God's existence; for to the Buddhist, the problem whether God exists or not has no relation to the problem of man's suffering. The way within is the sole discovery, necessary to solve all problems, and so the Buddha's message to all men was, "Work out your salvation with diligence".

In a similar manner, Confucianism builds an ethical system which ignores God. It is only as a man strives to be perfect, to be the "superior man", by embodying in himself all that is best in the moral code of his ancestors, that man achieves his goal of perfect peace and freedom.

It is this same doctrine of the God within that we have once again proclaimed to-day by Krishnamurti. He never uses the word God, and the conception of a Personal God, an extra-cosmic God, a Deity who is in some manner different from man, is alien to his thought. He proclaims the existence of an absolute Perfection, but he terms this "the Beloved", and he ever insists that Liberation means to become one with "the Beloved". To "see the Goal", to be "one with Life", "to enter the Kingdom of Happiness" are phrases which ho uses to describe the *summum bonum* for all men; and those familiar with the Upanishads realise that the ancient teaching of the Atman proclaimed of old by the Rishis to the few as a "Rahasya", as a "Secret", is now being proclaimed by Krishnamurti today to the whole world.

Are these two groups of solutions, one which proclaims the God without, and the other the God within, contradictory one of the other? It would certainly appear so. If in man, if in all men, the Perfect Godhead exists *even now* in His perfection, as the Upanishads teach, what has an evolutionary process of births and deaths to do with the souls liberation? What is the use of the gathering of experience, the acquirement of virtues, the performing of duties and the aspiring after ideals, if the goal of them all, which is to become one with God, Is already accomplished?

There is no use whatsoever in the world process, asserts boldly the Sankhya philosophy; and the same reply is given by the Advaita or Pure Vedanta. The wheel of births and deaths, the climbing from imperfection to perfection, all these are purely Maya, an illusion which envelops us. Let us but tear aside the stifling folds of the illusion which enwraps us, and we shall swiftly find ourselves once again as our true self, the Atman, the Godhead who never descended from his pure and perfect serenity and happiness into an imperfect evolutionary world. The only God who exists is in man himself, say the Upanishads; and they go so far as to assert that the Divine Nature *is* all things, not merely in all things. God is not *in* the stone as a Divine Immanence, but *is* the stone itself-this is the esoteric teaching of Hinduism.

In the light of these teachings, which proclaim everything a Maya, except the eternal and unchanging Spirit, there is no practical value to the soul in the process of evolution. Why the soul ever allows himself to be entangled in it is a mystery which is not explained; what forces all souls to put on the mantle of matter is a problem to which no solution is offered in the Vedanta.

It is quite clear, when one arrives at the logical conclusion from the premisses of esoteric Hinduism, that there is no such thing as evolution or progress, so far at least as the soul is concerned. The soul is always Atman, and needs only to step outside the illusion which hypnotises it to believe that it is not Atman at all. Ever the serene spirit, pure Sat, Chit and Ananda, it is the power of Maya which deludes the soul to regard itself as an evolving soul who is struggling to pay his debts to Karma.

The insistence by Krishnamurti that Liberation or Perfection is possible, *even now*, to every individual, however ignorant or however primitive and simple-minded, almost leads one to imagine that he too, like the Upanishads and the Vedanta, ignores the bonds of helpfulness and compassion which in the minds of the humanitarian bind all men in a common destiny. In the doctrine of the pure Vedanta, man's sole duty is to himself; he has but one work, which is to tear the veil of illusion. Such ideals as Brotherhood and Social Service are mere sentiment, compared to the supreme task before each soul of Liberation.

It is true that charity is enjoined on all, but such teachings are a compromise offered to our limited human nature. Men suffer-and so need charity-only because they insist on being bound on the wheel of birth and death; to shod tears over a soul who prefers to remain bound is sheer sentimentality. What he needs is not sympathy but to be led towards illumination so that he discovers that he is not bound.

Similarly in Buddhism, where the sole task is to escape from the "wheel", the doctrine of compassion seems illogical. It is Avidya or ignorance which drives a soul to drink deep at the well of sensation; and though intense compassion is inculcated as a virtue, no clue is given how compassion can help in the acquisition of wisdom.

In the list of virtues, with which the Buddha is described in one of the most famous of Buddhist verses, compassion is not mentioned. He is called "that Blessed One, Exalted, Omniscient, Endowed with knowledge and virtue, Auspicious, Knower of worlds, a Guide incomparable for the training of individuals, Teacher of Gods and humans, Enlightened and Holy". But not a word about Him as full of pity for all mankind.

Yet Buddhist tradition asserts that so great was His compassion even as long ago as in the dispensation of the Buddha Dipankara-the fourth in the list of twenty-eight Buddhas which closes with the Buddha Gautama-that He determined to tread the long and painful road to Buddhahood in order to lead men to Liberation.

Buddhism however does insist that compassion is necessary, as in some way stilling the craving to live, which is at the root of misery. But both in the Vedanta and in Buddhism, the emphasis laid upon understanding, contemplation and withdrawal as requisite for Liberation has led to an overemphasis upon individual salvation, to such an extent indeed as to lead sometimes to an ignoring of the collective betterment of mankind.

Krishnamurti's teachings, at first sight, would also appear to ignore collective salvation, because he is so insistent upon what be terms the "direct path". He insists that there is no need for any organisation of spiritual effort into such gradations as of teacher and pupil-the one to instruct, the other to learn, the science which teaches where is the "Way". Since within each man resides the power to see "the Goal", no external aid is necessary, if only the seeker will believe that he can come to the Goal unaided.

Above all, his insistent declaration that "the individual problem is the world problem" is being construed as a warning to desist from activities which hide their meddlesome and wasteful nature under the guise of philanthropy and service. But though Krishnamurti calls upon us to go the direct road, and to seek no other God but the God within, it is very clear that the thought of the Liberation of the soul is not dissociated in his mind from that of the service of all men.

While in one sentence he sternly challenges: "What have you, with your phrases, with your labels, with your books, achieved?", in the sentences immediately following, he tells us what we should have done.

*"How many people have you made happy, not in the passing things, but in the ways of the Eternal?"*

*"Have you given the Happiness that lasts, the Happiness that is never failing, the Happiness that cannot he dimmed by a passing cloud?"*

*"In what way have you created a protecting wall, so that people shall not slip into pitfalls?"*

*"How far have you built a railing along that deep river into which every human being is liable to fall?"*

*"How far have you helped these people who want to climb?"*

*"How far has it been your ambition to lead someone to that Kingdom of Happiness, that garden where there is unchanging light, unchanging beauty?"*

*"But, if you are all these things, have you saved one from sorrow?"*

*"Have any of you given me happiness-'me' the ordinary person?"*

*"Have any of you given me the nourishment of heaven when I was hungry?"*

*"Have any of you felt so deeply that you could throw yourself into the place of the person who is suffering?"*

*"What have you produced, what have you brought forth?"*

*"In what manner have you brought forth that precious jewel, so that it shall shine and guide the whole world?"*

These words of Krishnamurti show that his gospel is not a gospel of isolation. While he challenges us as to our ways of service, he insists that he who is truly intent on Liberation is equally bent on service. He tells us that when we shall enter the Kingdom of Happiness that then "you will lose the identity of your separate self; and there you will create new worlds, new kingdoms, new abodes for others". Again he insists,

*And because I really love,*
*I want you to love;*
*Because I really feel,*
*I want you to feel;*
*Because I hold every thing dear,*
*I want you to hold all things dear;*

*Because I want to protect,*
*You should protect.*
*And this is the only life worth living,*
*And the only happiness worth possessing.*

When, in another address, he asks us to "open the gate of your hearts that you may enter into Liberation", he makes clear that the individual who liberates himself can have but one motive, which is to "become in yourselves the true redeemers of mankind, so that you will go out and show to the people that are in sorrow and pain that their salvation, their happiness, their Liberation, lies within themselves".

It is this inseparableness of Liberation and Service which has ever been the theme of Theosophy as a code of ethics. Modern Theosophy has used less the word "Liberation" and more the word "Perfection", but the thought is the same. The value of the study of Theosophy lies in that each student can construct for himself a frame work of the world's events of the past, the present and the future, into which he can set in an appropriate setting whatsoever he examines of events in the domains of religion and science, philosophy and art, philanthropy and world development.

Thus it is that, with the aid of Theosophy, we can synthesise truth after truth out of the contradictions between those religions and cults which proclaim the God without, and the philosophies and sciences which proclaim the God within. And the way of that synthesis is as follows.

The first great truth which must never for one instant be obscured or forgotten is that the Divine Nature resides in man. Call that Divine Nature by any name we will-God, Atman, the Christ, Sammasambodhi, the Perfect Wisdom-its totality resides in man. In the wickedest sinner that Godhead resides in the inmost heart of his being, with as perfect a fulness of the Godhead as in the heart of the greatest of saints.

Brahmana and Pariah are equally divine; and the Brahmana who spurns the Pariah but spurns the Godhead dwelling in his own self. This is the supreme truth of Theosophy, which, as applied to daily conduct, is the soul and essence of Brotherhood.

To find the God within is the sole task of life; for when that Godhead is found in stone and in plant, in sinner as in saint, all life's processes are linked into one meaning, which ever guides to happiness and peace.

But there is a second truth which is less easy to understand; it is, that the Divine Nature is as if imprisoned in man, and not utterly free to manifest in freedom all its perfections. That Divine Nature abides equally in the sinner as in the saint. Yet there is a difference as the Divine Nature energises or operates in the encasement which holds it. When the Hindu Sadhu intent on God saw the British soldier coming to bayonet him, and said, "Even thou art He !", he truly saw the Divine Nature in all things, even in his assassin.

But yet surely there was a difference as that Divine Nature energised in the heart of the Sadhu and in the heart of the soldier? We can, if we will, say with the Upanishad, "If slayer thinks he slays, if slain thinks he is slain, both these know naught; THIS slays not, nor is slain"; but we are also forced by our moral conscience to say that the Sadhu did good and the soldier did evil. But since both Sadhu and soldier are, in their inmost natures, God, how can the one indivisible Divine Nature be at one and the same time good and evil?

Unless we adopt the solution of a Maya, which makes the Divine Nature appear other than it truly is, there is only one other line of solution, so far as I know. That solution is what Theosophy offers-that the world process, even if it enshrines a Maya, is of use to the Divine Nature, in enabling it to release Itself from Its imprisonment.

Strangely enough, this conception, that the world process is a releasing of perfection from an imprisonment, is suggested by modern Biology. As the Mendelian theory of heredity came to the front, one of its leaders, Bateson, said at the meeting of British Association in 1914 that Shakespeare lived in a pinhead of protoplasm.

All that we know as the genius of Shakespeare existed in the first speck of protoplasm; but it existed there as if imprisoned. Now, without a particular arrangement of Mendelian "factors" in the first cell which was the embryo of Shakespeare, his creative ability could not manifest; therefore rearrangement after rearrangement had taken place of the "factors" in every one of the myriads of cells which were the successive progenitors of that one zygote or embryo cell which finally became Shakespeare.

An evolutionary process stretching over millions of years was necessary for this continuous rearrangement of "factors", which was needed to bring about just that one grouping of factors which alone could produce Shakespeare. Yet, all the time, in the first speck of protoplasm, which somehow arose by a chance juxtaposition of certain colloidal substances, Shakespeare was sleeping, waiting to be awakened. The God within, Shakespeare, was there in the protoplasm; but the God without, that is, all Nature's processes which we term evolution, was also necessary in order to make Shakespeare dynamic and creative.

It is this conception which Theosophy gives-that there is a God without, a process of evolution in a foreordained Divine Plan, calling to a God within, the Divine Nature of the soul—which enables us to harmonise all the contradictory theories of the religions among themselves, and of modern science which stands opposed to all religions.

From the moment we accept that the Divine Nature in man, the God within, is imprisoned at the beginning of time, our next problem is to understand what is the process of his release. The answer can be summed up in one word-Life. It is Life, in all its forms, in all its kingdoms visible and invisible, Life manifesting from eternity to eternity; it is this Life which ever strives to create, and to destroy in order to create again, that is the instrument of release of the imprisoned Godhead.

The long process of the release of Divinity by Life is the theme of all Theosophical study. That study describes the details of the process, using special technical terms-a "jargon" if you like-such as Life and Form, Karma, Reincarnation, Root and Sub-races, Principles, Planes, Rays, Discipleship, Initiation, Adeptship, and others. But all such terms are like the terms of any other study like Chemistry or Botany. They serve to arrange into categories those facts which must be examined in order to come to a broad grasp of the subject.

True, Life's activities can be watched with the eye of the poet or artist, and not with the eye of the analytical observer like the Theosophist. Then no "jargon" of technical terms is required; then it is that we have such a description of Life as Krishnamurti gives in his poems.[The Search, pp. 9-12.]

*I have been a wanderer long*
*In this world of transient things.*
*I have known the passing pleasures thereof.*
*As the rainbow is beautiful,*
*But soon vanishes into nothingness,*
*So have I known,*
*From the very foundation of the world,*
*The passing away of all things*
*Beautiful, joyous and pleasurable.*
*In search of the eternal*
*I lost myself in the fleeting.*
*All things have I tasted in search of Truth.*
*In bygone ages*
*Have I known the pleasures of the transient world-*
*The tender mother with her children,*
*The arrogant and the free,*
*The beggar that wanders the face of the earth,*
*The contentment of the wealthy,*
*The woman of enticements,*
*The beautiful and the ugly,*
*The man of authority, the man of power,*
*The man of consequence, the bestower and the guardian,*
*The oppressed and the oppressor,*
*The liberator and the tyrant,*
*The man of great possessions,*
*The man of renunciation, the sannyasi,*
*The man of activity and the man of dreams.*

*The arrogant priest in gorgeous robes and the humble worshipper,*
*The poet, the artist and the creator.*
*At all the altars of the world have I worshipped,*
*All religions have known me,*
*Many ceremonies have I performed,*
*In the pomp of the world have I rejoiced,*
*In the battles of defeat and victory have I fought,*
*The despiser and the despised,*
*The man acquainted with grief*
*And agonies of many sorrows,*
*The man of pleasure and abundance.*
*In the secret recesses of my heart have I danced,*
*Many births and deaths have I known,*
*In all these fleeting realms have I wandered,*
*In passing ecstasies, certain of their endurance,*
*And yet I never found that eternal Kingdom of Happiness.*

But why must the soul thus wander from life to life, urged on by the God-given instinct for Liberation, and yet miss time after time the entrance to the true path? There are indeed some philosophies, like that of Christianity, Zoroastrianism and Muhammedanism, which insist that the soul does not so wander, and that within the brief period of one life the ultimate goal of Liberation or Redemption can be achieved.

For this, an utter subservience to the will of God is necessary; a perfect life so subservient to God gains the recompense of an eternal heaven. But such a solution, which denies to Life its repeated transformations by Reincarnation, brings in its train a host of problems which are difficult of solution.

The doctrine of a perfection which must be achieved in one life-time promptly raises question after question, such as, why God permits evil to exist, why if He is good some souls must be condemned to perdition, why if He is omnipotent He does not arrange for all to be born in an environment favourable to the building of their character towards perfection.

I cannot myself think of any scheme of things which is just-and here I can speak for all Theosophists-unless Reincarnation is a part of that scheme. It is far easier for me to believe that God's love and compassion are real, just because Reincarnation is a fact, than to believe that there is no Reincarnation, and yet that God expects all in one life-time to understand His will and to co-operate with it.

I said a while ago, Why must the soul wander from life to life, missing the entrance to the true path? But in reality that question of mine is not based on fact. For, the moment we realise that Life is a dual process, that of the God without knocking at the door of the God within, then every experience *is* an entrance on the path. It is this which Theosophy makes clear.

The intricate scheme describing the soul's evolution and unfoldment which is found in theosophical text-books can easily be swept aside by saying that in order to be good and noble, it is not necessary to have experience after experience. For goodness is innate in man, because the God within resides in man. Whence then the need to struggle in order to be good, when goodness is of the very nature of the soul?

Here each of us must determine what line of thought he will follow; no one, least of all a Theosophist, desires to impose a particular creed as the one and only solution. I can only say, speaking for most Theosophists, that every scrap of reason disappears from the universe if evolution is considered unnecessary. On the other hand, a most inspiring sweet reasonableness is clearly seen in the world process, when we admit that evolution by experience is the way to Liberation. William James once defined experience as "becoming expert by experiment". If we accept Life as the laboratory for the soul's experiments in order to be liberated, then, the environment which surrounds the soul in its many migrations begins to have a meaning.

Like as the dull uncut diamond dug from the bowels of the earth, so is the God within before experience moulds him; but like as the cut diamond flashing all the colours of the rainbow, so is the God within when he has undergone experience after experience which the God without sends him. This is Life, deep calling unto deep. Within our inmost nature is "the Way, the Truth and the Life"; within ourselves are all the Kingdoms-the Kingdom of Happiness of Krishnamurti, the Kingdom of Heaven of the Christ, and the Kingdom of the Law of the Buddha. But it is only when a Buddha, or a Christ, or a Krishnamurti reveals the Kingdom in which Hewells, that then we are aware that we too are God, and that every possible Kingdom dwells within us also.

Deep calling unto deep, Godhead calling to Godhead, this is the solution of the mystery of misery dogging at the heels of joy, of death ever the shadow of life. But life and death, joy and misery, the friend and the enemy, are not contrasted opposites; they are the one and the same Godhead, both equally divine when we understand.

So experience, coming with the message of the God without, knocks at the doors of the soul, the God within. When the soul's dwelling place is the savage, then experience brings hatreds and battles, in order to call out from the God within his hidden attributes of courage and decision. When the soul passes to dwell as the civilised man, then experience knocks to release the virtues of industry and efficiency, of learning and judgment, of comradeship and self-sacrifice. As child, as youth, as maid, as man, as woman, as husband and father, as wife and mother, at each stage some hidden capacity within the soul is released, at the bidding of the environment and of the experiences which it brings.

So, in the long pilgrimage of the soul to discover himself as the God, each, religion comes to him in turn to teach one word of the Mantram with which the God without created the world. Science reveals the framework of that creation, Art the joy which it conceals, and Philosophy the inspiration which it brings. No fact in life, no event anywhere in the world but has a meaning for the soul; that meaning is that the God without ever calls to the God within to be one.

This is the lesson which we all have to learn. And it is difficult, because the trend of our thinking and feeling is to make a duality of what we are, contrasted with what we are not. It is far easier to divide the world into what "I like" and what "I do not like" than to be beyond both like and dislike, and to contemplate the world as it is, irrespective of its relation to oneself. It is far easier to divide life into good and evil than to see life just as it is, and place no labels whatsoever on it. It is only as we "cast out the self "and see things "as they are", and so pass on to see "the things-in-themselves", the Archetypes of Plato, that for the first time we gain a glimpse of our true self.

It is such a glimpse of the truth that reveals to man that the suffering which crushes him is only himself at work, purifying himself. The moment we enter a world of duality and say, when we suffer, that it is God who sends us suffering, suffering does not end. For then suffering, as it discharges its force, creates new force to issue later in new suffering. But when we refuse to accept any duality, and say either, "It is Life releasing Life",-or "It is I the God without releasing myself the God within", then for the first time peace enters the heart.

It is then that we shall know that Liberation is not an event at the end of time, but a continuous happening which steadily brings nearer and nearer the God without to the God within. When once these two poles of Being commence to approach each other, Liberation has begun. Thenceforth 'the time factor is within the soul, and is the soul's agent, not the soul's master. Less important is when the soul shall achieve Mukti or Nirvana, and more important the fact that the soul shall know, and never cease from rejoicing, that the twain are becoming one. This is the most direct of all paths, and none can prevent the swiftness of the union except the soul himself.

This truth is our Ariadne's thread in the maze of life. And we shall learn this truth in myriads of ways, according as we have eyes to see, and ears to hear. Thus speaks *Light on the Path.*

Inquire of the earth, the air and the water, of the secrets they hold for you.

Inquire of the Holy Ones of the earth of the secrets they hold for you.

Inquire of the inmost, the One, of its final secret, which it holds for you through the ages.

And as we attempt to understand the meaning of it all, none can help us or guide. When Krishnamurti says that no Guru or teacher is needed for the soul who is intent on Liberation, he is only uttering once again what other teachers have said before him. "THAT art thou" is the axiom of esoteric Hinduism, and the Upanishads which proclaim this teaching have not insisted on any need of a Guru in order to achieve the Unity.

You know the immemorial tradition in India-first the student, then the householder, then the hermit, lastly the sannyasi, the "renouncer" of ceremonies and creeds, who goes out alone into the world, without a Guru, to find the Unity directly for himself. So too, during the forty-five years of service rendered by the Lord Buddha, never once did He put Himself as a Guru whose aid was necessary in order to enter on the Path. His last charge to His Sangha or Order was to emphasise the "individual uniqueness" of each who treads the Way.

As He lay dying, He said: "It may be, Ananda, that some of you will think. 'The word of the Teacher is a thing of the past; we have now no Teacher.' But that, Ananda, is not the correct view. The Doctrine and Discipline, Ananda, which I have taught and enjoined upon you is to be your teacher when I am gone."And His last words were", And now, O monks, I take my leave of you; all the constituents of being are transitory; work out your salvation with diligence".

It is never the Guru who says "Guru is Brahma, Guru is Vishnu, Guru is Maheshvara"; that is the phrase invented by the Sishya or pupil. No Guru has claimed to be what the pupil in his gratitude asserts of his teacher.

*tvam eva mata ca pita tvam eva,*
*tvam eva bandhuscha sakha tvam eva;*
*tvam eva vidya dravinam tvam eva,*
*tvam eva sarvam mama deva deva.*

Thou art verily my mother, Thou art the father indeed, my friend also art Thou, and companion as well. Thou indeed art my learning and possessions, Thou art my all in all, O God of Gods.

But all this is what the disciple says as to the Guru, but not what the Guru says concerning himself. What, then, does the Guru say? We have that in what the Guru of H. P. Blavatsky, H. S. Olcott and Annie Besant once said concerning Himself, and these are His words: "I am as I was, and as I was and am, so am I likely always to be-the slave of my duty to the Lodge and mankind; not only taught, but desirous to subordinate every preference for individuals to a love for the human race'" That even a Guru himself, even when liberated, is still striving for a yet larger love for the human race is shown in the words of the same Master: "The mark of the adept is kept at [Shamballa] not at Simla, and I try to keep up to it." It is His brother, the Master K.H., who has described Him as a man as stern for himself, as severe for his shortcomings, as he is indulgent for the defects of other people, not in *words* but in the innermost feelings of his heart".

And I desire here to give my testimony that the Master whom I have followed this life for the last forty-one years has never been to me a "crutch" on which I could lean in any one of my weaknesses. Never once has he made my path easier for me, nor helped me to climb over stiles and obstacles; never once has he prevented me from committing mistakes due to my stupidity or selfishness.

But he has ever been to me what a lighthouse is to a ship in a stormy sea-a flashing blinding beam cleaving the dark of the storm clouds to show that the harbour is not far away, and so not to despair but to take courage.

If I offer Him all my love and service, it is because He is the living symbol of what I hope to become someday; if I bend the knee before Him in gratitude and utmost reverence, it is because He is to me the glorious promise that I too shall some day love all mankind with the wondrous intensity of love with which He loves all men to-day. He is the God without rousing the God within me to be aware of my destiny, which is to strive through the ages to establish a Kingdom of Joy for all men.

I close this dissertation on the theme of the God without and the God within by reading to you two extracts from the Upanishads, one describing the God without, and the other the God within.

***The God Without***

Shvetashvatara Upanishad.(Mead's translation).

This God, in sooth, in all the quarters is long. long ago, indeed, he had his birth, he verily is now within the germ. He has been born, he will be born; behind all who have birth he stands, with face on every side.

He hath eyes on all sides, on all sides surely hath faces, arms surely on all sides, on all sides feet. With arms, with wings, he tricks them out, creating heaven and earth, the only God.

Whose faces, heads and necks, are those of all, who lieth in the secret place of every soul, spread o'er the universe is He, the Lord. Therefore as all-pervader, He's benign.

Blue fly, green bird, and red-eyed beast, the cloud that bears the lightning in its womb, the seasons, and the seas, art thou. In omnipresent power thou hast thy home, whence all the worlds are born.

Eternal of eternals, the consciousness which every being's consciousness contains, who, one, of many the desires dispenses-knowing that cause, the God to be approached by sacred science and holy art, the mortal from all bonds is free.

I know this mighty Man, sun-like, beyond the darkness; Him and Him only knowing, one crosseth over death; no other path at all is to go.

***The God Within***

[Kenn̆, Taittiriya, Mundaka and Mandukya Upanishads]

What no word can reveal, what revealeth the word, that know as Brahman indeed, not this which I they worship below.

What none thinks with the mind, but what thinks-out the mind, that know thou as Brahman indeed, not this which thy worship below.

What none sees with the eye, whereby seeing is seen, that know thou as Brahman indeed, not this which they worship below

Who knows this thus, indeed, destroying sin, in endless highest heaven-world he stands immovable, immovable he stands.

From whom the whole world comes, to whom indeed it goes again, by whom this is supported surely too-to Him, the Self that knows, all honour be!

*Truth, wisdom, endless, Brahm,*
*Source of all bliss, immortal, shining forth,*
*Peaceful, benign, and secondless !*
*Om ! Peace, Peace, Peace! Om !*

The amorphous collection of texts that might be labeled "Hindu scripture" consists of millions of lines of text written over thousands of years in several languages. Known as the Vedas, the holy writings of India are central to contemporary religion, though their authority is in no way analogous to that of the Bible or the Qur'an in Christian and Islamic communities.

Hindu scripture includes nearly every genre of literature, some hardly religious at all, and some incredibly irreligious, at least from a Christian perspective. Philosophical treatises, folk medicine, erotic poetry, and grammar tomes, as well as devotional hymns, liturgical manuals, and ethical instructions all find a niche in the immense and labyrinthine world of Hindu scripture. Most of the scripture was written by poets, priests, and philosophers, though some of the later traditional texts were composed by low-caste devotees. The oldest text, the *Rig Veda,* dates back to c. 1400 B.C., while the most recent authoritative works hail from the sixteenth century A.D. (though some accept as scripture the writings of gurus up to the present century). Vedic scripture includes the longest single literary work in the world, the *Mahabharata*, which weighs in at 110,000 couplets (seven times the length of Homer's *Iliad* and *Odyssey* combined), as well as the *sutra* literature, collections of aphorisms so brief that it is said that the author of such a text would sell his grandson to save a syllable.

Hindu scripture often is referred to collectively as the *Vedas*, a Sanskrit word meaning "knowledge" (from the root *vid*-"to know"; cognate to *wit*, wisdom). In one sense, Veda refers only to the most ancient writings of the Indo-Aryan community. This includes the four Vedic collections (*samhitas*): *Rig Veda*, *Yajur Veda*, *Sama Veda*, and the *Atharva Veda*. The *samhitas* consist primarily of odes to the gods; most resemble biblical psalms. On the foundation of these four venerable collections rests the remainder of vedic literature. To each *samhita* are attached inspired commentaries: the Brahmanas, Aranyakas, and the Upanishads. Thus, there are four traditions (*Rig, Yajur, Sama, Atharva*) and four categories of text (Samhitas, Brahmanas, Aranyakas, Upanishads) in the Veda proper.

The historical origin of the Vedas is unknown. Internal evidence suggests that they were written by Brahmin priests sometime between 1500 and 1200 B.C., though the ethnic persuasion of those priests and the ideas they recorded remain a mystery. Similarities between rituals and deities in the religion of Vedic Hinduism and that of Persia and ancient Europe have led some scholars to attribute the composition of the Vedas to Aryan migrants from central Asia. Other scholars acknowledge the Aryan influence, but credit indigenous North Indians with the production of the Vedas. Theories abound, and the issue has been politicized and is hotly debated, but insufficient linguistic and archeological evidence prevents satisfactory conclusions at the present.

The hymns themselves hint at their historical source. It seems that many were composed by mercenary poet-priests for wealthy patrons: several Vedic hymns describe transactions between composers and clients. "With wisdom I present these lively praises of Bhavya dweller on the bank of Indus; For he, unconquered King, desiring glory, has furnished me a thousand sacrifices" (*Rig Veda* 1.126.1).

There are also prayers recorded for the well-being of the priests' source of income: "O Agni, God, preserve our wealthy patrons with your succors" (*Rig Veda* 1.31.12). These hymns produced for individual patrons were probably then collected and edited by the Brahmin priests for use in the ritual sacrifice

(Mitchell, 1897, p. 17). Over time, Vedas were assigned to different Brahminical families for preservation through memorization. The texts were transmitted orally for at least a thousand years before they were written down. Several methods of memorization were used so that the words and sounds would be preserved exactly; rote memorization was supplemented with complex mnemonic devices, such as *ghanapatha* ("dense text"), in which the order of words is ab, ba, abc, cba, abc, bc, cb, bcd, and so forth (Goodall, 1996, p. x). By this method, Genesis 1:1 would be memorized: in the, the in, in the beginning, beginning in the, in the beginning, the beginning, beginning the, the beginning God.

The *Rig Veda* is the most authoritative of all Hindu scripture, if not for its content, then for its great antiquity. The *Rig Veda* ("Veda of Hymns") is among the world's oldest literature—some scholars date its composition to 3000 B.C., though most estimate the final recension to have occurred in 1000 B.C. (Basham, et al., 1997, p. 522). Arranged in ten books, or *mandalas*, the *Rig Veda* contains 10,028 verses, and is about one and a half times the size of the New Testament. The six oldest *mandalas* are linked to six priestly families who composed, memorized, and handed down the hymns; books one, and eight through ten, are anthologies of hymns by various independent poet-priests, and were written later.

The *Rig Veda* resembles a hymnal more than a Bible. If pressed to compare the *Rig Veda* to Christian scripture, it would most closely parallel the Psalms, though without the historical and moralistic tenor. The *Rig Veda* assumes a common knowledge on the part of the reader as to the origin of the Universe and the identity of the gods (*devas,* cognate to divine and devotion), and, like our own church hymnals, contains no introduction or narrative framework to orient the reader. One could not pick up a copy of the *Rig Veda* and understand modern Hinduism or even the Vedic rituals without significant explanation.

The bulk of the songs in the *Rig Veda* are addressed to the chief gods Indra, Agni, and Soma as petitions for success in battle, protection, and material prosperity. This hymn addressed to the entire pantheon is typical of a vedic chant: Not one of you, ye Gods, is small, none of you is a feeble child: all of you, verily, are great.

Thus be ye lauded, you destroyers of the foe, you thirty-three Deities, the Gods of man, the Holy Ones. As such defend and succor us, with benedictions speak to us: lead us not from our fathers' and from Manu's path into the distance far away. You Deities who stay with us, and all you Gods of all mankind, give us your wide protection, give shelter for cattle and for steed (*Rig Veda* 8.30).

Though many gods are recognized (according to this passage, there are 33, but the number of names mentioned throughout the Veda·exceeds that figure), each one is lauded as if it were the highest god, a phenomenon Max Müller called henotheism, and that some modern scholars call "serial monogamy" (Sarma, 2003b). These superlative descriptions inevitably overlapped, and in later passages the gods are identified with one another or with all. In time, the confusion led to the belief that the many gods and goddess were but manifestations of one indivisible transcendental Ultimate Reality. The pantheism of later texts is foreshadowed in a late Vedic passage: "To what is One, sages give many names—they call it Agni, Yama, Matarisvan" (*Rig Veda* 1.164.46).

At the heart of the Veda Samhitas lay the ritual sacrifice (*yajña*). Like the *Rig Veda*, the *Sama Veda* ("Veda of chants") and the *Yajur Veda* ("Veda of sacrificial prayers") served as liturgical manuals for the sacrifice; each of the three was used by one of the orders of Brahminic priesthood, a sacerdotal system similar in structure to the Mosaic system described in Numbers 4.

The primary purpose of the collections of hymns was to "propitiate the gods by praises accompanying the offering of malted butter poured on the fire and of the juice of the Soma plant placed on the sacrificial grass" (Macdonell, 1917). The songs and chants and prayers of the Samhitas were read over the sacrifice as part of the ritual. Incidentally, the sacrifice was not performed for the atonement of sin, as was the Mosaic sacrifice, but to obtain magically the favour of the gods, and ultimately, salvation in heaven (*svarga*). The fourth Veda, the *Atharva Veda* ("Veda of the Fire Priests"), differs in content from the other three, and was not used in the sacrifice. Drawing on ancient folk material, the fourth Veda consists of spells against sickness, sorcery, snakebite, and bad dreams, as well as incantations to bring about love, good luck, rain, fertility, and a multitude of other things. It also includes instructions for wedding and funeral rites.

To each of the four Samhitas was appended a body of inspired commentary. The Brahmanas ("exposition on the meaning of the sacred word"), the first layer of commentary composed about 900 B.C., are prose descriptions and explanations of various sacrificial rites. Named for the Brahmin priests who wrote them, the Brahmanas wax philosophical—evidence that the priests wanted not only to enact, but to understand, the rituals they performed. Unfortunately, any profundity in the Brahmanas is undercut by rambling mythology and asinine digressions. In the introduction to his translation of the Brahmanas, Oxford Sanskritist Max Müller railed:

> *No one would have supposed that at so early a period, and in so primitive a state of society, there could have risen up a literature which for pedantry and downright absurdity can hardly be matched anywhere These works deserve to be studied as the physician studies the twaddle of idiots and the raving of madmen. They will disclose to a thoughtful eye the ruins of faded grandeur, the memories of noble aspirations. But let us only try to translate these works into our own language, and we shall feel astonished that human language and human thought should ever have been used for such purposes. (as quoted in Robson, 1905, pp. 23-24)*

The Aranyakas ("forest teachings") followed the Brahmanas without introducing much new material. Their name derives from the esoteric nature of the texts—the mystic teachings were handed down from teacher to disciple in the seclusion of the forests. The Aranyakas reflect an increasingly abstract conception of the sacrifice—the literal fire of the sacrifice began to be internalized and symbolically represented as the "fire" of digestion and the "fire" of sexual intercourse (for the fully developed doctrine, see *Chandogya Upanishad* 5.18.2 and *Brhadaranyaka Upanishad* 6.2.13).

The Aranyakas transition almost seamlessly into the final layer of Vedic commentary, the Upanishads, between 800-600 B.C. These books are seen as the fulfillment of the Vedas, and consequently are known as the Vedanta, the "end of the Vedas." The Upanishads are the culmination of hundreds of years of reflection, and are much more rationalistic than the Vedas and Brahmanas. Their influence is felt even to the present.

The Upanishads supply the basis of later Hindu philosophy; they alone of the Vedic corpus are widely known and quoted by most well-educated Hindus, and their central ideas have also become a part of the spiritual arsenal of rank-and-file Hindus, while the earlier Vedic texts remain largely the special reserve stock of priests and scholars (O'Flaherty, 1988, p. 2).

Upanishads ("sitting close to a teacher") are, like the Aranyakas, secret teachings transmitted from guru to student. Unlike the Samhitas (the function of which was essentially restricted to sacrificial rites) and the other two commentaries (which expounded on those rites), the Upanishads expanded speculation to the entire Universe, especially the absolute basis of reality (*brahman*) and the self or soul (*atman*). The most famous teaching of the Upanishads is "that you are" (*tat tvam asi*), which means that the essence of the self is the absolute. An early Hindu sage illustrated this by pointing to a hive of bees collecting nectar. As nectar is collected from many different plants and reduced by the bees to honey, he explained, so all souls are part of the larger, indivisible essence of being (*Chandogya Upanishad* 6.9). The Universe is within the self, and the self is the Universe. Those who know this essential truth possessed great cosmic power.

The Upanishadic sages realized that this power of knowledge far excelled the power of the sacrifice: if the soul is identified with the Universe, then whoever controls their own soul controls the cosmos. Sacrifice affected the gods only indirectly, but esoteric knowledge was the key to omnipotence (Edgerton, 1965, p. 29). These books also contain the seeds of the doctrine of transmigration of souls (*samsara*), the laws of *karma* that govern the transmigration process, mental training associated with Yoga, and ascetic renunciation (Olivelle, 1996, p. xxiii).

Together these sixteen branches of literature are known as *œruti*, meaning "what is heard" (from the root *sru-*, "to hear"). It was "heard" by inspired sages who received this primary revelation from Brahma, the Supreme Lord. As divine revelation, *œruti* literature is considered to be "eternal, intrinsically powerful, and supremely authoritative" (Coburn, 1989, p. 119).

Despite the aura of holiness ascribed to the Vedas, the majority of Hindus have little access to these writings; they are massive, technical, and written in an archaic tongue. Much more familiar to the average Hindu are the colloquial *smrti* writings, a secondary set of scriptures considered to be of human authorship and subordinate to divinely delivered *œruti*.

"While the *œruti* texts have retained their authority as holy sources for Brahmanic ritual, philosophical speculation, and recitative *mantras*, the functional scriptures of the masses in India have been other texts, most of which are categorized as *smrti* rather than *œruti*" (Graham, 1989, p. 139). *Smrti* ("what is remembered") explains and elaborates the *œruti*, making them more understandable and meaningful to the general population—it is an "easier" form of truth. A mythological story of the origin of the theatrical art describes the role of *smrti*:

The gods asked: "Since it is not proper that the Vedas be heard by those of low birth, you should create a fifth Veda for all classes of people."

Brahma replied: "I shall compose a fifth Veda, called the Theatrical Art, based on history, which will convey the meaning of all the Scriptures and give an impulse to the arts. It will give good advice and moral lessons, rich in meaning, that lead to good conduct, prosperity, and fame. It will show the line of proper conduct to the future world" (*Natya Úastra* 1.4.13-15).

*Smrti* texts were intended to simplify the Vedas for the masses, and to elucidate Vedic teachings in a practical way. *Smrti* was written for the people's admonition, to illustrate dramatically through the lives of gods, sages, and kings the proper path of good conduct (*dharma*).

The Samhitas speak of salvation through ritual sacrifice, a ceremony only the wealthiest patrons could afford; the Upanishads refer to salvation through knowledge, an avenue inaccessible to all but the most educated men. *Smrti* offered scriptures and a means of salvation through devotion (*bhakti*) to people of all castes and both genders. In this category of scripture, Hinduism attained its most mature stage. Most prominent among the *smrti* texts are the Puranas, the Epics, the Dharma literature, and the Agamas, as well as other miscellaneous works.

Puranas ("ancient lore") are narrative works in the *itihasa* ("thus verily happened") tradition, a mythistorical genre describing the creation of the Universe, the origin of evil, and a history of Indian civilization focusing on legendary kings, sages, and gods. Woven into the central narrative are various religious instructions concerning caste laws, customs, ceremonies, pilgrimage, and temple construction. If the Vedic *samhitas* are like the Psalms, then the Puranas resemble the historical books of Samuel, Kings, and Chronicles.

The *Bhagavata-Purana* is one of the most popular of the eighteen principle Puranas, describing in an entertaining and endearing fashion the childhood of Krishna, who would later become one of the most worshiped gods in the pantheon. The mythological stories of young Krishna stir feelings of adoration within the devotee, the pursuit of which can lead to salvation. There also exist eighteen lesser Puranas of basically the same narrative structure, called Upapuranas, and numerous other books called *sthala* Puranas, which record legends of particular locations and temples. The eighteen most prominent Puranas alone contain about 375,000 verses—approximately the size of two *World Book* encyclopedias.

Also part of the *itihasa* are the great epic poems, the *Ramayana* and *Mahabharata*, written between 400 B.C. and A.D. 200. Together containing about 124,000 verses, the epics comprise some of the longest literary works in human history—

five times as long as the Bible. The *Ramayana* tells the story of Rama, a god-king who rescues his kidnapped wife Sita with the help of the monkey king. The *Mahabharata* relates a civil war between two groups of cousins that occurred in the mythical age before the present. Characters in both epics exemplify proper conduct for kings, soldiers, and persons wishing to attain rebirth. Many Hindus consider these epics to be the Veda of the masses, the books that "in all of history have influenced the largest number of people for the longest time" (Krishnamurthy, 1999).

Book six of the *Mahabharata* contains the *Bhagavad Gita*, the "Song of the Lord." This short text (about the size of John's gospel), though technically part of the *smrti* literature, is popularly considered to be among the holiest revelation (Coburn, 1989, p. 116). Many compare it to the New Testament as the definitive piece of Hindu scripture. Ghandi read it once daily. Written by an unknown sage, the *Gita* tells the story of Arjuna, a general in the civil war on the eve of battle, and his chariot driver, Krishna, who is actually an incarnate form of God. Arjuna expresses his reservations about fighting his cousins to Krishna, who encourages him by explaining the principles of *dharma* and revealing himself as the celestial lord.

About the same period as the sages Vyasa and Valmiki were composing the Epics to provide concrete examples of the dharmic code of conduct, the more formal *dharma shastra*s were being assembled. A *shastra* is simply a systematic treatise, though *dharma* is more difficult to translate: the word "subsumes the English concepts of 'religion', 'duty', 'law', 'right', 'justice', 'practice', and 'principle' "(Doniger and Smith, 1991, p. xvii). *Dharma shastra*s are thus books of law and duty. In this category, the Laws of Manu have been very influential, as have the more concise Laws of Yajñavalkya.

The Laws of Manu alone is as long as the four gospel accounts, yet it is just one treatise among about 5,000. In many respects these books resemble the Levitical code, minus the consistency and ethicality. The *agamas*, also known as the Tantras, are sectarian manuals for the worship of particular gods. They cover the three major traditions—*Œaivism*,

*Vaishnavism*, and *Œaktism*—and are usually associated with heterodox rites involving sexual intercourse and the consumption of alcohol and meat.

These are only the most influential parts of the *smrti* category: there are many more. According to Coburn, "the very concept of *smrti* is that of an authoritative, but open-ended Word" (1989, p. 120). The size and difficulty of the current body of Hindu scripture is compounded by the fact that authoritative works are added to the canon on a regular basis. "To see Hinduism in proper perspective we must remember that from the time of the Buddha till now, the composition of religious literature in India has been almost uninterrupted and that almost every century has produced works accepted by some sect as infallible scripture" (Eliot, 1968, 1:lxxiv). Surveying this vast, ever-expanding collection of Hindu sacred writings, it is no wonder that Sir William Jones remarked: "Wherever we direct our attention to Hindu literature, the notion of infinity presents itself "(as quoted in Londhe, 2001).

### Hindu Conception of the Vedas

While recognizing the role that sages have had in the preservation and transmission of the Vedas, Hindus generally reject the notion that the Vedas are the production of human ingenuity. Swami Vivekananda, the man credited with introducing Hinduism to the West, explained the Hindu outlook on revelation to the 1893 World Parliament of Religions:

> *The Hindus have received their religion through revelation, the Vedas. They hold that the Vedas are without beginning and without end. It may sound ludicrous, that a book can be without beginning or end. But by the Vedas no books are meant. They mean the accumulated treasury of spiritual laws discovered by different persons at different times. Just as the law of gravitation acted before its discovery by humanity, and would continue to act if all humanity forgot it, so is it with the laws that govern the spiritual world. The discoverers of these laws are called Rishis, and we honour them as perfected beings (as quoted in Londhe, 2001).*

Vivekananda summarily stated the orthodox Hindu view of scripture: scripture is eternal, it is impersonal, and it is much more than letters written on a page. These qualities apply primarily to *œruti* scripture, but depending on one's definition of *veda*, they may also qualify other scripture.

The Mimamsa school, a sect devoted to Vedic exegesis, established these principles over two thousand years ago in the *Purva Mimamsa Sutra*s (c. 200 B.C.). There they affirmed the Vedas to be eternal (*nitya*) and impersonal (*apauruseya*). To understand these two propositions, insight must be gained into the Hindu conception of Veda. As Vivekananda pointed out, the Vedas are more than a mere book—they are eternal knowledge, without author, beginning, or end.

The *Purva Mimamsa Sutra* likewise asserts that "the sacred Sanskrit-language Scripture known as the *Veda* is not a 'book' to be read, nor a source of information about a world exterior to itself "(Clooney, 1987, p. 660). One 18th-century pundit characterized Veda as "that which pertains to religion; books are not Veda" (*Vedam est, quidquid ad religionem pertinet, vedam non sunt libri*) [Graham, 1989, p. 139]. These increate truths have occasionally been perceived by humans and recorded in books, but the Vedas are much more than what is written. Vedic knowledge hangs in the atmosphere as a sort of ether exuded by the gods; the truth needs only to be grasped by enlightened disciples whose heightened senses allow them to perceive it. This is why the most sacred Vedas are called *œruti*—they have been heard by holy men. Hence the description of Vedas as sound vibration in the air:

> *I (Krishna) personally establish the Vedic sound vibration in the form of* omkara *within all living entities. It is thus perceived subtly, just like a single strand of fiber on a lotus stalk. Just as a spider brings forth from its heart its web and emits it through its mouth, the Supreme Personality of Godhead manifests Himself as the reverberating primeval vital air, comprising all sacred Vedic meters and full of transcendental pleasure (Bhagavata-Purana 11.21.38-39).*

Krishna (a primary Hindu god, conceived as a manifestation of Vishnu) declares that the Vedas are within. They are the "reverberating primeval vital air" that must be heard. Many seek the truth in the hope that they might grope for it and find it, though, according to this passage, it is not far from each one of us. Though Christians believe scripture to be the complete, written record of specific truths revealed by God, Hindus consider scripture to be the whole of universal truth that may be discovered. Only fragments of this everlasting knowledge are revealed in the written Vedas (Danielou, 1991, p. 280).

Vivekananda also stated that the Vedas are eternal, even preexisting the gods. This means something significantly different to a Hindu than it would to a Western Christian with his linear notions of time and space. To the Hindu, time and space exist only in relation to perception; when perception is altered (through religious rites such as meditation) and the Cosmos is seen as it really is, distinctions in time and space melt away into the Absolute. "Absolute time is an ever-present eternity" (Danielou, p. 15).

Thus, the Vedas and the gods both were created, but they both have also always existed. It is not inconsistent in the Hindu mind to hold that the Vedas are uncreated—that they were delivered to *brahman* at the dawn of creation by the "source of all beings" (*Úvetaúvatara Upanishad* 6.18)—and to believe that they were created from fire, wind, and Sun by the god Prajapati (*Chandogya Upanishad* 4.17.2). These sophisticated beliefs developed over time, however, and some of the most ancient hymns attribute revelation to the highest god. "The *Rig*, *Sama*, *Yajur* and *Atharva*, became manifest from the Lord, along with the Puranas and all the *Devas* [gods] residing in the heavens" (*Atharva Veda* 11.7.24). The scripture and the gods sprang from the "Lord," Brahma, who is the manifestation of the Absolute principle of the Universe. Later passages elaborate this same theme.

The influential *Bhagavad Gita* grounds all things, including the Vedas, in Brahma: "From food are born (all) creatures; from rain is the production of food; rain is produced by sacrifices; sacrifices are the result of action; know that action has its source in the Vedas; the Vedas come from the Indestructible [the Supreme Being]" (3.15). Likewise, the *Brahmanda Purana* depicts a four-headed Brahma emitting the four Vedic books from his four mouths (1.2.8). Ultimately, the Vedas derive from the Absolute Being, the Immense One.

This Absolute god-principle did not create the scriptures, but as eternal truth they are part of his essence. They are thought to have co-existed with the Absolute, and pre-existed in the Absolute. He created the gods and manifested the truth of his presence to them; they in turn created the written books of the Veda for the humanity they also made. The eternal Vedas were thus received by the gods, who entrusted them to humans.

According to the *Brhadaranyaka Upanishad*, the method of transmitting the Vedas from heaven to Earth is similar to the biblical conception described in 2 Timothy 3:16, wherein Scripture is described as being "god-breathed."

As clouds of smoke billow from a fire lit with damp fuel, so indeed this Immense Being has exhaled all this: Rig Veda, Yajur Veda, Sama Veda, the Atharva-Angirasa, histories, ancient tales, sciences, hidden teachings (Upanishads), verses, aphorisms, explanations, and glosses–it is that Immense Being who has exhaled all this (2.4.10).

God, known here as the Immense Being, breathed out the Vedas, not into specific men, but into the Universe. There the scripture remains, as smoke lingering from an extinguished fire, waiting to be perceived by humans. Seven men served as interlocutors between the Supreme and humanity—men of extraordinary perspicacity who distinguished themselves by their asceticism and acts of renunciation (see Mitchiner, 2000). These men were not chosen to be inspired; they were gifted sages with keen insight into spiritual matters.

Their sensitivity allowed them to perceive those eternal truths that permeate the fabric of space and time. The revelation they perceived was not confined to a particular time or place, and if it were to be forgotten, other sages would comprehend those truths again. The seven, called *rsis*, or "seers," perceived the *œruti* vibrating in the Universe and recorded what they heard/saw. Coburn notes that the use of two metaphors—hearing and seeing—is intentional; it represents an attempt to "convey the holistic and supremely compelling nature of that experience" (1989, p. 109).

According to Hindu tradition, the *rsis* recorded their experience because of the coming Age of Kali, a dispensation when men would be hardened against spiritual matters. The seven *rsis*, along with Vyasa, the compiler of the scripture, are generally considered to be perfected beings, greater than humans but less than divine.

The eternal Vedas came from the impersonal Absolute. They were not personally delivered from God to man, but impersonally manifested. The Veda was not received by humans, as was the Bible, but perceived by sages. Though impersonal, the Hindu philosophy of the word is not unlike that of the Bible. One of the Brahmanas states: "[In the beginning] was the only Lord of the Universe. His Word was with him. This Word was his second. He contemplated. He said, 'I will deliver this Word so that she will produce and bring into being all this world' "(*Tandya Maha Brahmana* 20.14.2).

Though written centuries before, this passage sounds remarkably like John 1:1: "In the beginning was the Word, and the Word was with God, and the Word was God." Just as Christ, the Word, is the ground of all that exists, so Hindus believe that the impersonal Veda is the source of the Universe. The Atharva Veda reads: "From the bosom of the sacred Word he brought forth the world" (4.1.3). A paraphrase of a modern Hindu prayer states: "Those who are versed in the Vedas know that the universe is the transformation of speech. It was out of the Vedas that this universe was first evolved" (Eickler, p. 24). Maharishi Mahesh Yogi (of transcendental mediation and Beatles fame) explained this process in more detail:

> Atma, *the Self, is the ground from where the steps of evolution begin. The first step is Œruti, the speech value of expression,* Veda. *The second step of evolution is from the speech level to the material level where the frequencies of sound, frequencies of speech in the Language of*

> *Natural Law, evolve into frequencies of matter which construct the whole physiology of the ever-evolving material universe,* Viœva *(Eichler, p.1).*

The material Universe did not come into being by omnipotent fiat, or the intentional will of a purposeful Deity, but by spontaneous evolution from the eternal Veda. The sounds of the Veda (the Veda is sound) became the fabric of the Cosmos. This view is not foreign to Christianity; by the Word, "all things were created that are in heaven and that are on earth, visible and invisible" (Colossians 1.16). Yet in contrast to the impersonal Hindu word, the Christian Word is a living and personal Being, Who willed the Universe into existence for His own purposes, Who delivered a temporal revelation to humanity for the express purpose of imparting saving knowledge, and Who revealed Himself to man as the ultimate divine knowledge.

### *Faith Comes by Hearing*

It is important to remember that the majority of India's population has been illiterate for the greater part of its history (as has been most of the world). As a result, Hindus typically have relied on the spoken word to a greater degree than any written text. "The Veda was not primarily a written text, but the powerful speech that came forth from the mouths of Brahmans" (Carpenter, p. 63). Words and sounds were very important in the Vedic tradition, and even in the earliest Vedas the smallest syllables and intonations were thought to be of divine origin. "In the actual sounded syllables of the Veda lie the points of contact with transcendent reality" (Graham, p. 138). Vac is the female personification of speech, and might be compared to the personification of Wisdom in Proverbs 4 (also perceived as feminine).

The relationship between Vac and Dame Wisdom is interesting, though perhaps a more accurate comparison from the Hindu perspective is the Word of John 1:1. Just as that passage equates the Word with God, several vedic passages divinize the Veda in the form of Vac. Depicting Vac as both a personification of the Vedas and as their progenitor, the *Aitareya Aranyaka* states: "She 'enters into the seers.' She gives power and intelligence to those she loves. She is the 'mother of the Vedas,' the consort of the lord-of-heaven (Indra), containing all the worlds within herself. 'Hence Vac is everything'" (3.1.6). Alain Danielou defined speech (Vac) as the ground and being of the Universe:

> *Speech has the power to evoke images and ideas. The process through which a thought, at first indistinct, gradually becomes definite and exteriorizes itself is similar to the process through which the divine thought becomes the universe. The difference is only one of degree. If our power of thought, our power of expression, was greater, things we speak of would actually appear. With our limited powers only their image is evoked. Speech can therefore be represented as the origin of all things. The cosmos is but the expression of an idea, a manifested utterance. Supreme Divinity can be represented as the causal word (sabda-brahman) [1991, p. 38].*

The words of the Veda are intrinsically powerful. Every syllable is sacred, and the repetition of the scripture is auspicious in and of itself. Eliot notes that it "is sacred sound not a sacred book which is venerated" (1968, 1:lxxi). The books of the Veda are cherished not for their great wisdom or moral instruction, but for the holy sounds contained within. Understanding the text is unnecessary; scriptures' value lies in its oral repetition. The Veda's "sanctity often appears to be inversely related to comprehensibility" (Coburn, p. 112). Peculiarly, it is not the message of the Vedas that transcends time, but the words themselves, even "the particular sounds and their precise verbal order in the corpus (including the variants)" (Lipner, 1994, p. 46).

Christians may be skeptical of this oral approach to scripture, but they would do well to remember the supremacy of the spoken word in their own religion. The spoken word indicates presence, while the written word implies absence. Christ, as the Word, was present among us, and he represents the highest form of revelation. His ascension to the right hand of the Father necessitated the written words of the New Testament so that the disciples might be "guided into all truth"

(John 16:13). Those written words are "living and powerful" (Hebrews 4:12), and reflect the continuing presence of God in the person of the Holy Spirit. It is not the immediacy of the Word that sets Christianity apart from Hindu scripture, however, nor the respect for the spoken word, but the content.

The Bible contains clear statements that must be affirmed prerequisite to salvation. Some are of a historical nature, such as "Jesus was born of a virgin in Bethlehem." Others are ethical: "Love your neighbor as yourself." There are also what might be characterized as theological or doctrinal truths, which include "Jesus is Lord" and "There will be a day of judgment." The power of these statements of scripture derives from a comprehension of, and conformation to, those truths—not from their repetition. For instance, Jesus gave the model prayer (Matthew 6:9-13) to His disciples as an example of prayer that was pleasing to God. To repeatedly recite the exact words of that prayer today would be of little use because the effectiveness of the prayer is linked to a comprehension of the words uttered as well as compliance with certain moral requisites (such as forgiving others their trespasses, Matthew 6:14-15).

### *Significance of the Scripture*

Though the Hindu scriptures are immensely significant to the tradition, they exert surprisingly little influence in the religious life of the average Hindu devotee. Deepak Sarma stated in an introductory lecture on Hinduism that "all Hindus orient themselves in relation to the Vedas" (2003). This is not to say that all Hindus accept the scriptures. It might accurately be said that atheists orient themselves in relation to the Bible, yet their position is opposite that of a Christian. Similarly, Hindus are defined by the degree to which they accept or reject the Vedic scriptures.

Some renounce the holy books on principle: most notable among these is Gautama Buddha, an Indian prince who abandoned the Vedas because they reinforced the caste system. Many reject them for more pragmatic reasons; Lipner observed that "in practice most Hindus have had no direct access to the Vedas, either in written form or aurally" (p. 26). The mammoth size and obsolete script of traditional Sanskrit scriptures renders them inaccessible to the majority, and even vernacular translations are unintelligible to a predominately illiterate population.

This is true among the clergy as much as the laity—some of the greatest Hindu practioners of the past centuries, such as Sri Ramakrishna, spoke not a word of Sanskrit. "Even in the most orthodox domains, reverence to the Vedas has come to be a simple 'tip of the hat' made in passing to an idol with which one intends no longer to be encumbered" (Renou, as quoted in Carpenter, 1992, p. 57). Gupta lamented: "In the present age we take pride in the mere mention of the Vedas without caring to know about their contents" (1979).

### *Elasticity*

Nonetheless, the majority's abandonment of the Vedic scriptures does not diminish the significance of the Vedas to the religion. In the Laws of Manu, the Veda is held in highest regard:

> *The root of religion is the entire Veda, and (then) the tradition and customs of those who know (the Veda), and the conduct of virtuous people, and what is satisfactory to oneself. Whatever duty Manu proclaimed for whatever person, all of that was declared in the Veda, for it contains all knowledge. So when a learned man has looked thoroughly at all of this with the eye of knowledge, he should devote himself to his own duty in accordance with the authority of the revealed canon. For the human being who fulfils the duty declared in the revealed canon and in tradition wins renown here on earth and unsurpassable happiness after death.*

The Veda should be known as the revealed canon and the teachings of religion as the tradition. These two are indisputable matters, for religion arose out of the two of them. Any twice-born man who disregards these two roots (of religion) because he relies on the teachings of logic should be excommunicated by virtuous people as an atheist and a reviler of the Veda (*Manusmrti* 2.6-11, emp. added).

The sage Manu elaborates the hierarchy of authority in this passage: Vedas or *œruti* literature, secondary or *smrti* literature, and one's own preferences. The Vedas are the most authoritative texts, and ought to be called the "revealed canon."

Contemporary Western and Indian scholars also acknowledge the centrality of the Vedas to Hindu religion. Brian Smith emphasized the role of scripture when he defined Hinduism as "the religion of those humans who create, perpetuate, and transform traditions with legitimizing reference to the authority of the Veda" (as quoted in Flood, 1996, p. 226, n. 26). Lipner points out that "*in theory* at least, the Vedas are the source of saving knowledge" (1994, p. 26, italics in orig.). Sarvepalli Radhakrishnan, Hindu philosopher and first president of India, identified the Vedas as "the standard of thought and feeling for Indians" (as quoted in Sawhney, 1999).

One might expect something as important as the "source of saving knowledge," the "standard of thought and feeling," and the "legitimizing reference" of a world religion to be well defined, yet, in the words of Wendy O'Flaherty, a revealed canon as mentioned in the Laws of Manu "is a concept with little meaning for a religion as pluralistic as Hinduism" (1988, p. xi). Lipner added that "the boundaries of the Vedic scriptures as they have come down to us are not particularly neat" (1994, p. 42). Jayaram, a Hindu scholar, admitted that Hinduism "does not rely exclusively upon any particular source" (2000), and Princeton professor Donald Lopez noted that it has "no single text that can serve as a doctrinal point of reference" (1995, p. 5).

As noted above, Hindus do not unanimously accept any single text, or group of texts, as the authoritative body of eternal truth. Judaism, Christianity, and Islam each cherish a holy book containing everything that pertains to life and godliness, but Hindus have no analogous monolithic text. According to Mahatma Gandhi, "Hinduism does not rest on the authority of one book or one prophet, nor does it possess a common creed" (1991, p. 120). As frustrating as this may be from a comparative religions standpoint, the lack of a definitive text is a source of pride for many Hindus who feel that tolerance and pluralism are the primary themes of the twenty-first century incarnation of the religion. Absolute scriptures lead to dogmatic beliefs, they reason, and dogmatic beliefs lead to strife and violence.

Nonetheless, it already has been shown that most Hindus have a high regard of the *œruti* texts, most broadly referred to as the Vedas. If any canonical scripture exists, it is the Vedas, which have been considered a gauge of orthodoxy (see *Manusmrti* 2.6-11, quoted above). During the Indian renaissance of the 19th century, various reform movements such as the Brahmo Samaj and the Arya Samaj sought to return to the Vedas as the ground of Hindu spirituality. Nolini Gupta, a Hindu scholar, summed up the view of one such school of Hinduism: "He who defies Veda is an atheist, a non-Hindu, an untouchable and a non-Aryan. All the various religious systems and scriptures of the Hindus look upon the Veda as the sole authority. What is inconsistent with the Veda is false and unacceptable" (1979). Veda here is used in the sense of a canon, yet that canon is left undefined.

Traditionally, the Vedas includes either the four Samhitas or all sixteen branches of texts (Sarma, 2003a). The texts themselves, however, list only the *Rig Veda, Sama Veda,* and the *Yajur Veda* as canonical; originally, the priests rejected the *Atharva Veda* from the *trayi vidya*, or "triple veda" (*Bhagavad Gita* 9.20; *Manusmrti* 1.23; 4.125). Limiting scripture to a few books tends to be the exception, not the rule; books are more often added to the Veda and deemed sacred. In the *Chandogya Upanishad* (a text within the *œruti* collection), the Puranas and Itihasa are described as the "fifth veda" (7.1.2). Vallabha, a 15-century theologian, proposed a fourfold canon embodying Veda, *Brahma Sutra*, *Bhagavad Gita*, and *Bhagavata Purana* (Lipner p. 60).

The Law Book of Yajñavalkya established the Vedas, the Puranas, the philosophical system called Nyaya, the exegetical school of Mimamsa, treatises on moral duty (*dharmaúastra*s), and the six classes of work that are auxiliaries to the Veda (pronunciation, prosody, grammar, word-derivation, astronomy, and ritual) as "the fourteen bases of knowledge and moral duty"

(1.3). A more contemporary interpretation of Veda comes from the International Gita Society, which considers not only Hindu texts, but also the Bible and the Qur'an as scriptures from the Supreme Being. Coburn points out that "*œruti* must be seen as ongoing and experientially based feature of the Hindu religious tradition" (1989, p. 112).

Many other passages could be noted, each having a different opinion on what texts are sacred and should thus be listed under the name "Veda." How does the average Hindu view this dilemma? "The average man – even the average priest—regards all these as sacred works without troubling himself with distinctions as to *œruti* and *smriti*, and the Vedas and Upanishads are hardly within his horizon" (Eliot, 1968, 1:lxxv).

Coburn, in his essay "'Scripture' in India," expands further on the Hindu conception of scripture. He argues that Indian scripture exceeds written texts—the written word is only one revelatory medium. "[T]he holy words that are *œruti* must be seen alongside other transforming, sacramental activities, such as philosophical argumentation, the worship of the divine image form, and the highly nuanced moods (*bhavas*) of Krishna devotees" (p. 112). He also cites Diana Eck's book, *Darœan*, in which she elaborates the thesis that Hindu images (which some would refer to as idols) are actually "visual scriptures" (1998). David Carpenter suggests further that the conduct and judgment of those Brahmin priests who have memorized the Vedas is considered Vedic, "even when they went beyond the known Vedic teachings" (1992, p. 62).

### *Why the Bible is Superior to Hindu Scripture?*

The corpus of Hindu scripture is enormous. A person could spend a lifetime sorting through the millions of pages of sacred and semi-sacred texts. Even the most orthodox sections of scripture are many times larger than the Bible. Clarke, in an essay on Hindu scripture, defended his limited treatment of the Vedas with this description of his subject: "How large, how difficult to understand! So vast, so complicated, so full of contradictions, so various and changeable, that its very immensity is our refuge!" (1875, p. 81). Recall that the four

Veda Samhitas are about the size of the Old Testament, and the Upanishads number over 100. Among the *smrti* literature, the Epics are five times the length of the entire Bible, each of the 18 principle Puranas is about the size of the Old Testament, and over 5,000 texts of varying length belong to the *dharmaúastra* tradition.

The Bible seems concise in comparison, containing only 23,314 verses in the Old Testament and 7,959 verses in the New. An average Western library or bookstore stocks some abridged compilation of the Vedic Samhitas, the 13 principle Upanishads, and the *Bhagavad Gita,* but only the most specialized libraries carry full versions of even the major scriptures. A Hindu equivalent of the Gideon missionary society would have to donate an entire library of books to hotels rather than a single volume to each room. Of course, Hindus have little interest in proselytizing, so it is not really a problem.

If the size were insufficient to deter an honest seeker of truth, the incomprehensibility of the scripture certainly would. The Bible was written originally in Hebrew, Aramaic, and Greek. Though Bible students rarely master the original languages, sufficient lexical aids exists so that the original meaning can be understood with relatively little difficulty. Hindu students are not so fortunate. Since the Vedas were delivered from an impersonal source (the "Absolute") there can be no original meaning. "[T]he Veda has no author, no meaning beyond the words and the sacrificial actions themselves; one cannot appeal to a pre-verbal intention to get beyond the words" (Clooney, 1987, p. 660). Incidentally, as Clooney points out in his essay, postmodernists find this approach to understanding texts refreshingly in line with their own views.

English translations are available for the primary scriptures, yet even the most careful translations are difficult to understand. Most English translations of the Bible are on the reading level of a 6-12th grader, yet the same cannot be said of the Vedas. "Many [of the Vedas] are written in a style which even educated men find very difficult to understand; and, if they have to be studied in the original, only a very small part of them can possibly be mastered by one man" (Mitchell, 1897, p. 247).

Archaic Sanskrit (also called Vedic), the language of the *Rig Veda*, is a dead language, and inaccessible to most Hindus. Other scriptures are written in classical Sanskrit, Prakrit, Tamil, and other regional dialects. The possibility of interpretation is further hampered by the belief that the Vedas consist of sacred sound, not written text.

Were the language difficulties to be sorted out, the problem of incomprehensibility would remain. Hindu scripture contradicts itself time and time again. One might expect works separated by thousands of years to disagree (and they do), but these contradictions are found even within individual texts. There are logical contradictions, conceptual contradictions, and even factual contradictions. This may be explained partially by the Hindu conception of scripture, as explained by Eliot: "The Hindu approaches his sacred literature somewhat in the spirit in which we approach Milton and Dante.

The beauty and value of such poems is clear. The question of whether they are accurate reports of facts seems irrelevant" (1968, 1:lxxi). Apparently, contradiction is not regarded as evidence against the Vedas' divine origin. Hindu scripture confirms this suspicion, and actually embraces the contradictions. The Laws of Manu recommends that both sides of a contradiction in the Veda be accepted as authoritative: "But where the revealed canon is divided, both (views) are traditionally regarded as law; for wise men say that both of them are valid laws" (*Manusmrti* 2.14). Regarding the contradictions inherent in the Upanishads, the collection of texts considered by Olivelle to be the "vedic scripture *par excellence* of Hinduism" (1996, p. xxiii), Robson remarked: "It is hard to say what philosophical opinion might not be supported from the Upanishads, for the most contradictory statements find a place in them" (1905, p. 28). Likewise the Puranas, so holy as to be called "the fifth veda" (*Chandogya Upanishad* 7.1.4), are "for the most part intensely sectarian; one denounces beliefs and rites which another enjoins" (Mitchell, p. 260). Coburn stated that, when it comes to Hindu scripture, "sanctity often appears to be inversely related to comprehensibility" (p.112).

Hindu scripture is for all practical purposes useless to the average Hindu for these and other reasons. This, of course, assumes that all Hindus have access to the scripture. Traditionally, Hindu society is divided into four castes, the Brahmin (priestly class), Kshatriya (ruling class), Vaiúya (merchant class), and Úudra (outcastes). The first three classes are known as the twice-born, and only the males of those classes are allowed to read the Vedas.

All women and males of the Úudra class are excluded because of their "impurity" (*Manusmrti* 2.164-172). These restricted groups do have access to the *smrti* writings and devotional literature, but the most sacred *œruti* texts are forbidden. The religion itself restricts to a select few the scripture that purportedly contains saving knowledge. There is much morally reprehensible material within the Vedic literature. One 19th-century writer, speaking specifically of the Puranas, underlined the true nature of the Hindu scripture: "The instructions which it professes to give are useless, where they are not scandalous and criminal.

The only things clearly to be understood, are the profane songs, the obscene ceremonies, and the other indecencies connected with the prescribed festivals" (as quoted by Goodall, 1996, p. xxxviii). The immoralities endorsed by Hindu scripture range from racial prejudices and rigid social hierarchies to rape and murder. For instance, the earliest Vedic texts, which are traced back to the Aryan invasion of the Indian subcontinent, reflect the racial biases of the invaders. It seems that the Aryans were a fairer-skinned people of Persian descent, whereas the indigenous peoples (Dasas) whom they subjugated were of a darker skin colour and Negro-Australoid features. One prayer directed to the warrior god Indra petitioned him to "give protection to the Aryan colour" (*Rig Veda* 3.34.9).

Another passage lauds Indra's victory over the dark-skinned natives: "He, much invoked, has slain Dasas and Simus [dark-skinned natives], according to his will, and laid them low with arrows. The mighty Thunderer [Indra] with his fair-complexioned friends won the land, the sunlight, and the waters"

(*Rig Veda* 1.100.18). According to Mitchell, the "language in which the Vedic poets speak of these enemies is uniformly that of unmingled, vehement hatred" (1897, p. 19). Critics might observe that the Old Testament is also guilty of ethnic cleansing; however, the Israelite battles were drawn over moral lines, not ethnic or racial (see Bass, 2003). Though the historical picture is unclear, it seems that the Dasas were incorporated into the Aryan social hierarchy as the lowest class (*Rig Veda* 10.90.12). Evidence for this comes from the Sanskrit word for class, *varna*, which means "colour" (cognate to the English varnish).

More disturbing than the Vedic treatment of race are the pervasive references to sex, and the its role in the religious ritual. The *Kama Sutra* of Vatsayayana is one of the most infamous Hindu texts. Known as the "Aphorisms on Love," or more popularly as the "Sex Manual," the *Kama Sutra* celebrates sexual love (*Kama* is the god of love, in many ways similar to Cupid).

In addition to explicit information for use between husbands and wives, there are also sections entitled "Concerning the Wives of Other People" and "Concerning Prostitutes," both providing advice on how to procure such forbidden fruit. The *Kama Sutra* is but one text among many. One entire category of *smrti* literature known as Tantras is dedicated to the worship of the goddess principle, *Œakti*. The esoteric teachings within that body of texts describe various sexual rites that represent the spiritual union of the worshipper's soul with the goddess. Violence and sexual perversion penetrates even the most orthodox scripture. The *Brhadarankyaka Upanishad*, for instance, condones rape:

> *Surely, a woman who has changed her clothes at the end of her menstrual period is the most auspicious of women. When she has changed her clothes at the end of her menstrual period, therefore, one should approach that splendid woman and invite her to have sex. Should she refuse to consent, he should bribe her. If she still refuses, he should beat her with a stick or with his fists and overpower her, saying: "I take away the splendor from you with my virility and splendor" (6.4.9,21).*

Bestiality is likewise advocated. A particularly solemn rite for the early Vedic religion was the horse sacrifice. Though it probably was performed rarely, it is mentioned frequently in the Vedic commentaries. Note one section from the *Úatapatha Brahmana*: "Then they draw out the penis of the horse and place it in the vagina of the chief queen, while she says, 'May the vigorous virile male, the layer of seed, lay the seed'; this she says for sexual intercourse" (13.5.2.1-10). Examples such as this could be multiplied. To the list of atrocities in the Vedic scripture may be added human sacrifice (*Aitaraya Brahmana* 7.13-18), as if pornography, bestiality, rape, racism, inequalities were not enough.

The Bible is the authentic, authoritative, and final revelation of the true God. Though written over a period of 1,400 years by forty very diverse men on two continents, The Book is completely unified and free from error. A single theme is expanded upon throughout—the redemption of man through the Messiah. The Bible was confirmed by predictive prophecies and the miracles of the inspired men who wrote it.

The moral laws contained within are more reasonable and consistent than that of any other religious or naturalistic system. By contrast, the Hindu scriptures have no final, objective authority; according to one Hindu, "all scriptural knowledge is lower knowledge" (Jayrama, 2000). Subjective religious experiences are generally preferable to written texts. Hindu scripture contains little that is noble, just, pure, lovely, virtuous, or praiseworthy. Allegedly a progressive revelation, Hindu scripture contradicts itself both within particular texts and as a body of literature. The Bible, also a progressive revelation, never corrects itself, but only compliments and fulfils that which has been written. Different Hindu scriptures present completely different paths to salvation (liberation)—*karma-yoga* (the path of action), *jaña-yoga* (path of knowledge), and *bhakti-yoga* (path of devotion). The Vedas contain no predictive prophecy and offer no miracles to confirm the revelation supposedly sent from God. Thus the Hindus have no accessible ground of truth, no normative written word, and no objective moral or religious instruction.

# 9

# Philosophy of Rituals

***Aarti:*** Aarti, arti, arathi, or arati is a Hindu ritual, in which light from wicks soaked in ghee (purified butter) or camphor is offered to one or more deities. It is said to have descended from the Vedic concept of fire rituals, or *homa*. The word may also refer to the traditional Hindu devotional song that is sung during the ritual. Aarti is performed and sung to develop the highest love for God. "Aa" means "towards", and "rati" means "the highest love for God" in Sanskrit.

Aarti is generally performed twice or three times daily-usually, in the morning and in the evening, and at the end of a puja or bhajan session.

Aarti is also a common name for Hindu females.

The assembled devotees in the temple sing various types of *kirtana* and *bhajans* during the arati ceremony. Although exact rituals vary, aarti follows roughly the following steps. The pujari performing arati first purifies his hands with sacred water from the *achamana* cup. He then sprinkles three spoonfuls of water over a conch, and blows it three times. He then lights an odd number of incense sticks (usually three) from a ghee lamp standing beside the altar. While ringing a small bell, he waves it seven times around the deities, and then he waves it once to the assembled devotees.

The pujari next lights a five-wick ghee lamp from the large lamp and offers it; four circles to the deities' feet, two to their navel, three to their face, and then he waves it seven times around the deities' whole bodies. This allows the devotee to focus on all parts of the deity. He then gives it to another devotee, who presents the lamp to each devotee in the temple room. When offered the ghee lamp, devotees touch the flame with their hands, and then touch their hands to their foreheads in a gesture to embrace the warmth and devotion towards the God.

The pujari then takes a smaller conch and fills it with water. He offers it by waving it three times around the deities' heads and seven times around their bodies. He then pours the water into a shaker; which another devotee takes and walks around the temple room shaking it, ensuring that everyone has been touched by the water.

The next item offered is a cloth, offered seven times around the deities. After the cloth has been offered, the pujari takes a plate with flowers on it and offers it seven times around the deities' bodies. The plate is then taken by another devotee and offered to the rest of the devotees, who each sniff the flowers.

Pujari concluded the aarti by waving a chamara (yak-tail whisk) at the altar in a gesture of fanning the deities. In warm weather, he will also wave a peacock fan before the deities.

## Aarti Lyrics

While any devotional song or bhajan can be sung during aarti, the following song is very popular. If the aarti is specifically ascribed to a particular deity, then, of course, the corresponding special song of praise is offered.

*Om Jaya Jagadeesha hare*
*Swami Jaya Jagadeesha hare*
*Bhakta janon ke sankata*
*Daas jano ke sankata*
*Kshana mein door Kare*
*Om Jaya Jagadeesha hare*
*Jo Dhyaave Phala Paave*
*Dukha Vinase Mana kaa*
*Swami Dukha Vinase Mana kaa*
*Sukha Sampati Ghara Aave*

*Sukha Sampati Ghara Aave*
*Kashta Mitey Tana kaa*
*Om Jaya Jagadeesha hare...*
*Maata Pitaa Tum Merey*
*Sharana Gahoon main kiski*
*Swami Sharana Gahoon main kiski*
*Tum Bin Aur Na Doojaa*
*Prabhu Bin Aur Na Doojaa*
*Aash karoon main Jiski*
*Om Jaya Jagadeesha hare...*
*Tuma Purana Paramaatmaa*
*Tuma Antaryaami*
*Swami Tuma Antaryaami*
*Par Brahma Parameshvara*
*Par Braḥma Parameshvara*
*Tuma Sabake Swami*
*Om Jaya Jagadeesha hare...*
*Tuma Karunaa Ke Saagar*
*Tuma Paalana Kartaa*
*Swami Tuma Paalana Kartaa*
*Main moorakh khal-kaami*
*Main Sevaka Tum Swami*
*Kripaa Karo Bharataa*
*Om Jaya Jagadeesha hare...*
*Tum Ho Ek Agochara*
*Sabkey Praanapati*
*Swami Sabkey Praanapati*
*Kisa Vidhi Miloon Dayaamaya*
*Kisa Vidhi Miloon Gosai*
*Tuma ko main kumati*
*Om Jaya Jagadeesha hare...*
*Deena Bandhu Dukha Harataa*
*Thaakur Tum merey*

*Svaami Rakshaka tum Mere*
*Apney haath uthaao*
*Apney charan lagaao*
*Dwaar para main terey*
*Om Jaya Jagadeesha hare...*
*Vishaya Vikaar Mitaao*
*Paap Haro Devaa*
*Swami Paap Haro Devaa*
*Shraddhaa Bhakti Badhaao*
*Shraddhaa Prem Badhaao*
*Santan Ki Sevaa*
*Om Jaya Jagadeesha hare...*
*Tan Man Dhan Sab Hai Tera*
*Swaami Sab Kuchh Hai Tera*
*Tera Tujhko Arpan*
*Tera Tujhko Arpan*
*Kyaa Laagey Mera*
*Om Jaya Jagadeesha hare...*

***Other Arti Lyrics:*** There are other very popular arti lyrics, based on a shloka from the Vedas:

*Guru brahma*
*Guru vishnu*
*Guru devo maheshwarah*
*Guru sakshat parabrahma*
*Tas mai Shri Guru vai namaha.*

Translation: *Guru is Lord Brahma, Lord Vishnu and Lord Maheswara, Guru is nothing but the Supreme Brahman devoid of attributes.* That is the reason why we bow to the Guru.

This version was sung by George Harrison on the song My Sweet Lord.

***Aarti in South Indian Temples:*** Aarti performed at South Indian Temples mostly follows the above mentioned rituals except that they are often more elaborate in the way they are performed. Aarti is also referred to as Deepa Aaradhanai in Tamil.

The following Sanskrit Shlokha accompanies the ritual of Aarti:

*Rajadhi Rajaya Prasahya Saahine,*
*Namo Vayamvai Shravanaya Kurmahe,*
*Tumekam Kamakamaya Mahyam,*
*Kamesharovai Shravano Thathathu,*
*Kuberaya Vai Shravanaya,*
*Maha Rajaya Namaha*

***Bhajan:*** A bhajan or kirtan is basically a Hindu or Sikh devotional song, often of ancient origin. Great importance is attributed to the singing of bhajans within the Bhakti. It is also one of the paths of Sikhism and in that context refers to the singing of the Sacred Hymns from the *Sri Guru Granth Sahib*, or "SGGS". The Sikhs place huge value on this type of singing and a Sikh is duty bound to listen to and/or sing Guru-Kirtan as frequently as possible. In Surat Shabd Yoga, bhajan means listening to the inner sounds of the Shabd or the Shabd Master.

### *Music of India*

***Bhajan Bhangra Filmi Ghazal-Genres:*** Classical (Carnatic and Hindustani)-Rock-Pop-Hip hop

***Awards:*** Bollywood Music Awards-Punjabi Music Awards

### *Charts*

***Festivals:*** Sangeet Natak Akademi–Thyagaraja Aradhana–Cleveland Thyagaraja Aradhana

***Media:*** *Sruti*, *The Music Magazine*

***National Anthem:*** "Jana Gana Mana", also national song "Vande Mataram"

### *Music of the States*

Andaman and Nicobar Islands-Andhra Pradesh – Arunachal Pradesh – Assam – Bihar – Chhattisgarh– Goa – Gujarat – Haryana – Himachal Pradesh – Jammu – Jharkhand – Karnataka – Kashmir – Kerala– Madhya Pradesh – Maharashtra – Manipur – Meghalaya – Mizoram – Nagaland–Orissa – Punjab– Rajasthan – Sikkim – Tamil Nadu – Tripura–Uttar Pradesh – Uttaranchal – West Bengal.

Kirtans are deeply rooted in the Vedic tradition. Bhajans are simple songs in soulful language expressing the many-splendored emotions of love for God; a complete submission or self-surrender to Him through singing.

Traditionally, the music has been Indian classical music, which is based on ragas and tala (rhythmic beat patterns) played on the harmonium and tabla (traditional Indian instruments). The Sikh Scripture contains 31 ragas and 17 talas which form the basis for kirtan music compositions.

***Mantras and Prayers:*** A mantra is a sacred syllable, word or verse, often rooted in sanskrit or revealed to a sage in deep meditation. A mantra, when recited with devotion, concentration and understanding, revitalizes the body and mind with mystic power, and harmonizes thought and action.

A mantra, when repeated constantly during meditation, first loudly and then through silent and mental chanting, relieving the mind of any stress.

Prayer is uplifting inspiring and fascinating for the mind and it has great power. Therefore, it is very important that each of you learns to pray. Through prayer you purify your mind and gain spiritual strength. Thus prayer is the foundation of success.

***History and Origin:*** The groundwork for the bhajans was laid in the hymns found in Sama Veda, the third Veda in the Hindu scriptures. They are distinguished from the Sanskrit *shlokas* by virtue of their easy, lilting flow, their colloquial renderings and their profound appeal to the masses. Bhajans are sung in a group of devotees, with a designated lead singer. The simple tunes, repetition of words (particularly the various Names with which God is addressed) and phrases lend the hymns a kind of tonal mesmerism. Anecdotes, episodes from the lives of Gods, preachings of saints and descriptions of God's glories have been the subject of bhajans. The Dhrupad style is a famous form of bhajan. Another well-known form of the bhajan is the keertan/kirtan, or, song in the Haridas tradition.

***Types of Bhajans:*** A look into the past reveals that bhajans as a genre have come a long way; weaving a home for themselves into the core of human hearts. Traditions of bhajan — singing, such as Nirguni, Gorakhanathi, Vallabhapanthi, Ashtachhap and Madhura-bhakti, have been formed over the ages. Each sect has their own sets of bhajans and methods of singing.

The traditional form of bhajan in south india is known as Sampradya Bhajans. In the past few decades, this has seen a lot of upswing in popularity thanks mainly to Swami Haridhos Giri.

***Great Exponents:*** The medieval age saw devotees like Tulsidas, Surdas, Meera, Narottama Dasa (founder of Garanhati style), Kabir and others composing bhajans. In the modern times, composers like Pt. V. D. Paluskar and Pt. V. N. Bhatkhande have tried to mingle Raga Sangeet or Indian classical music-which had been an exclusive domain of the elite-with bhajans, thereby democratizing the Raga tradition. Chanting of bhajans and kirtan continues to be a favourite mode of worship in the Bhakti tradition of Hinduism, a tradition often regarded as far more accessible to the average person. This popularity is also reflected in the emphasis of many different gurus on chanting. For instance, devotees of Sathya Sai Baba of Puttaparthi all over the world perform bhajans on every Thursday (and Saturday or Sunday) wherein they refer to God with various names, such as: Rama, Krishna, Waheguru, Buddha, Mahavir, Zoroaster, Sathya Sai Baba himself, and other names.

***Popularity with the Masses:*** The common masses indulge in bhajan-singing without realizing that such traditional methods of invoking the divine can have a tremendous stress-removing impact. Bhajan *mandalis*, or gatherings, that have existed in the Indian villages since the beginning of the Bhakti era, have proved to be great social levelers, where individuals unhesitatingly participate in the singing, relegating their petty differences to the background. This participatory action elicits recreation and consequently a kind of mental relaxation. They close their eyes to ensure that they concentrate on God and nothing else.

***Modern Forms:*** While most Hindus devoutly sing bhajan in its more traditional form, there are smaller groups that experiment with incorporation of non-Indian instruments like the guitar and interspersing Western themes like jazz.

***Mixture of Modern and Traditional Forms:*** Bhajan in a traditional form popularised by the name "Sringeri Bhajans" and "Jyothirbhajan" since 50 years by Sri.R.V. Krishnabhat in Bangalore besides his teacher profession. Bhajans with the flavour of classical ragas and touch of tala perfection is the speciality of Sringeri bhajans. It also has mix of modern bhajans, kirtans and traditional bhajans. Jyothirbhajan is the most important part of it which has gained popularity besides the usual bhajans.

***Usage in Surat Shabd Yoga:*** In Surat Shabd Yoga, the spiritual exercises (sadhanas) include repetition, particularly silent repetition of a mantra given at initiation), and bhajan (listening to the inner sounds of the or the Shabd Master).

***Darshan:*** Darshan is a Sanskrit and Hindu (also used to some extent in Urdu) term meaning sight (in the sense of an instance of seeing something or somebody), vision, apparition, or a glimpse. It is most commonly used for visions of the divine; that is, of a god or a very holy person or artifact. One could receive "darshan" of the deity in the temple or from a great saintly person, such as the Spiritual Master.

1. In India people will travel hundreds of kilometres for the darshan, the look, of a holy man or woman because this look is to confer blessings. Conversely, looks of anger or envy are widely feared.
2. "Darshan" means *Seeing*, derived from the root *drsh*= "to see" (compare Greek *derkomai*). To see with reverence and devotion. The term is used specifically for beholding highly revered people with the intention of inwardly contacting and receiving their grace and blessings. "By doing darshan properly a devotee develops affection for God, and God develops affection for that devotee."
3. In Indian culture, the touching of the feet (*pranam* or *charaoasparsh*) is a show of respect and it is often an integral part of darshan. Children do touch the feet of

their family elders while people of all ages will bend to touch the feet of a great guru or the icon of a Deva (angel) or a form of God (such as Rama or Krishna).

4. Vedanta darshan is also the philosophy of life as revealed in the Upanishads

***Diksha:*** In Hinduism, diksha is the ritual of initiation into the worship of some deity by a guru (diksha guru) who bestows mantra(s) and takes the karma of the initiate-at least in case of Vaishnava diksha, as per Hari Bhakti Vilasa 1.70:

*raji catmatyaja dosah patni-papam sva-bhartari*
*tatha sisyartjitam papam guruh prapnoti niscita*
*"The faults of the counselor fall on the king, and the sins of a wife fall on her husband. In the same way a spiritual master attains the sins of his disciple. That is certain."*

Diksha primarily means a transfer of spiritual knowledge. Vishnu Yamala (tantra) says:

*divyam jnanam yato dadyat kuryat papasya sanksayam*
*tasmad dikseti sa prokta desikais tattva-kovidaih*
*"The process that bestows divyam jnanam (transcendental, spiritual knowledge) and destroys sin (papa), the seed of sin and ignorance, is called diksha by the spiritual persons who have seen the Truth (desikais tattva-kovidaih)."*

Vaishnava pancaratrika system requires a sadhaka to undergo the process known as pancha samskara consisting of pancha (five) stages of samskara (purification):

*tapah pundram tatha nama mantro yagas ca pancamah*
*ami hi panca-samskarah paramaikanti-hetavah*
*"Tapah, pundra, nama, mantra, and yaga; these five items comprise pancha samskara. They are the cause of intense devotion to Lord Hari."*
*yatha kancanatam yati kamsyam rasa-vidhanatah*
*tatha diksa-vidhanena dvijatvam jayate nrnam*
*"As bell metal is turned to gold when mixed with mercury in an alchemical process, so one who is properly trained and initiated by a bona fide spiritual master becomes*

*a brahmana immediately." (Tattva-sagara, quoted in Hari-bhakti-vilasa 2.12)*

Other sampradayas use different procedures.

Another type of diksha, into a monastic order, involves a vow of celibacy, renunciation of all personal possessions and of all worldly duties, including family ties. Diksha has the same meaning in Jainism. Diksha is also called *Charitra* or *Mahanibhiskraman* in Jainism.

An organization called Oneness University in South India, founded by Sri Bhagavan and Sri Amma teaches diksha as a process by which divine energy can be transmitted. They explain that this will lead to individual enlightenment and eventually by the year 2012 to collective enlightenment. At present the movement has educated thousands of diksha givers in the western world and millions of followers in India.

***Mantra:*** A mantra is a religious syllable or poem, typically from the Sanskrit language. Their use varies according to the school and philosophy associated with the mantra. They are primarily used as spiritual conduits, words or vibrations that instill one-pointed concentration in the devotee. Other purposes have included religious ceremonies to accumulate wealth, avoid danger, or eliminate enemies. Mantras originated in India with Vedic Hinduism and were later adopted by Buddhists, Sikhs and Jains, now popular in various modern forms of spiritual practice which are loosely based on practices of these Eastern religions.

***The Sanskrit Word Mantra:*** Consists of the root *man-* "to think" (also in *manas* "mind") and the suffix-*tra* meaning, tool, hence a literal translation would be "instṛument of thought". Mantras are interpreted to be effective as sound (vibration), to the effect that great emphasis is put on correct pronunciation (resulting in an early development of a science of phonetics in India). They are intended to deliver the mind from illusion and material inclinations. Chanting is the process of repeating a mantra.

Mantras have some features in common with spells in general, in that they are a translation of the human will or desire into a form of action. Indeed, Dr. Edward Conze, a scholar of Buddhism, frequently translated "mantra" as "spell". As symbols, sounds are seen to effect what they symbolise. Vocal sounds are frequently thought of as having magical powers, or even of representing the words or speech of a deity. For the authors of the Hindu scriptures of the Upanishads, the syllable Aum, itself constituting a mantra, represents Brahman, the godhead, as well as the whole of creation. Merely pronouncing this syllable is to experience the divine in a very direct way.

Kukai suggests that all sounds are the voice of the Dharmakaya Buddha—*i.e.* as in Hindu Upanishadic and Yogic thought, these sounds are manifestations of ultimate reality. We should not think that this is peculiar to Eastern culture, however. Words do have a mysterious power to affect us. Accepted scholarly etymology links the word with "manas" meaning "mind" and 'trana' for protection so that a mantra is something which protects the mind—however in practice we will see that mantra is considered to do far more than simply protect the mind.

For many cultures it is the written letters that have power the Hebrew Kabbalah for instance, or the Anglo-Saxon Runes. Letters can have an oracular function even. But in India special conditions applied that meant that writing was very definitely inferior to the spoken word. The Brahmins were the priestly caste of the Aryan peoples. It was they that preserved the holy writings — initially the Vedas, but later also the Upanishads. For years, they were the only ones who knew the mantras or sacred formulas that had to be chanted at every important occasion.

However, with the advent of egalitarian Hindu schools of Yoga, Vedanta, Tantra and Bhakti, it is now the case that intra-family and community mantras are passed on freely as part of generally practiced Hindu religion. Such was the influence of the more orthodox attitude of the elite nature of mantra knowledge that even the Buddhists, who repudiated the whole idea of caste, and of the efficacy of the old rituals, called themselves the shravakas, that is, "the hearers". A wise person in India was one who had "heard much". Mantras then are *sound symbols*. What they symbolise and how they function depends on the context, and the mind of the person repeating them. Studies in sound symbolism suggest that vocal sounds have meaning whether we are aware of it or not. And indeed that there can be multiple layers of symbolism associated with each sound. So even if we do not understand them, mantras are not simply meaningless mumbo jumbo — no vocal utterance is entirely without meaning. We can look at mantra as a range of different contexts to see what they can mean in those contexts: *Om* may mean something quite different to a Hindu and a Tibetan Buddhist. The analysis of Kukai, a 9th century Japanese Buddhist is revealing. See below.

While Hindu tantras eventually came to see the letters as well as the sounds as representatives of the divine, it was when Buddhism travelled to China that a major shift in emphasis towards writing came about. China lacked a unifying, ecclesiastic language like Sanskrit, and achieved its cultural unity by having a written language that was flexible in pronunciation but more precise in terms of the concepts that each character represented. In fact the Indians had several scripts which were all equally serviceable for writing Sanskrit.

Hence the Chinese prized written language much more highly than did the Indian Buddhist missionaries, and the writing of mantras became a spiritual practice in its own right. So that whereas Brahmins had been very strict on correct pronunciation, the Chinese, and indeed other Far-Eastern Buddhists were less concerned with this than correctly writing something down. The practice of writing mantras, and copying texts as a spiritual practice, became very refined in Japan, and the writing in the Siddham script in which the Sanskrit of many Buddhist Sutras were written is only really seen in Japan nowadays. However, written mantra-repetition in Hindu practices, with Sanskrit in any number of scripts, is well-known to many sects in India as well.

***Mantra in Hinduism:*** Mantras were originally conceived in the great Hindu scriptures known as the Vedas. Within practically all Hindu scriptures, the writing is formed in painstakingly crafted two line "shlokas" and most mantras follow this pattern, although mantras are often found in single line or even single word combinations.

***Aum:*** The most basic mantra is *Aum*, which in Hinduism is known as the "pranava mantra," the source of all mantras. The philosophy behind this is the Hindu idea of nama-rupa (name-form), which supposes that all things, ideas or entities in existence, within the phenomenological cosmos, have name and form of some sort. The most basic name and form is the primordial vibration of Aum, as it is the first manifested nama-rupa of Brahman, the unmanifest reality/unreality. Essentially, before existence and beyond existence is only One reality, Brahman, and the first manifestation of Brahman in existence is Aum. For this reason, Aum is considered to be the most fundamental and powerful mantra, and thus is prefixed and suffixed to all Hindu prayers. While some mantras may invoke individual dieties or principles, the most fundamental mantras, like 'Aum,' the 'Shanti Mantra,' the 'Gayatri Mantra' and others all ultimately focus on the One reality. In Hinduism mantra is also used to worship One God, and it is worshiped as God. It is used as a vehicle to attain liberation.

In the Hindu tantras the universe is sound. The supreme (para) brings forth existence through the Word (Shabda). Creation consists of vibrations at various frequencies and amplitudes giving rise to the phenomena of the world. The purest vibrations are the var.na, the imperishable letters which are revealed to us, imperfectly as the audible sounds and visible forms.

Varnas are the atoms of sound. A complex symbolic association was built up between letters and the elements, gods, signs of the zodiac, parts of the body — letters became rich in these associations. For example in the Aitrareya-aranya-Upanishad we find:

"The mute consonants represent the earth, the sibilants the sky, the vowels heaven. The mute consonants represent fire, the sibilants air, the vowels the sun? The mute consonants represent the eye, the sibilants the ear, the vowels the mind."

In effect each letter became a mantra and the language of the Vedas, Sanskrit, corresponds profoundly to the nature of things. Thus the Vedas come to represent reality itself. The seed syllable Om represents the underlying unity of reality, which is Brahman.

***Mantra Japa:*** Mantra Japa was a concept of the Vedic sages that incorporates mantras as one of the main forms of puja, or worship, whose ultimate end is seen as moksha/liberation. Essentially, Mantra Japa means repetition of mantra, and has become an established practice of all Hindu streams, from the various Yoga to Tantra. It involves repetition of a mantra over and over again, usually in cycles of auspicious numbers (in multiples of three), the most popular being 108. For this reason, Hindu malas (bead necklaces) developed, containing 108 beads and a head "meru" bead. The devotee performing japa using his/her fingers counts each bead as he/she repeats the chosen mantra. Having reached 108 repetitions, if he/she wishes to continue another cycle of mantras, the devotee must turn the mala around without crossing the "meru" bead and repeat.

It is said that through japa the devotee attains one-pointedness, or extreme focus, on the chosen deity or principal idea of the mantra. The vibrations and sounds of the mantra are considered extremely important, and thus reverberations of the sound are supposed to awaken the prana or spiritual life force and even stimulate chakras according to many Hindu schools of thought.

Any shloka from holy Hindu texts like the Vedas, Upanishads, Bhagavad Gita, Yoga Sutra, even the Mahabharata, Ramayana, Durga saptashati or Chandi are considered powerful enough to be repeated to great effect, and have therefore the status of a mantra.

A very common mantra is formed by taking a deity's name. Called Nama japa and saluting it in such a manner: "Aum namah—" or "Aum Jai (Hail!) —" or several such permutations. Common examples are "Aum namah Shivaya" (Aum I bow to Lord Shiva), "Aum Namo Narayanaya"; or "Aum Namo Bhagavate Vasudevāya," (Salutations to the Universal God

Vishnu), "Aum Shri Ganeshaya Namah" (Aum to Shri Ganesha) and "Aum Kalikayai Namah" and "Aum Hrim Chandikãyai Namah." (*i.e.*, mantras to Devi.)

***Some Hindu Mantras:*** The most representative mantra of all the Hindu mantras is the famed Gayatri Mantra:

*Om Bhur Buva Sva*
*Tat Savitur Varenyam*
*Bhargo Devasya Dhimahi*
*Dhiyo Yo Na Prachodayat*

It is considered one of the most universal of all Hindu mantras, invoking the universal Brahman as the principle of knowledge and the illumination of the primordial Sun.

Lead me from Ignorance to Truth

asato Ca sat gamaya / tamaso Ca jyotir gamaya / Crityor-Ca amritam gamaya / Om uanti uanti uanti

"from non-being to being lead me, from darkness to light lead me, from death to immortality lead me."

Mantra to Worship the Guru

*Guru brahma*
*Guru vishnu*
*Guru devo maheshwarah*
*Guru sakshat parabrahma*
*Tas mai Shri Guru vai namaha*

***Translation:*** I bow to that Guru who is Lord Brahma (the creator of the comos), Lord Vishnu (the sustainer of the cosmos) and Lord Maheswara (the destroyer of the cosmos). Indeed the Guru is nothing but the Supreme Brahman (the God).

### *The Shanti Mantras*

*Om sahanaavavatu*
*Sahanau bhunaktu*
*Saha viiryan karavaavahai*
*Tejasvi naavadhiitamastu*
*Maa vidvishhaavahai*
*May we be protected together.*

*May we be nourished together.*

*May we work together with great vigor.*

*May our study be enlightening*

*May no obstacle arise between us.*

*Om shaantih shaantih shaantih*

*Om peace, peace, peace.*

*—Black [krishna] Yajurveda Taittiriya Upanishad 2.2.2*

***Universal Prayer***

*Sarveuaam Svastir Bhavatu*

*Sarveuam Santir Bhavatū*

*Sarveuam· Purgam Bhavatu*

*Sarveuam Cangalam Bhavatu*

(May good befall all, May there be peace for all, May all be fit for perfection, and· May all experience that which is auspicious.)

*Sarve Bhavantu Sukhinaha*

*Sarve Santu Giramayaha*

*Sarve Badragi Pasyantu*

*Ca Kascidh-dhuhkha Bhaga-Bhavet*

(Om, May all be happy. May all be healthy. May we all experience what is good and let no one suffer. Om, Peace, Peace, Peace!)

***Hare Krishna Maha Mantra:*** A mantra comprising of the names *Hare*, *Krishna* and *Rama*. It appears originally in the Kali-saoþaraoa Upanisad (Kali Santarana Upanisad):

*Hare Krishna Hare Krishna*

*Krishna Krishna Hare Hare*

*Hare Rama Hare Rama*

*Rama Rama Hare Hare*

In the 16th century, Chaitanya Mahaprabhu (considered an incarnation of Krishna), founder of Gaudiya Vaishnavism, along with his followers, spread this mantra across India through public congregational chanting (kirtan). Mahaprabhu and his followers had traveled from town to town singing this mantra, said to bring salvation to whoever happens to hear it. It is often referred to as the 'Maha Mantra' by practitioners. When A.C. Bhaktivedanta Swami Prabhupada established ISKCON (the International Society for Krishna Consciousness), a branch of the Brahma Madhva Gaudiya Vaishnava sampradaya, he brought the "Hare Krishna" mantra to the West and spread it around the world as an easy yet sublime way of liberation in the Age of Kali.

***Other Examples***

- *Tat Twam Asi* "Thou Are That"
- *Aham Brahmasmi* "I am the Creater"
- *Sohum* "That I am"
- *Tryambakam.*
- *Surya Namaskara*

***The Hindu Bija Mantra:*** The most revered of all Bija mantras is Om/Aum which is the starting point of many other mantras. (see below for an example)

*Aum Krim Krim Krim Hoom Hum:*

*Krim Krim Krim Hum Hum Hrim Hrim Swaha*

***Hindu Philosophy and Religion***

Sanatan (eternal) Dharma as a universal tradition has room for all faiths and all religious and spiritual practices regardless of the time or country of their origin. Yet it places religious and spiritual teachings in their appropriate place relative to the ultimate goal of Self-realization, to which secondary practices are subordinated.

Sanatan Dharma also recognizes that the greater portion of human religious aspirations has always been unknown, undefined and outside of any institutionalized belief. Sanatan Dharma thereby gives reverence to individual spiritual experience over any formal religious doctrine. Wherever the Universal Truth is manifest; there is Sanatan Dharma—whether it is in a field of religion, art or science, or in the life of a person or community. Wherever the Universal Truth is not recognized, or is scaled down or limited to a particular group, book or person, even if done so in the name of God, there Sanatan Dharma ceases to function, whatever the activity is called. — *Dr. David Frawley*

By the laws of Dharma that govern body and mind, you must fear sin and act righteously. Wise men by thinking and behaving in this way become worthy to gain bliss both here and hereafter. — *Natchintanai Scripture.*

***The Significance of the Symbol Om:*** The symbol Om (also called Pranava), is the most sacred symbol in Hinduism. Volumes have been written in Sanskrit illustrating the significance of this mystic symbol. Although this symbol is mentioned in all the Upanishads and in all Hindu scriptures, it is especially elaborated upon in the Taittiriya, Chandogya and Mundaka Upanishads.

The goal, which all Vedas declare, which all austerities aim at, and which human desire when they live a life continence, I will tell you briefly it is Om. The syllable Om is indeed Brahman. This syllable Om is the highest. Whosoever knows this symbol obtains all that he desires. This is the best support; this is the highest support. Whosoever knows this support is adored in the world of Brahman. *Katha Upanishd I, ii, 15-17*

The symbol of Om contains of three curves, one semicircle and a dot. The large lower curve symbolizes the waking state; the upper curve denotes deep sleep (or the unconscious) state, and the lower curve (which lies between deep sleep and the waking state) signifies the dream state. These three states of an individual's consciousness, and therefore the entire physical phenomenon, are represented by the three curves. The dot signifies the Absolute (fourth or Turiya state of consciousness), which illuminates the other three states.

The semicircle symbolizes maya and separates the dot from the other three curves. The semicircle is open on the top, which means that the absolute is infinite and is not affected by maya. Maya only affects the manifested phenomenon. In this way the form of Om symbolizes the infinite Brahman and the entire Universe.

*Uttering the monosyllable Om, the eternal world of Brahman, One who departs leaving the body (at death), he attains the superior goal.* — Bhagavad Gita, 8.13

***Mantra in Buddhism:*** History of Buddhism Time line of Buddhism Buddhist councils.

Foundations Four Noble Truths Noble Eightfold Path The Five Precepts Nirvna • Three Jewels:

*Key Concepts Three marks of existence Skandha • Cosmology • Dharma Samsara • Rebirth • Shunyata Pratitya-samutpada • Karma.*

***Mantra in Shingon Buddhism:*** *Kkai* advanced a general theory of language based on his analysis of two forms of Buddhist ritual language: *dharani* (dharani) and *mantra*. Mantra is restricted to esoteric Buddhist practice whereas dharani is found in both esoteric and exoteric ritual. Dharanis for instance are found in the Pali Canon see below. The term "shingon" (lit true word) is a Japanese translation of the Chinese term for mantra, chen yen.

The word *dharani* derives from a Sanskrit root dhr which means to hold, or maintain. Ryuichi Abe suggests that it is generally understood as a mnemonic device which encapsulates the meaning of a section or chapter of a sutra. This is perhaps related to the use of verse summaries at the end of texts as in the Udana which is generally acknowledged as being in the oldest strata of the Pali Canon. Dharanis are also considered to protect the one who chants them from malign influences and calamities.

The term *mantra* is traditionally said to be derived from two roots: "man", to think; and the action oriented (krt) suffix "tra". Thus a mantra can be considered to be a linguistic device for deepening ones thought, or in the Buddhist context for developing the enlightened mind. However it is also true that mantras have been used as magic spells for very mundane purposes such as attaining wealth and long life, and eliminating enemies.

The distinction between dharani and mantra is a difficult one to make. We can say that all mantras are dharanis but that not all dharanis are mantras. Mantras do tend to be shorter. Both tend to contain a number of unintelligible phonic fragments such as Om, or Aum which is perhaps why some people consider them to be essentially meaningless. Kukai made mantra a special class of dharani which showed that every syllable of a dharani was a manifestation of the true nature of reality — in Buddhist terms that all sound is a manifestation of shunyata or emptiness of self-nature.

Thus rather than being devoid of meaning, Kukai suggests that dharanis are in fact saturated with meaning — every syllable is symbolic on multiple levels. One of Kukai's distinctive contributions was to take this symbolic association even further by saying that there is no essential difference between the syllables of mantras and sacred texts, and those of ordinary language. If one understood the workings of mantra, then any sounds could be a representative of ultimate reality. This emphasis on sounds was one of the drivers for Kukai's championing of the phonetic writing system, the kana, which was adopted in Japan around the time of Kukai. He is generally credited with the invention of the kana, but there is apparently some doubt about this story amongst scholars.

This mantra-based theory of language had a powerful effect on Japanese thought and society which up until Kukai's time had been dominated by imported Chinese culture of thought, particularly in the form of the Classical Chinese language which was used in the court and amongst the literati, and Confucianism which was the dominant political ideology. In particular Kukai was able to use this new theory of language to create links between indigenous Japanese culture and Buddhism.

For instance, he made a link between the Buddha Mahavairocana and the Shinto sun Goddess Amaterasu. Since the emperors were thought to be descended form Amaterasu, Kukai had found a powerful connection here that linked the emperors with the Buddha, and also in finding a way to integrate Shinto with Buddhism, something that had not happened with Confucianism. Buddhism then became essentially an indigenous religion in a way that Confucianism had not. And it was through language, and mantra that this connection was made. Kukai helped to elucidate what mantra is in a way that had not been done before: he addresses the fundamental questions of what a text is, how signs function, and above all, what language is. In this he covers some of the same ground as modern day Structuralists and others scholars of language, although he comes to very different conclusions.

In this system of thought all sounds are said to originate from "a" — which is the short *a* sound in father. For esoteric Buddhism "a" has a special function because it is associated with Shunyata or the idea that no thing exists in its own right, but is contingent upon causes and conditions. (See Dependent origination) In Sanskrit "a" is a prefix which changes the meaning of a word into its opposite, so "vidya" is understanding, and "avidya" is ignorance (the same arrangement is also found in many Greek words, like *e.g.* "atheism" vs. "theism" and "apathy" vs. "pathos"). The letter a is both visualised in the Siddham script, and pronounced in rituals and meditation practices. In the Mahavairocana Sutra which is central to Shingon Buddhism it says: Thanks to the original vows of the Buddhas and Bodhisattvas, a miraculous force resides in the mantras, so that by pronouncing them one acquires merit without limits".

***Mantra in Indo-Tibetan Buddhism:*** Conze distinguishes three periods in the Buddhist use of mantra. Initially, like their fellow Indians, Buddhists used mantra as protective spells to ward of malign influences. Despite a Vinaya rule which forbids monks engaging in the Brahminical practice of chanting mantras for material gain, there are a number of protective for a group of ascetic monks. However, even at this early stage, there is perhaps something more than animistic magic at work. Particularly in the case of the Ratana Sutta the efficacy of the verses seems to be related to the concept of "truth". Each verse of the sutta ends with "by the virtue of this truth may there be happiness".

Later mantras were used more to guard the spiritual life of the chanter, and sections on mantras began to be included in some Mahayana sutras such as the White Lotus Sutra, and the Lankavatara Sutra. The scope of protection also changed in this time. In the Sutra of Golden Light the Four Great Kings promise to exercise sovereignty over the different classes of demigods, to protect the whole of Jambudvipa (the India subcontinent), to protect monks who proclaim the sutra, and to protect kings who patronise the monks who proclaim the sutra.

The apotheosis of this type of approach is the Nichiren school of Buddhism that was founded in 13th century Japan, and which distilled all Buddhist practice down to the veneration of the Lotus Sutra through recitation of the daimoku: "Nam myoho renge kyo" which translates as "Homage to the Lotus Sutra".

Then mantra began, in about the 7th century, to take centre stage and become a vehicle for salvation in their own right. Tantra started to gain momentum in the 6th and 7th century, with specifically Buddhist forms appearing as early as 300CE. *Mantrayana* was an early name for the what is now more commonly known as *Vajrayana*, which gives us a hint as to the place of mantra in Indo-Tibetan Buddhism.

The aim of Vajrayana practice is to give the practitioner a direct experience of reality, of things as they really are. Mantras function as symbols of that reality, and different mantras are different aspects of that reality — for example wisdom or compassion. Mantras are almost always associated with a particular deity, with one exception being the Prajnaparamita mantra associated with the Heart Sutra. One of the key Vajrayana strategies for bringing about a direct experience of reality is to engage the entire psycho-physical organism in the practices.

In one Buddhist analysis the person consists of body, speech and mind. So a typical sadhana or meditation practice might include mudras, or symbolic hand gestures, or even full body prostrations; the recitations of mantras; as well as the visualisation of celestial beings and visualising the letters of the mantra which is being recited. Clearly here mantra is associated with speech. The meditator may visualise the letters in front of themselves, or within their body. They may pronounced out loud, or internally in the mind only.

***Om Mani Padme Hum:*** Probably the most famous mantra of Buddhism is Om mani padme hum (renounced the same way), the six syllable mantra of the Bodhisattva of compassion Avalokiteshvara (Tibetan: *Chenrezig*, Chinese: *Guanyin*). This mantra is particularly associated with the four-armed Shadakshari form of Avalokiteshvara. The Dalai Lama is said to be an incarnation of Avalokiteshvara, and so the mantra is especially revered by his devotees. Donald Lopez gives a good discussion of this mantra and its various interpretations in his book *Prisoners of Shangrila: Tibetan Buddhism and the West*. Lopez is an authoritative writer and challenges the stereotypical analysis of the mantra as meaning "The Jewel in the Lotus", an interpretation that is not supported by either a linguistic analysis, nor by Tibetan tradition, and is symptomatic of the Western Orientalist approach to the 'exotic' East.

He suggests that Manipadma is actually the name of a bodhisattva, a form of Avalokiteshvara who has many other names in any case including Padmapani or *lotus flower in hand*. The Brahminical insistence on absolutely correct pronunciation of Sanskrit broke down as Buddhism was exported to other countries where the inhabitants found it impossible to reproduce the sounds. So in Tibet, for instance, where this mantra is on the lips of many Tibetans all their waking hours, the mantra is pronounced *Om mani peme hung*.

***Some other Mantras used by Tibetan Buddhists:*** The following list of mantras is from Kailash-Journal of Himalayan Studies, Volume 1, Number 2, 1973. (pp. 168-169) (augmented by other contributors). It also includes renderings of *Om mani padme hum*.

Please note that the word *swaha* is sometimes shown as *svaha*, and is usually pronounced as 'so-ha' by Tibetans. Spellings tend to vary in the transliterations to English, for example, *hum* and *hung* are generally the same word. The mantras used in Tibetan Buddhist practice are in Sanskrit, to preserve the original mantras. Visualizations and other practices are usually done in the Tibetan language.

- *Om wangishwari hum:* This is the mantra of the Mahabodhisattva Manjusri, Tibetan: Jampelyang (Wylie "'jam dpal dbyangs")... The Buddha in his wisdom aspect.
- *Om mani padme hum:* The mantra of Chenrezig, Mahabodhisattva, the Buddha in his compassion aspect.
- *Om vajrapani hum* The mantra of the Buddha as Protector of the Secret Teachings. ie: as the Mahabodhisattva Channa Dorje (Vajrapani).
- *om vajrasattva hum:* The short mantra for Vajrasattva, there is also a full 100-syllable mantra for Vajrasattva.
- *Om ah hum vajra guru padma siddhi hum:* The mantra of the Vajraguru Guru Padma Sambhava who established Mahayana Buddhism and Tantra in Tibet.
- *Om tare tuttare ture swaha:* The mantra of Jetsun Dolma or Tara, the Mother of the Buddhas.
- *Om tare tuttare ture mama ayurjnana punye pushting svaha:* The mantra of Dölkar or White Tara, the emanation of Tara representing long life and health.
- *Om amarani jiwantiye swaha:* The mantra of the Buddha of limitless life: the Buddha Amitayus (Tibetan Tsépagmed) in celestial form.
- *Om dhrum swaha:* The purificatory mantra of the mother Namgyalma.
- *Om ami dhewa hri:* The mantra of the Buddha Amitabha (Hopagmed) of the Western Buddhafield, his skin the colour of the setting sun.
- *Om ah ra pa tsa na dhih:* The mantra of the "sweet-voiced one", Jampelyang (Wylie "'jam dpal dbyangs") or Manjusri, the Bodhisattva of wisdom.
- *Hung vajra phat:* The mantra of the Mahabodhisattva Vajrapani in his angry (Dragpo) form.
- *Om muni muni maha muniye sakyamuni swaha:* The mantra of Buddha Sakyamuni, the historical Buddha
- *Om gate gate paragate parasamgate bodhi swaha:* The mantra of the Heart of the Perfection of

***Wisdom Sutra:*** *Om maitri maitreya maha karuna ye:* The Maitri mantra, bija mantra of MahaBodhisattva Maitreya.

- *Namo bhagavate Bhaishajya-guru vaidurya-praba-rajaya tathagataya arthate samyak-sambuddhaya tadyata OM bhaishajye bhaishajye bhaishajya-samudgate svaha:* The mantra of the 'Medicine Buddha', from Chinese translations of the Master of Healing Sutra.

***Mantra in Sikhism:*** In the Sikh religion a "Mantar" or "Mantra" is a Shabad (Word or hymn) from Gurbani to concentrate the mind on God and the message of the Ten Gurus.

Mantras have two components of primary importance-Meaning and Sound. First is the actual meaning of the word or words and the second is the effective sound (vibration). For the mantra to be effective, great emphasis is put on correct pronunciation and the level of concentration of the mind on the meaning of the word or words that are recited.

Due to this emphasis, some care has to be taken regarding the place and surrounding in which the mantras are recited; the way in which these are delivered-ie, a loud; quietly; in a group; with music; without music; etc. The purpose to mantras is to deliver the mind from illusion and material inclinations and to bring concentration and focus to the mind.

- Chanting is the process of the continuous repeating a mantra.

***The Main Mantras of Sikhism are:***

- The Gurmantar, which is Waheguru
- The Mool Mantar which start Ek-onkar, Satnam ....

***Mantra in other Traditions or Contexts:*** Transcendental Meditation, also known simply as 'TM', uses what the group refers to as 'simple mantras'-as a meditative focus. TM was founded by Maharishi Mahesh Yogi. According to the practice can result in a number of material benefits such as relaxation, reduced stress, better health, better self image; but it can also benefit the world by reducing violence and crime, and generally improve quality of life. The founder was well versed in Hindu tradition, but TM attempts to separate itself from that tradition these days. Simple two-syllable mantras are used.

Mantra practice has also been enthusiastically taken up by various New Age groups and individuals, although this is typically out of context, and from the point of view of a genuine Hindu or Buddhist practitioner lacks depth. The mere repetition of syllables can have a calming effect on the mind, but the traditionalist would argue that mantra can be an effective way of changing the level of one's consciousness when approached in traditional way.

Some forms of Jewish meditation use mantras, although they do not call them by that name. Hasidic Jews sing phrases from the Hebrew Bible over and over, in a form of rhythmic chant, often accompanied by drumming on the table. They also use wordless sacred meditation tunes called niggunim, which are revealed through the higher consciousness of the Rebbes (Hasidic leaders, similar to gurus). Some subgroups of the Breslov Hasidic movement use the mantra Na Nach Nachma, based on the name of their founder, Rabbi Nachman of Breslov. All of these practices are done to achieve deveikut which means "cleaving (holding on) to God." Lubavitch Hasidim of the messianic faith use the mantra of Yechi to draw on the power of their Rebbe.

The spiritual exercises of Surat Shabda Yoga include simran (repetition, particularly silent repetition of a mantra given at initiation), dhyan (concentration, viewing, or contemplation, particularly on the Inner Master), and bhajan (listening to the inner sounds of the Shabda or the Shabda Master).

In the Islamic Sufi tradition, chants of the 99 Names of Allah are popular invocations of attibutes as are the names of the Prophet.

In Neo-Pagan ritual, deities may be invoked by a recitation of their many names or aspects.

In Christianity, repetitive prayer using prayer beads such as a rosary or chotki includes well known mantras such as the Jesus prayer and Hail Mary. A form of Christian meditation was taught by Dom John Main that involves the silent repetition of a mantra.

## Puja

Puja (alternative transliteration pooja, Sanskrit: reverence or worship) is a religious ritual that Hindus perform on a variety of occasions to pray or show respect to God (or gods).

Most practicing Hindus pray once or twice a day. Puja's are reserved for special occasions like house warming. Puja is often done after a shower or bath and it is recommended that rites be performed before food intake to ensure sattvic qualities and full concentration (dhyan). Puja is also performed on special occasions beside of the daily ritual. These include Durga Puja, Pongal and Lakshmi Puja and other religious occasions. Puja or Pooja is also a Hindu female first name.

***Puja Rituals:*** A puja can be performed to honour worship God in one of his many forms, one of the demigods (Deva's), a Guru, cows (Go-Puja), or other sacred personalities or objects. The worship consists of offering various articles to the object of worship, such as flowers and vegetarian food, and usually includes lighting a candle or incense. The puja may also represent the welcoming ceremony and thus is also performed for prominent guests to one's home. In the Vedic tradition a guest is considered a form of God (*atithi Narayana*).

Puja ceremonies consist of meditation (dhyana), austerity (tapa), chanting (mantra), scripture reading (svadhyaya), offering food (thaal) and prostrations (panchanga or ashtanga pranama, dandavat). The individual also applies a tilaka mark on the forehead with sandalwood paste, and then a vermillion (kumkum) dot (chandlo) in its centre. This signifies submission to the Almighty and also His Omnipresence. Puja is usually concluded with aarti to the Lord.

Puja may be performed by an individual worshipper or in gatherings. The ritual may be observed in silence or accompanied by prayers. Sometimes a puja is done for the benefit of certain people, for whom priests or relatives ask blessings. A Hindu priest (called a Pundit) will chant prayers in Sanskrit or some other language while performing puja. Large pujas request the presence of fellow believers and pray to the god or goddesses in question. This usually involves a full day ritual where people are present for the actual puja ceremony and have puja prasad (blessed food that should not be thrown out), followed by bhajans (religious prayer songs) and an all-vegetarian dinner.

***27 Steps of a Puja***

A puja generally takes the form of the Lord as your guest:

1. Dhyaanam Samarpayami (Think or meditate on the Lord)
2. Aawaahanam Samarpayami (Invite the Lord into your home/heart)
3. Aasanam Samarpayami (Offer a seat)
4. Paadyam Samarpayami (Offer water to wash the feet)
5. Arghyam Samarpayami (Offer water to wash the hands)
6. Aachamaneeyam Samarpayami (Offer water to drink)
7. Snaanam Samarpayami (Give bath)
8. Maha Abhishekam Samarpayami (Main head bath)
9. Pratishtaapayaami (Make Him seated)
10. Vasthram Samarpayami (Offer clothes)
11. Yajnopaveetham Samarpayami (Offer the Holy Thread)
12. Gandham Samarpayami (Offer sandlewood paste/ powder)
13. Akshatham Samarpayami (Offer Akshatha (rice))
14. Pushpam Samarpayami (Offer flowers)
15. Ashthothtra Poojam Samarpayami (Say the holy names of the Lord)
16. Dhoopam Aaghraapayaami (Offer fragrance)
17. Deepam Darshayaami (Offer light)
18. Neivedyam Samarpayami (Offer food)
19. Phalam Samarpayami (Offer fruits)

20. Taamboolam Samarpayami (Offer betel nut and leaves)
21. Dakshinam Samarpayami (Offer wealth)
22. Maha Nirajanam Samarpayami (Perform aarti)
23. Pradakshinam Samarpayami (Continue aarti)
24. Namaskaram Samarpayami (Prostrate before Him)
25. Mantra Pushpam Samarpayami (Offer incantations and flowers)
26. Praarthanaam Samarpayami (Offer prayers, request your desires)
27. Xamaapanam Samarpayami (Admit wrongdoings and ask for forgiveness)

***The Role of the Priest:*** Often, temple priests conduct pujas on behalf of sponsors. The sponsors either bear expenses of the puja ingredients or provide ingredients and *dakshina*.

***Satyanarayana Puja:*** The Satyanarayana Puja is unique in that it does not require a brahman to perform. The Satyanarayana Pooja is usually done on the *Poornima* day of every month (full moon day). It is also done on special occasions and during times of achievements as an offering of gratitude to the Lord. These occasions include marriage, graduation, and the purchase of a new home to name a few. In addition, it is said that a devotional performance of this pooja will bear children to infertile couples.

The pooja starts by a prayer to Lord Ganesha, the elephant God and remover of all obstacles that may occur as a result of incorrectly performing the pooja. This is done by chanting all the names of Lord Ganesha and offering *prasad* (a food offering, usually consisting of one of Lorg Ganesha's favourite foods-*modak*, a sugar and coconut mixture, or *lhadu*) and the showering of flower petals.

Another part of the prayer involves a prayer to the Navagraha's, which are the 9 important celestial beings, in the universe. They consist of Surya (the Sun), Chandra (the moon), Angaaraka/Chevaai (Mars), Budha (Mercury), Guru aka Bruhaspati (Jupiter), Shukra (Venus), Sani (Saturn), Rahu (the head of Demon snake), and Ketu (the tail of Demon snake).

The rest of the prayer consists worship to Lord Satyanarayana, an extremely benevolent form of Lord Vishnu. Again, names of Lord Satyanarayana are chanted along with offering of a variety of *prasads* (including a mixture of milk, honey, ghee/butter, yogurt, sugar) and flower petals.

Another requirement of the pooja is that the story of the pooja be heard among all those observing and partaking in the pooja. The story involves the origin of the pooja, the benefits of it, and the potential mishaps that may occur with the careless performance of the pooja.

The prayer concludes with an *Aarti*, which consists of revolving a small fire-lit-lamp in the vicinity of an image of the Lord. After the pooja is over, participants and observers of the pooja are required to injest in the *prasad* that was offered and blessed by the Lord.

### *Satsang*

Satsang (sanskrit sat = true, sanga = company) describes in indian philosophy 1) the company of the "highest truth"; 2) the company of a guru; 3) the company with an assembly of persons who listen to, talk about, and assimilate the truth. This practice also takes the form of listening to or reading scriptures, reflecting on, discussing and assimilating their meaning, meditating on the source of these words, and bringing their meaning into one's daily life. Especially in the tradition of advaita-vedanta, satsang with an "enlightened" master is considered to be a prerequisite. Contemporary satsang-teachers in the west sometimes mix traditional eastern knowledge with methods of modern psychology.

During a satsang with a teacher students are likely to ask questions. Satsangs also may contain elements like lectures, meditations, or recitations. The purpose of a satsang is not primarily to be found in the transmission of a mental teaching, but in the experience of the presence of an "awakened" or "enlightened" being, in which students are meant to come to the same level of inner freedom through the effect of an energetic resonance-phenomenon.

***Satsang in the West:*** The modern satsang masters have freed their teachings from the strict expectations of traditional advaita-teachers toward their followers. The masters assert that rituals or meditations are not necessary for inner freedom. Enlightenment is the ever-present truth that is being found beyond any conditions and spiritual states.

As attachment to thoughts and to unresolved emotions are considered to be the hindrances to this cognition, many teachers emphasize the importance of accepting emotions unbiased as they are, with no attempt of changing or dissolving them. This, they say, will take the energy away from the stories of the mind, and thus from the stream of thoughts. Others recommend to permanently "return to the moment" in order to reach the same result. Because these practices are aimed at experiencing freedom in the presence, they are not regarded as "techniques" with an outcome to be found in the future. The worldwide fast-growing satsang movement has its roots in H. W. L. Poonja, a student of Ramana Maharshi.

***Stotras***

Stotras are Hindu prayers that praise aspects of God, such as Devi, Siva, or Vishnu. Stotras, according to Swami Tapasyananda, are invariably uttered aloud and consist of chanting verses conveying the glory and attributes of God. The three most famous and sacred stotras in Hinduism are Lalitha Sahasranama, Shri Rudram Chamakam, and Vishnu Sahasranama. Other famous Stotras are: Sri Ramraksha Stotra, Sri Maruti Stotra.

## Hindu Wedding

Hindu wedding (*vivah* 5 or *shadi* in Hindi, *panigrahana* in Sanskrit, other terms are also used) ceremonies are traditionally conducted in Sanskrit, the language in which most holy Hindu ceremonies are conducted. They have many rituals that have evolved since traditional times and differ in many ways from the modern western wedding ceremony and also among the regions and caste. The Hindus attach a lot of importance to weddings and the ceremonies are very colourful and extend for several days. By the Hindu Marriage Act of 1955 passed by the Union Parliament of India, for all legal purposes, all Hindus of any caste, creed or sect, Sikh, Budhhists and Jains are considered as Hindus for the sake of the Hindu marriage Act— and can hence intermarry. By the Special Marriage Act, 1954, a Hindu can marry with a non-Hindu employing any ceremony provided certain legal conditions are fulfilled.

The pre-wedding ceremonies include engagement (involving vagdana or oral agreement and lagna-patra written declaration), and arrival of the marriage party at the brides residence, often in the form of a marriage procession. The post-marriage ceremonies involve welcoming the bride to her new home.

An important thing to note is that despite the fact that the modern Hinduism is based on the puja form of the worship of *devas* as enshrined in the Puranas, a Hindu marriage ceremony is essentially a Vedic yajna (a fire-sacrifice), in which the Aryan deities are invoked in the archaic Indo-Aryan style. The primary witness of a Hindu marriage is the fire-deity (or the Sacred Fire) *Agni*, and by law and by tradition, no Hindu marriage is deemed complete unless in the presence of the Sacred Fire, seven encirclements have been made around it by the bride and the groom together.

***Important Marriage Ceremonies:*** The Hindu marriage ceremonies vary in different regions and according to family traditions. The major ceremonies are the following.

- Invoking Lord Ganesh (Ganesh Puja)
- Evoking the holy fire (Agni Puja)
- Kanyadhan-Giving away the bride to the groom
- Tying of holy necklace (Mangalsutra)
- The Seven Holy Steps ("Saptapadi"), circling the fire
- Bride steps on the stone (Shilarohana)

Many of the ceremonies involve the pandit (priest) chanting mantras of various prayers and blessings for the couple.

Though Mangalya dharanam (tying of the holy mangalsutra) is considered to be the important part of the marriage, the wedding is considered complete only after Saptapadhi. The hindu marriage ceremony consists of these major rituals as described below but every part of India have some variations in all the ceremonies. These are the main ceremonies but the explanation of these rituals here is typically North Indian or Punjabi style and are not the same for all Hindu marriages.

## Saptapadi

The bridegroom gets up from his seat holding his bride's right hand. He then goes around the Holy Fire (Agni) from the right side, by lifting his bride's right feet at each step. This is done for seven steps. With each step, he recites a mantra addressed to bride with the following meaning:

*Let Lord Maha Vishnu follow each one of your steps for the following specific purposes.*

*To give you unlimited food.*

*To give you excellent health and energy.*

*To make you perform your vrithas (rituals) as ordained in Vedas, during your life time.*

*To give you happiness in life.*

*To make your cows and good animals to grow in strength and in numbers.*

*To make all the seasons be beneficial to you.*

*To make the homams (sacrifices to be done in Holy Fire) to be performed by you in your life as ordained in Vedas, successful and free from hindrances.*

The idea behind this is to pray to Lord Vishnu, the protector of life, for his blessings in marital life.

The groom then recites a mantra to convey the following meaning:

*After crossing seven steps with me thus, you should become my friend. I too have become your friend now. I will never discord this friendship and you should not also do that. Let us be together always. Let us resolve to do things in life in the same manner and tread the same path. Let us lead a life by liking and loving each other, having good heart and thoughts, and enjoying the food and our strong points together. Let us have undivided opinions. We will perform the vrithas united. Let us have same and joint desires. I will be Sama (one of the vedas); you will be Rig (another Veda). Let me be the Heaven; you be the Earth. Let me be the Shukla (Moon) and you be its wearer. Let me be the mind and you its spokesman (Vak). With these qualities, you be my follower. You the sweet tongued, come to me to get good male children and wealth.*

This is the short version of the saptapadi, though "Yalgnavakya Smrithi" gives a much longer version of actual exchange of vows between the groom and the bride.

***Barni Bandhwana:*** Approximately 15 days prior to the actual wedding, on an auspicious day, the Panditji (priest) will perform a puja to Lord Ganesh (the remover of obstacles). During this puja, a piece of mauli (thread) is tied to the hands of the groom, and his parents. This puja is done to make a humble request to Lord Ganesh that the wedding happen without any problems. After that day, the family performs a puja to Lord Ganesh every day until after the wedding is complete.

***Byaha Hath:*** These are ritualistic ceremonies signifying the cleansing of one's mind, body and soul before embarking on the path of marriage. This daytime ceremony prepares both of them for the nuptials. 'Uptan' is a paste made from sandalwood, turmeric and rose water and is applied by seven married female members of the families, to the faces, hands and feet of the bride and groom. After this ceremony the bride and the groom are barred from stepping outdoors until after the wedding ceremony.

***Mudda-Tikka:*** On an auspicious day, decided by an astrologer, the bride's family call on the groom, taking with them, a platter filled with rice, jaggery, dry fruits, sweetmeats, and sometimes a garland for the 'tikka'. They also carry gifts for the groom, which may include clothes and other items.

***Bari:*** The bride is considered to be a form of the goddess of wealth (Goddess Laxmi). As such, she always wears jewelry and is decorated with nice clothes. At this time, the groom's parents gift the bride jewelry with this in mind.

***Barna:*** The groom is considered to be a form of Lord Vishnu. As such, the parents of the bride come to the groom's house. The parents of the bride go to the groom's house and perform a puja to Lord Ganesh. Then, considering the groom as a form of Lord Vishnu, they perform the puja of the groom's feet. This is followed by gifting the groom clothes and tying a headdress on the groom.

***Mayara:*** The mayara is an important ceremony, common to both the bride and the groom's families. This ceremony is performed by the maternal uncle of the groom/bride, who, along with his wife and family, arrives with much fanfare, and is received by the bride/groom's mother with the traditional welcome. The clothes that the uncle gives are than worn by the family during the wedding.

***Sangeet Sandhya:*** The sangeet sandhya is an evening of musical entertainment. The groom's family puts on a show for the groom and bride. Included as part of this event is an introduction of all the family members for the bride.

***Tilak Ceremony:*** Tilak is a mark of auspiciousness. It is put on the forehead using Kumkum, a red turmeric powder. The male members of the bride's family, like her father, brother, uncles place a tilak on the forehead of the groom.

***Mehendi Lagwana:*** Another name for "Vivaah" is "haath ppila karna" or simply translated, making your hands yellow. (There is probably a better meaning for this phrase but it escapes me at the moment). Mehendi (henna) is applied to the groom's hands and feet. In the right hand, a round spot is left open for Hathlewa.

***Biradh Morcha:*** The groom's family's elder members go to the bride's house. There Lord Krishna's Deity is decorated and aarti is performed. This is ended by some hymns.

***Barat Nikasi:*** The groom leaves for the wedding venue riding a decorated horse. This is a very colorful and grand ceremony. The groom is dressed in a sherwani (long jacket) and 'churidars' (fitted trousers). On his head he wears a 'safa' (turban) with a 'kalgi' (brooch) pinned onto it. Before he departs all his relatives apply the ceremonial 'tilak' on his forehead. The baraat is headed by the dancing of the congregated folks. Accompanied by the rhythm of the north Indian dholak the baraat finally reaches the place of the wedding.

Upon arriving at the venue of the wedding, the groom is welcomed by a welcome song. This is called "talota." Then the groom knocks on the door with his sword and enters.

***Ver Mala:*** The groom is led to a small stage where is he "attacked" by the bride with flowers. A close family member of the groom defends him with a shield. The bride does this while circling the groom four times. Following this, the groom and bride exchange garlands (these are the "ver mala") signifying their acceptance of each other as husband and wife. Than, the groom's mother-in-law measures the groom's chest, and pokes and prods him to make sure he is tough enough to defend her daughter. She than puts kajal on the groom to ward off evil spirits. This is followed by aarti.

***Aarti:*** The 'baraatis' (groom's party) are received by the bride's family and at the entrance to the wedding venue. The bride's mother welcomes the groom by performing the 'aarti' (traditional Indian welcome ritual with a lamp or 'diya' placed on a platter or 'thali') to welcome her son-in-law and placing a tilak on his forehead.

***Hathlewa:*** After being led to the wedding mandup, the bride and groom have their hands tied together. The Panditji does a puja to Lord Ganesh and than puts a coin & mehendi on the groom's right hand where the round empty spot is (where no mehendi was put) and ties his hand with the brides. This puja is done schedule in advance based on an auspicious time & date.

***Havan:*** The ritual connotes the actual marriage, for the very meaning of the word "vivaah" is-marriage. The priest ties the end of the groom's dhoti or the kurta; whichever he is wearing, with that of the bride's saree, the knot signifying the sacred wedlock. The groom and the bride then circle the holy fire seven times, making seven promises to be fulfilled in the married life, after which they are considered to be 'married' to each other. This ritual is called "phere".

***Saat Phere (Wedding Vows)***

1. With the first step, the couple invokes the gods for plenty of pure and nourishing food. "With God as our guide, let us take the first step to live with honour and respect. Let us walk together so we get food," the couple prays.
2. With the second step, the couple prays to the Gods to give them the mental, physical and spiritual strength to lead a healthy life. "Let us be happy and enjoy life. Let us walk together so we grow together in strength," they pray.
3. The third step is for preserving wealth and prosperity in life. The chant at this stage means, "let us share joys and pains together. Let us walk together so we get wealth."
4. With the fourth step, the bride and groom invoke the gods for attainment of happiness and harmony by mutual love and trust in all walks of life. "Let us not forget parents and elders. Let us walk together so we get happiness by sharing our joys and sorrows," they say.
5. With the fifth step, they pray for the welfare of all living beings in the Universe and pray for virtuous, noble and heroic children." Let us observe all acts of charity. Let us walk together so we have family," the mantras say.
6. With the sixth step, they ask the gods to give them a long, joyous life and togetherness forever. "Let us live a long and peaceful life. Let us walk together so we have joy," the couple prays.
7. With the seventh, and last, step, the couple prays for understanding, companionship, loyalty and unity. "Let us be friends with love and sacrifice. Let us walk together so we have friendship," the holy chants signify.

8. After the seventh step, the groom says to the bride: "With seven steps we have become friends. Let me reach your friendship. Let me not be severed from your friendship. Let your friendship not be severed from me."

Only after the 7 steps, are the couple pronounced husband and wife.

***Kanya Daan:*** Kana Danam is performed by the father of the bride in presence of a large gathering that is invited to witness the wedding. The father pours out a libation of sacred water symbolizing the giving away of the daughter to the bride groom. The groom recites Vedic hymns to Kama, the God of love, for pure love and blessings. As a condition for offering his daughter for marriage, the father of the bride requests a promise from the groom for assisting the bride in realizing the three ends : dharma, artha, and kama. The groom makes the promise by repeating three times that he will not fail the bride in realizing dharma, artha and kama. Vidaai:

*This is considered to be the most emotional ritual, when the bride leaves her parents' home and makes her way to her husband's. Family and friends, who also shower her with blessings and gifts, give her a tearful farewell. The male members of the bride's family bid farewell to the groom by applying the traditional 'tilak' (vermilion) on his forehead and shower him with gifts. The couple leaves in a decorated car.*

***Baasi-Jawari:*** This event takes place the day after the wedding. The groom along with some friends and family (but not parents or people senior to him in relation) go to his father-in-law's house where they eat lunch. During this time, the sisters of the bride will steal the groom's shoes and demand a ransom. The groom's company are responsible for preventing this from happening. After this, the bride accompanies the groom back to the groom's house.

***Dwar-Rokai:*** After leaving the groom's father-in-law's house, the couple come home. They are stopped at the entrance of the house by either the groom's sister or his father's sister.

There, in a earthen vessel, the sister/aunt uses a mixture of salt and water to ward off evil spirits from the groom. After this, the pot is thrown on the ground and destroyed. After this, the couple enter the house.

***Griha Pravesh:*** When the bride arrives at her new home, her mother-in-law, who welcomes her with the traditional 'Aarti'.. At the entrance, she puts her right foot onto a tray of vermilion powder mixed in water or milk, symbolizing the arrival of good fortune and purity. With both her feet now covered in the red powder paste, she kicks over a vessel filled with rice and coins to denote the arrival of fertility and wealth in her marital home.

***Mooh Dikhai:*** The family now indulges in a series of games and post-wedding rituals, amidst much laughter to make the new member feel comfortable. One such ritual is the Mooh dikhai. Literally translated, Mooh Dikhai means 'show your face', but this is a ritual, which helps to introduce the newly wed to members of her husband's family! Each member of the groom's family comes in turn to make an acquaintance with the new bride.

***Modern Hindu Weddings:*** Modern Hindu weddings are often much shorter and do not involve all of the rituals of the traditional ceremony which sometimes were for 5 days. Instead certain ceremonies are picked by the families of the bride and the groom, depending on their family tradition, caste, jati etc. Hence the ceremonies vary among the various ethnic groups that practice Hinduism. The wedding is normally conducted under a mandap, a canopy traditionally with four pillars, and an important component of the ceremony is the sacred fire (Agni) that is witness to the ceremony.

***Yajna:*** In Hinduism, Yajna also anglicized as Yagna or Yagya) is a Vedic ritual of sacrifice (Monier-Williams gives the meanings "worship, prayer, praise; offering, oblation, sacrifice"), performed to please the Devas, or sometimes to the Supreme Spirit Brahman. It involves pouring oblations into the divine Agni (the sacrificial fire). Everything that is offered in the divine Agni is believed to reach the Devas. A yajna is typically performed by a hotar, with a number of additional priests playing a supporting role, chanting Vedic verses. Often there will be a fire in the centre of the stage and items are offered into the fire. Among the items offered as *ahuti* in the Yajna include many coconuts, large quantities of ghee, sandalwood shavings and even quantities of clothing.

A yajna can go on for several hours, typically with a large number of people in attendance. Yajna,where milk products (ghee or yogurt), fruits, flowers, cloth, and money are offered, is also termed *homa* or *havan*. A typical Hindu marriage essentially consists of a yajna, because the fire deity Agni is supposed to be the witness of all pious marriages. Brahmins and certain other castes receive a yagnopavitham at their Upanayanam. The yagnopavitham symbolizes the right of the individual to carry out yagnas or homams. The mode of temple worship is termed agamic, while communication to divinity through the fire god, Agni, is considered Vedic. Temples of today are generally a combination of both Vedic and Agamic rituals.

***Pancha Mahayajnas:*** Hindu tradition has the *Pancha Mahayajnas* ("Five Great Yajnas", Taittiriya Aranyaka 2.10) namely:

- Devayajna-consists of offering *ahutis* to *devas*
- Pitruyajna-consists of offering libations to ancestors or pitrus
- Bhutayajna-consists of offering *bali* or foodstuffs to all creatures
- Manushyayajna-consists of feeding guests
- Brahmayajna-consists of chanting Vedas, namely Rigveda, Yajurveda, Samaveda and Atharvaveda

### *Three Kinds of Shrauta Yajnas*

Those yajnas explicitly described in the Vedas are known as *Shrauta* yajnas. The Vedas describe 400 Yajnas. In the category of nitya-karma there are 21 sacrifices. There is no compulsion with regard to the rest of the 400 Yajnas. But the 21, included in the forty samskaras, are required to be performed at least once in a lifetime of a Dvija. These are divided into groups of seven-*paaka-yajnas*, *havir-yajnas*, and *soma-yajnas*.

***Pakayajnas:*** *Pakayajnas* are minor sacrifices and are performed at home. On every Prathama (first day of the lunar fortnight), a pakayajna and a haviryajna have to be performed in the grhyagni and srautagni respectively. The first is called sthalipaka. "Sthali" is the pot in which rice is cooked and it must be placed on the aupasana fire and the rice called "caru" cooked in it must be offered in the same fire.

***Haviryajnas:*** The *haviryajnas* are more elaborate, though not so large in scale as the somayajnas. The haviryajna performed on every Prathama is "darsa-purna-isti", "darsa" meaning the new moon and "purna" the full moon. So the "istis" or sacrifices conducted on the day following the new moon and the full moon (the two Prathamas) are together given the name of darsa-purna-isti. The two rituals are also referred to merely as "isti". This is the *prakrti* (archetype) for haviryajnas. The first four haviryajnas-adhana, agnihotra, darsa-purna-masa and agrayana-are performed at home. The last three haviryajnas-chaturmasya, nirudhapasubandha and sautramani-are performed in a yagasala.

***Somayajnas:*** The name *somayajna* is derived from the fact that the essence of the Soma plant, said to be *relished by the celestials*, is made as an oblation. For soma sacrifices "agnistoma" is the prakrti, the word "stoma" also meaning a sacrifice. Apart from this, animals are also sacrificed. Even so the Saman is sung. In such soma sacrifices there is the full complement of priests-the hota, the adhvaryu, the udgata and the brahma. Each priest is assisted by three others. So in all there are sixteen priests in a soma sacrifice. Agnistoma which is the first of the seven somayajnas is the *prakrti* (archetype) and the other six are its *vikrti*.

These six are: atyagnistoma, uktya, sodasi, vajapeya, atiratra and aptoryama. *Vajapeya* is regarded as particularly important. When its yajamana (sacrificer) comes after having had his ritual bath (avabhrtha snana) at the conclusion of the sacrifice, the king himself holds up a white umbrella for him.

"Vaja" means rice (food) and "peya" means a drink. As the name suggests, the vajapeya sacrifice is believed to bring in a bountiful crop and plentiful water.

The name is appropriate in another sense also. This sacrifice consists of soma-rasa homa, pasu-homa (23 animals) and anna- or vaja-homa. The sacrificer is "bathed" in the rice that is left over. Since the rice is "poured over" him like water the term "vajapeya" is apt.

# Bibliography


Agrawala, V.: *Shiva Mahadeva: The Great God*, Veda Academy, Varanasi, 1966.

Ahmad, Imtiaz: *State and Foreign Policy: India's Role in South Asia*, Vikas, New Delhi, 1993.

Aiyar, M.K.: *Advaita Vedanta, according to Sankara*, Asia Publishing House, New York, 1965.

Aiyar, R. Krishnaswami: *Outlines of Vedaanta*, Chetana, Bombay, 1978.

Arthur, B.: *The Religion and Philosophy of the Veda and Upanishads*, Harvard University Press, Cambridge, 1925.

Berreman, Gerald D.: *Hindus of the Himalayas*, University of California Press, Berkeley, 1963.

Bhattacharji, Sukumari: *Literature in the Vedic Age*, Kali Ram Press, Calcutta, 1988.

Boas, Franz: *Indian Myths and Legends from the North Pacific Coast of America,* Talonbooks, Vancouver, 2002.

Bruhn, Klaus: *The Jina-lmages of Deogarh*, MacMillan, Leiden, 1969.

Bryant, E.: *Poems to the Child-God: Structures and Strategies in the Poetry of Surdas* University of California Press, California, 1979.

Devaraja, N.K.: *An Introduction to Shankara's Theory of Knowledge*, Motilal Banarsi Dass, Delhi, 1962.

Frawley, David: *Tantric Yoga and the Wisdom Goddesses*, Passage Press, Salt Lake City, 1994.

Goetz, Hermann: *The Art of India*, MacMillan, New York, 1964.

Goldman, R.: *The Ramayana of Valmiki*, Berkeley Hills Books, New York, 2000.

Guenther, Herbert. V.: *Gampopa's Jewel Ornament of Liberation*, Rider and Co., London, 1970.

Harding, Elizabeth: *Kali: The Black Goddess of Dakshineshwar*, Nicolas-Hays, York Beach, 1993.

Harlan, B.: *From the Margins of Hindu Marriage*, Oxford University Press, New York, 2000.

Harman, William: *The Sacred Marriage of a Hindu Goddess*, Indiana University Press, Bloomington, 1989.

Jain, Girilal: *The Hindu Phenomenon*, UBSPD, Delhi 1994.

Krishnamurthy, Visvantha: *Essentials of Hinduism,* Narosa Pub. House, New Delhi, 1989.

Kuvalayananda, Swami: *Pranayama*, Science Press, Pennsylvania, 1972.

Maharishi, Yogiraj Vethathiri: *Journey of Consciousness*, MacMillan Limited India, Delhi, 1992.

Mahendranath, S.: *Comparative Studies in Vedaantism*, Humphrey Milford, Bombay, 1927.

McLeod, W. H.: *Guru Nanak and the Sikh Religion*, MacMillan, Delhi, 1976.

Mizuno, Kogen: *The Beginnings of Buddhism,* Richard L. Gage. Tokyo, 1980.

Mueller, Max: *My Autobiography*, Hind Pocket Books, Delhi, 1976.

Paramahansa, P.: *Autobiography of a Yogi,* Self-Realization Fellowship, Los Angeles, 1984.

Peter, Russell: *The Tantra*, Harper and Row, New York, 1978.

Pramathanath, M.: *Introduction to Vedanta Philosophy,* Basu Mallik Press, Calcutta: 1975.

Pratyagatmananda, Swami: *Science and Sadhana*, Sri K. P. Maitra, Calcutta, 1966.

Ramanujan, A. K.: *Hymns for Visnu by Nammalvar,* Motilal Banarsidass, Delhi, 1995.

Rao, K. B.: *Ontology of Adavita*, Mulki S. India, Delhi, 1996.

Reuchenbach, Hans: *The Philosophy of Space and Time*, Dover Publications, New York, 1958.

Richards, John F.: *The Mughal Empire*, Cambridge University Press, Cambridge,1993.

Richards, M.: *Meditation on the Lower Tantras*, Library of Tibetan Works and Archives, Dharamsala, 1983.

Rocher, L.: *The Puranas*, , Motilal Banarsidass, Delhi, 1984.

Rose, J.: *The Cybernetic Revolution*, Elek Science, London, 1974.

Rosen, Steven: *Vaisnavi: Women and the Worship of Krishna*, Motilal Banarsidass Publishers, Delhi, 1996.

Samdup, Lama Kazi, Dawa: *Chakrasambhara Tantra*, Luzac and Co., London, 1910.

Sankaia, H.D.: *Aspects of Indian History and Archeology*, B.R. Publishing, Delhi, 1977.

Sayyambhava, Arya: *Dasa Vaikalika Sutra,* Kastur Chand Lalwani. Delhi, 1973.

Schwartz, H.: *Reimaging the Bible: The Storytelling of the Rabbis,* Oxford University Press, New York, 1998.

Shearer, Alistair, and Peter Russell: *The Upanishads*, Harper and Row, New York, 1978.

Shukla, D. N.: *Vastu-Shastra,* Motilal Banarsidass, Delhi, 1966.

Singer, June: *Androgyny: Toward a New Theory of Sexuality*, Anchor Press/Doubleday, New York, 1976.

Singh, R.: *Kundalini: The Mother of the Universe*, Singh, California, 1930.

Sircar, Mahendranath: *Comparative Studies in Vedaantism*, Humphrey Milford, Bombay, 1987.

Smith, Bardwell L.: *Essays on Gupta Culture*, Motilal Banarsidass, Delhi, 1983.

Sushil, K.: *The Ethics of the Hindus*, Calcutta University Press, Calcutta, 1952.

Suzuki, S.: *Branching Streams Flow in the Darkness: Zen Lectures on the Sandokai*, University of California Press, Berkeley, 1999.

Swami Sivananda: *Kundalini Yoga for the West*, Shambala Publications, Boulder, 1994.

Trilok, C.: *Sadhus and Saints of India and Nepal*, Tecpress, Bangkok, 1996.

Trungpa, Chogyam: *The Dawn of Tantra*, Shambala, Berkeley, 1975.

Venkatarama, A.: *Advaita Vedanta, according to Sankara*, Asia Publishing House, New York, 1965.

Verma, S.: *Role of Reason in Sankara Vedanta*, Parimal Publication, Delhi, 1992.

Vidya, D.: *An Introduction to Tantric Buddhism*, National Museum, New Delhi, 1985.

Waley, Arthur: *The Analects of Confucius*, Allen & Unwin, London, 1938.

Walters, Donald: *The Path: Autobiography of a Western Yogi (Swami Kriyananda),* Ananda Publications, Nevada City, 1977.

Wendy, D.: *Karma and Rebirth*. Motilal Banarsidas, Delhi 1993 (1980).

Woods, J.: *The Yoga-System of Patanjali,* Motilal Banarsidass, Delhi, 1966.

Yogananda, P.: *Autobiography of a Yogi,* Self-Realization Fellowship, Los Angeles, 1946.

Zimmer, Heinrich. *The Art of Indian Asia*, Pantheon, New York, 1955.

Zimmer, Heinrich: *Myths and Symbols in Indian Art and Civilization*, Joseph Campbell, Delhi, 1946.

Zimmer, Heinrich: *Yogic and Tantric Medicine*, Joseph Campbell, Delhi, 1946.

Zion, Bokser: *Abraham Isaac Kook: The Lights of Penitence*, Paulist Press, New York, 1978.

# Index

## G



## H



## I



## J



## K

## L



## M



## N

## S

## W



## Y